T0300886

Transform BEHAVIORS, Transform RESULTS!

When trying to embed changes or new mindsets and behaviors, organizations tend to focus on following a particular methodology rather than clearly defining the underlying behaviors that will deliver the sustainable behavioral change and align the thought processes that drive the behaviors—whether the intent is to continuously improve safety or overall risk management or achieve a sustainable growth and improvement trajectory.

The key role of leadership teams is not to deliver results. It is to inspire and own the organizational culture that delivers the expected results. If culture is owned by HR, it is doomed to be another thing leaders have to do on top of their day job. Business leadership teams must oversee defining and managing organizational culture and have HR coach the capability of leaders to cast the right leadership shadow by role modeling the right behaviors, rewarding the right behaviors in their teams, and providing clarity on expectations around behaviors of all leaders and employees.

The most challenging part of any performance-improvement implementation is the identification of key behavioral indicators (KBIs). The purpose of this book is to assist with that challenge and make "behaviors" easier to understand and identify.

The book defines and describes the importance of focusing on the behaviors necessary for sustainable change rather than focusing on the tools and methodology behind change management. It discusses multiple lenses of change including Lean, Six Sigma, Agile, Risk, and Customer Experience and also addresses the weaknesses of complying solely with the methodology and tools. It proposes a behavioral framework to suit each particular lens.

This book begins with reasons most continuous improvement programs fail to deliver the expected results. More importantly, it discusses embedding the newly described mindsets and capabilities into the business. The book concludes by providing leaders a roadmap and a coaching framework on how to align and embed their new behavioral framework at all levels, starting from the front-line worker up to the CEO.

Essentially, this book leads the reader through the process of understanding the concept of defining behaviors and the difference between them and tools/methodology. It introduces KBI for leaders to define and drive the desired behaviors at all levels. This will increase the probability of sustainability of the improvement initiative by focusing on and maturing the behaviors these initiatives are trying to drive.

Transform BEHAVIORS, Transform RESULTS!
Identifying and Using Behavioral Indicators to Drive Sustainable Change and Improvement

By
Morgan L. Jones
Drew Butler
Gerhard Plenert

Routledge
Taylor & Francis Group

A PRODUCTIVITY PRESS BOOK

First published 2023
by Routledge
605 Third Avenue, New York, NY 10158

and by Routledge
4 Park Square, Milton Park, Abingdon, Oxon, OX14 4RN

Routledge is an imprint of the Taylor & Francis Group, an informa business

ISBN: 978-1-032-12476-6 (hbk)
ISBN: 978-1-032-12475-9 (pbk)
ISBN: 978-1-003-22474-7 (ebk)

DOI: 10.4324/9781003224747

Typeset in Garamond
by KnowledgeWorks Global Ltd.

Contents

Preface..xv

Acknowledgments xix

Foreword..xxi

About the Authors xxiii

1   **Review of CI Program Challenges** 1

    Reasons for CI Failure...2

        Implementing a Tool-Oriented Approach 3

        Focus on Performance 4

        Lack of Motivation..4

        Poor Communication 5

        Inexperienced Manager 6

        Inexperienced Team Members 6

        Inadequate Infrastructure 7

        Contextual Reasons..8

        Focus on Short-Term Results..8

    Previous Attempts at Continuous Improvement 9

    Change Management 10

    Summary 13

2   **Introduction to Desired Behaviors** 15

    Organization's Core Behaviors 17

        Why Define Core Behaviors?..17

        The Ideal Core Behaviors 18

    Ideal Results Require Ideal Behaviors...................................20

        KPIs and KBIs 21

        Habit Formation 22

    Purpose and System Drive Behavior.....................................24

Designing a System...26
    Internal and External Relationships for a Well-Designed System 26
    Structures and Hierarchies...26
Defining a Purpose for the System 27
Integrating Behaviors into Systems.....................................27
    Step 1: Identify Critical Business Systems 28
    Step 2: Prioritize Which System(s) Need to Be Addressed First..........28
    Step 3: Agree on a Purpose Statement for Priority Systems...........28
    Step 4: Agree on a High-Level System Map 28
    Step 5: Agree on KPIs and Targets for Each System.....................28
    Step 6: Use Value Stream Mapping (VSM) If Applicable 29
    Step 7: Use the Behavioral Deployment Process 29
    Step 8: Get Feedback 29
    Step 9: Refine the System...29
Principles Inform Ideal Behavior...30
    Cultural Enablers 30
        Respect Every Individual..30
        Lead with Humility..31
    Continuous Improvement 31
        Focus on Process..32
        Embrace Scientific Thinking.....................................32
        Pull and Flow Value 33
        Assure Quality at the Source 34
        Seek Perfection...34
    Enterprise Alignment 35
        Create Value for the Customer...................................35
        Create Constancy of Purpose 36
        Think Systemically 37
Risk-Taking Mindset and Behavior......................................38
    Anatomy of Key Indicators (KPIs, KBIs, and KAIs)....................39
Summary 39

3 **Change Management..41**
The Disconnected Bridge 42
    Systematic Approach Rather Than Tool-Based Approach 43
    Emphasis on People and Culture 43
Change Management Methodologies 44
    ADKAR Model..45
        Stage 1: Prepare Approach.......................................45

Stage 2: Transition 45

Stage 3: Future..46

Mckinsey 7-S Model 46

Style 46

Skills...47

Systems 47

Structure 47

Staff..47

Strategy 47

Shared Values 47

Kotter's Theory (Including Accelerate) 48

Create a Sense of Urgency..48

Build a Guiding Coalition 48

Form a Strategic Vision and Initiatives 49

Enlist a Volunteer Army 49

Enable Action by Removing Barriers....................................49

Generate Short-Term Wins 49

Sustain Acceleration 49

Institute Change 49

TFSD Model...50

Think 50

Feel...51

Say..51

Do 51

HRM Role in Continuous Improvement...................................52

KPIs and KBIs...52

Production 53

Relationship 53

Organizational Performance 53

Lag KPIs 54

Lead KPIs 54

Focusing on Results Only 54

Decision-Making 54

Variability of Measurement 55

Developing a Whole System 55

Step 1—Set the Principles...56

Step 2—Why Those Principles? 56

Step 3—Understand the Principles.......................................56

Step 4—Set the Behaviors 57

Step 5—Deploy the Behaviors 57
Step 6—Assess the Behaviors...57
Step 7—Diagnose..58
Step 8—Implement 58
Effective Communication for Change Management 58
Programmatic Communication 59
Participatory Communication 59
Barriers to Effective Change Management..65
Lack of a Plan..65
Lack of a Leader 65
Change Fatigue..65
Technology Issues 66
Existence of Multiple Cultures 66
Summary 71
Measuring Success 72

4 **Agile and Patterns** **73**
What Is Agile and Scrum..74
Leadership and Agile/Scrum...77
Agile/Scrum Patterns of Behaviors and Systems 80
Small Teams and Cross-Functional Team...80
Autonomous Teams...82
Small Items 82
Sprint Goal 82
Yesterday's Weather and Teams That Finish Early Accelerate.............83
Swarming—One-Piece Continuous Flow...84
Regular Product Increment 84
Happiness Metric..85
Chapter Conclusion 86
Summary 86
Measuring Success 91

5 **Case Study of CI in Financial Services** **93**
Suncorp Case Study 93
Suncorp's Previous Transformation Attempts.....................................94
BIP Achievements 94
Initiatives and Frameworks...95
Benefit Realization Framework 95
Governance Program 95
Claims Benefit Framework 96

Financial Outcomes..96
Process and Performance Optimization..............................97
Improved Business Performance and Services 98
Enhanced Customer Experience and Removal of Pain Points...........98
BIP Shortfalls...99
    Using Tools and Systems Only 100
    Focusing on the Benefits and Profits Only 100
    Leaders Did Not Show a CI Behavior..........................100
    Absences of Guiding Principles and Behavioral Framework 101
Lessons Learned from the BIP..101
BIP Competencies Behavioral Framework............................102
    Fosters a Culture of Continuous Improvement.............105
    Develops and Implements Solutions 105
    Leads Change 105
    Lives BIP and Continuous Improvement.....................106
    Understands Suncorp..106
    Understands the Industry 106
    Reaches Measured Decisions......................................106
    Enhances Brand Reputation..107
    Applies Good Judgment..107
Comprehensive CI Competency Framework 107
    Fosters a Culture of Continuous Improvement.............112
    Develops and Implements Solutions 112
    Leads Change 116
    Lives Productivity and Continuous Improvement.........117
Summary 117
Measuring Success 118

6 **Risk Behaviors.. 119**
What Is Behavioral Risk? 119
Background on Risk in Financial Service 120
    Compliance Governing and Management.......................121
    Cybersecurity..121
    Third Party 121
Process Risk Controls...121
A-B-C Model...122
Risk Behaviors..122
    Ethical Role Modeling 122
    Challenge Management..123

Nonblame Behavior 123
Risk Mindset 123
How to Develop a Risk Mindset 125
Risk Culture 125
Definition 125
Top-to-Bottom Approach 126
Bottom-to-Top Approach 127
How to Develop a Risk Culture 127
The Ideal Risk Behaviors 128
Framework 136
Defining Ideal Risk Behaviors 137
Benefits of Risk-Defining Behavior 138
A Practical Case 139
Risks Beyond Financial Services 141
Measuring Success 142
Banking Royal Commission 142
Summary 144
Measuring Success 145

7 Customer Experience 147
Which Flavor Is Your Customer Experience (CX)? 149
CX—A Sea Change in How Work Gets Done 150
The Justification and Benefits for Evolving to a Customer-Centric
View 152
Business Transformation via CX Thinking and Practice 153
A Strategy for CX Success 154
Step 1: CX Leadership—Organizing for Success 154
Step 2: A Total Experience Management Framework 155
Step 3: Migrating the Organization to True North Alignment 155
So What Is the Process to Define Your North Star Metric
Effectively? 157
Summary 158
Measuring Success 171

8 Safety 173
Physical Safety 174
Behavior-Based Safety 176
A Real-Life Example 177
Our Goal 177
Set Expectations and Observe 178

    Use Technology 178
    Coaching 178
    Leadership 178
  Keys to Success 179
    Psychological Safety 179
    Psychological Safety and the Lean Practitioner 186
  Summary 187
  Measuring Success 188

9 Personality Types and Behaviors 189
  Impact of Personalities on Behavioral Change 190
  Organizational Culture 190
    Artifacts 190
    Beliefs and Values 190
    Underlying Assumptions 191
  Big Five Personality Traits 191
    Extraversion vs. Introversion 191
    Agreeableness vs. Disagreeableness 192
    Conscientiousness vs. Unconscientiousness 192
    High Neuroticism vs. Low Neuroticism 193
    Openness vs. Closeness to Experience 193
    Predictions for Work Outcomes 194
  The Eight Personalities 195
    Champion 195
    Ambassador 195
    Challenger 196
    Skeptic 196
    Saboteur 196
    Thief 197
    Prisoner 197
    Passenger 198
  Myers & Briggs 16 Personalities 198
    Extraversion (E)—Introversion (I) 198
    Sensing (S)—Intuition (N) 198
    Thinking (T)—Feeling (F) 199
    Judging (J)—Perceiving (P) 199
    The 16 Personalities 199
    ISTJ (Logistician) 200
    ISFJ (Defender) 200

INFJ (Advocate) 200

INTJ (Architect) 200

ISTP (Virtuoso) 201

ISFP (Adventurer) 201

INFP (Mediator) 201

INTP (Logician) 201

ESTP (Entrepreneur)...202

ESFP (Entertainer) 202

ENFP (Campaigner)..202

ENTP (Debater) 202

ESTJ (Executive) 203

ESFJ (Consul)..203

ENFJ (Protagonist)..203

ENTJ (Commander)...203

Different Personalities and Imposing Change....................................204

Influences on Behavior...206

Messenger 206

Incentives...207

Norms 207

Defaults..208

Salience..208

Priming 209

Affect 209

Commitment...210

Ego...210

How to Persuade People 211

Arrogance...211

Stubbornness..211

Narcissism..211

Integrated Cultural Framework..212

Ability to Influence 212

Comfort with Ambiguity...212

Achievement Orientation 212

Individualism vs. Collectivism 213

Time Orientation..213

Space Orientation...213

Summary 213

Measuring Success 214

10 Fourth Stage of the Industrial Revolution: Industry 4.0, Internet of Things (IoT), and Artificial Intelligence (AI) **215**

Traditional Approach 216

Sensei Moment 224

Chapter Summary 225

Measuring Success 225

11 Leadership Responsibility **227**

Respect for the Individual 228

Lead with Humility 229

Decision-Making Framework 235

Summary 241

Measuring Success 241

12 Roadmap for Implementation **243**

Making Behavioral Change Real 244

Summary 254

Measuring Success 254

13 Wrap-Up **257**

Appendices—Summary of Behavior Frameworks **259**

Behavioral Truths

Continuous Improvement (Chapter 3—CI)

Judgment (Chapter 4—Risk)

Change Management (Chapter 5—Communication
    and Change Management)

Customer Focus (Chapter 6—Customer Focus
    and Customer Experience)

Agile Management (Chapter 7)

Safety (Chapter 8)

Drive for Results (Chapter 9—Leadership)

Fourth Stage of the Industrial Revolution (Chapter 10)

Leadership Responsibility (Chapter 11)

Roadmap for Implementation (Chapter 12)

References 309

Index 317

Preface

'Know-how' alone is not enough! You need to 'know-why'! All too
often people visit other organizations only to copy their systems
and tools or know-how and know-what.

> Shigeo Shingo (Shingo, S. Non-Stock Production:
> The Shingo System of Continuous Improvement.
> Portland OR, Productivity Press, 1988)

If you don't give your employees the appropriate tools that they need in
order to direct their behaviors, they won't know what's important to you.
These tools come in the form of systems and metrics which tell them what
they need to do in order to move the organization closer to its goals. If
you don't provide guidance, in the form of systems and metrics, employees
will decide for themselves what they think you are focusing on, which can
potentially be disastrous. Managers need to provide guidance, which in
turn influences behaviors. This book will help the reader understand how
important this guidance is and what is necessary in order to motivate the
behaviors that management feels is the most important.

When trying to shift mindsets and behaviors and embed changes,
organizations tend to focus on following a particular methodology or
process without context. They need clearly defined desired behaviors that
will deliver sustainable behavioral change to align the outcomes and context.
Moreover, many fail to consider the thoughts, emotions, and mindsets that
drive these behaviors. Whether it is continuously improving safety or overall
risk management through implementing continuous improvement, it is
critical to understand the role that mindset plays in driving behaviors and
the role behaviors play in creating and sustaining change in organizations.

Leaders play a key role in defining, role modeling, and reinforcing these
behaviors through the actions they take, or do not take, each day. The key

role of leadership teams is not to drive results, it is to model the way forward, inspire individuals, and nurture a culture within teams that deliver the expected results. They do this through the behaviors they demonstrate, the actions and outcomes they reward or choose to walk past, and the things they prioritize. If culture is seen as owned by the human resources department, it is doomed to be another thing leaders feel they "have to do" on top of their "day job." A leader's "day job" is to define, create, and nurture a positive culture through the supportive systems and metrics that they create, and this is the foundation from which results grow.

Most leaders are already aware of the potential that organizational culture has on the long-term success of an organization. These leaders perceive shared values and behaviors as the key factors determining how an organization conducts business. A successful embracement of a particular corporate culture can help an organization achieve high productivity based on reduced operational costs and enhanced execution of services. Additionally, employees are likely to become more creative when a firm's culture conforms to improving the value of both the organization and its workers. In other words, organizational culture provides employees with the appropriate tools to channel their productivity toward a particular direction that would draw an organization closer to accomplishing its goals.

Although leaders seem to acknowledge that organizational culture can improve the value of a firm, most of them have found it challenging to improve it. Both employees and leaders seem reluctant to change due to particular factors revolving around the complexity involved and perhaps the period it would take to achieve a successful transition. The latter weighs in more than the former in the sense that some leaders think that organizational change might take longer than their tenure or quite longer to the extent of finding it hard to balance with other priorities.

The reluctance portrayed by employees and leaders is a factor of mindset, which leads to a loss of interest, support, and passion, from the parties involved in the change process. Most of the time, the behavior employees portray in a work environment corresponds to how they will partake in the change. A clear behavioral framework enables the employees to embrace a mindset that can steer an organization to success. Quality leadership is essential in ensuring a workforce adopts behavioral uniformity aligned to the firm's core values. This uniform behavior can be achieved through various hiring, promotions, evaluations, and firing policies. By focusing on these areas, the guidance provided in this book emphasizes the significance of behavior in contributing to organizational change.

Several years ago, Dr. Gerhard Plenert, one of the authors of this book, was involved in a project for the Texas Office of the Attorney General. This required working with 80 branch offices throughout the state and analyzing their performance. The environment was unique in that each office had two bosses, an office manager and a lead attorney. Dr. Plenert would go to the offices one at a time and spend time there, analyzing flow, efficiencies, line balancing, employee satisfaction, participation, etc. Afterward, he would sit down with the two "bosses" and give them a report on the performance of their branch along with recommendations. He discovered things like the backlog of mail in someone's drawer that would exceed one year, work overlaps between employees, highly disruptive flows, and major redundancies.

The results were mixed; some locations paid attention to the recommendations and implemented changes. Others ignored the recommendations, feeling that they were either too busy to be bothered or that they did not feel the recommendations had merit. Because of the mixed level of interest, the reports received about any performance changes were also mixed. One of the Dallas offices excitedly called Dr. Plenert two weeks after his visit. They congratulated him and informed him that they immediately implemented all his recommendations, and in the two weeks, they were able to triple their throughput. Is this an anomaly?

Another interesting case is the NASA Space Shuttle. Was it a failure or was not it? Originally, the shuttle was to go into space several times a year. In the end, it was less than one time a year and sometimes a couple years between flights. The difference occurred in the safety checks that had to be performed between flights. Each manufacturer of a component was required to create a list of areas requiring inspection between flights. In addition, each of the inspection sheets must be completed. Unfortunately, the inspections, in and of themselves, were a good thing. However, the redundancies were enormous, and each redundant test had to be performed separately for each inspection sheet. Doing an inspection one time in order to satisfy all the times the inspection was required was not acceptable because different teams performed the inspections. The various inspections could require minutes to days to complete. The accumulative time required by all the redundant inspections increased the lead time between flights to the point where the space shuttle program was considered a failure in that it did not accomplish the desired number of trips each year. It could not be cost justified. You could say that quality killed the space shuttle program. However, in reality, it was a lack of enterprise excellence.

Countless organizations have, at one time or another, begun a "Lean journey" or they have implemented a continuous improvement initiative of some sort. At the foundation of these initiatives are plethora of tools that seem to promise exciting new results. While many organizations may initially see significant improvements, far too many of these initiatives meet disappointing ends. Leaders quickly find that Lean tools such as Six Sigma, judoka, SMED, 5S, JIT, quality circles, etc. are not independently capable of effecting lasting change. An integrated synergy occurs between these various tools built upon a set of eternal principles that creates an environment of lasting change. That is the topic of this book, How to create a ***sustainable culture of continuous improvement***.

> 94% of problems in business are systems driven and only 6% are people driven.
>
> **Dr. W. Edwards Deming**

This book is about behaviors. It teaches us how to achieve this sustainable culture of continuous improvement through a shift in culture. It teaches us that this shift occurs because of a shift in behaviors. In addition, it directs us to understand that these behaviors, when incorporated into properly designed systems, will drive us toward the excellence we are looking for. I hope you enjoy the read.

> It is not necessary to change. Survival is not mandatory.
>
> **Dr. W. Edwards Deming**

Acknowledgments

We would like to thank the thousands of people we have worked with over the years to change underlying behaviors to implement sustainable continuous improvement and transformations. We learn something from every conversation we have and have attempted to share these lessons throughout this book.

We would like to acknowledge the input from the following people in various chapters to improve the quality of this book: Brad Jeavons, Kevan Latty, Louise Phelan, Mark Ley, Neil Allen, Rob Telford, Shermonika Walker, and Steve Towers. We would also like to thank our families for their support during this endeavor, they make it all possible!

We would also like to acknowledge Nicole Gallant for her great work on initial editing.

The interactive effects of associative effects of associative response priming and response priming and personality traits on insight problem solving over time. *Journal of Global Education Research*, 4(1), pp. 14–32, DOI: https://www.doi.org/10.5038/2577-509X.4.1.1023

Ziapour A, Khatony A, Jafari F, and Kianipour N. 2017. Correlation between personality traits and organizational commitment in the staff of Kermanshah University of Medical Sciences in 2015. *Annals of Tropical Medicine and Public Health*, 10, pp. 371–376.

Foreword

I am Dr. Frank Koentgen, the CEO, owner, and founder (since 1999) of Ozgene Pty. Ltd. in Perth, Australia (www.ozgene.com) where I developed Geneoz VMS, the revolutionary Vivarium Management Solution. I am also a Professor at the University of Notre Dame Australia. I have been on the board of the Shingo Institute since 2015.

I find it incredible how many companies struggle with behavior management within their organizations. Behavior management is at the root of success or failure, and it can be managed with either a carrot or a stick. Far too many companies choose the stick, as you will see as you consider the many stories and examples that are highlighted in this book. The benefit of using the stick often offers short-term results, but it also results in long-term struggles and failures forcing the stick to repeatedly be deployed to the pain and frustration of the employees. The Shingo methodology teaches us how to manage behaviors in such a way that you will achieve not just short-term results, but you will also accomplish a long-term sustainable transformation throughout your organization, which should ultimately be the goal of every enterprise.

This book draws the connection between behaviors and results using the Shingo methodology. It teaches the reader what desired behaviors should look like within successful enterprises. It talks about continuous improvement and change management with a focus on the Shingo methodology when driving toward enterprise transformations. It teaches the reader how to achieve these transformations, while at the same time achieving structural goals like safety, agility, a successful customer experience, and a strong, motivational leadership. This book is filled with examples of the same tools that I have used throughout my own personal highly successful business practices, and which I continue to teach to organizations around the world. Many books provide a concept and give one or two examples of the application of the tool. The authors demonstrate their deep experience in applying this across many different lenses including customer focus, continuous improvement, agile, etc., and then at the end of the chapter give practical key indicators for the lens.

Most organizations struggle with defining ideal behaviors; then, many leaders define what their managers and front-line staff have to do and say. This book not only shows behaviors for front-line associates but also for senior leaders and CEOs so they can actually role model these behaviors in their context. The chapter on defining measures for measuring behavioral change in the form of key behavioral indicators (KBIs), they also introduce a new pragmatic approach for front-line associates in the form of key activity indicators to make it front line practical. The anatomy of constructing good key indicators is excellent and is then demonstrated with examples at the end of each chapter.

I strongly recommend this book, not just because of its valuable content and its examples but also because of its authors, each of which has a strong background and a long record of experience, implementing exactly the methodologies discussed in this book at companies within the United States and Europe, but also in locations as remote as Malaysia, Saudi Arabia, China, and the Philippines. Between them, these authors have over 30 published books, many of which discuss various aspects of the Shingo methodology, including books like, ***Why Bother? Why and How to Assess Your Continuous-Improvement Culture***, ***Driving the Enterprise to Sustainable Excellence: A Shingo Process Overview***, and of course the first book in the Shingo Model series, ***Discover Excellence: An Overview of the Shingo Model and Its Guiding Principles***. Between them, the authors have taught at universities all over the world and have taught all the Shingo courses numerous times. But most important is their success including cultural transformations within the companies they work for but also in their various consulting engagements. They bring this experience to life by subtle use of language in the frameworks to illicit an emotional response in the reader. Just enough to inspire the reader into action and create behavioral frameworks for their organizations. Also great for the many consultants out there to work with their clients.

I hope you enjoy exploring the behaviors within your own enterprises as you explore the concepts and principles discussed in this book, and I look forward to hearing your thoughts and comments as make the various described transformations.

Dr. Frank Koentgen

About the Authors

Dr. Morgan Jones has over 30 years' experience in transformations using Lean and Six Sigma, a pragmatic and experienced improvement leader, delivering over $2.1B in hard savings to organization, improving customer, staff experiences, and improved health and safety. The legacy capabilities of business improvement have resulted in over 26 international awards and chairing 28 international conferences around business improvement. Morgan is an international award-winning author and has written five books. He has led a business unit with overall P&L accountability of $167M and led an organization to be the first bank to win the Shingo Award. He is also a Chartered Engineer, Certified Master Black Belt, Lean Master, and Executive Coach. Morgan has leadership experience in marine, manufacturing, government, military, mining, utilities, telecommunications, oil and gas, banking, and supply chain.

Drew Butler is currently the Head of Corporate Operational Excellence for Digital room, an e-commerce printing business and former Vice President of Operations at Signs.com, one of the fastest-growing tech companies in Utah where he was responsible for daily operations, operational excellence, as well as strategic planning to support their future growth plans.

Prior to this Butler worked at Curtiss Wright as Senior Corporate Director of Operational Excellence. He joined Curtiss Wright in September 2013. With over 30 years of operations experience, he was responsible for the implementation of Lean Operational systems and controls, methods, and strategies in the Oil & Gas Division and in 2014 transitioned into the role of Corporate Director of Operational Excellence for Curtiss Wright. As CW Corporate OPEX Director, Butler was responsible for leading the development and implementation of the CW Way Lean Operating System throughout Curtiss Wright globally.

Before Curtiss Wright, Butler was the Plant Manager with Boart Longyear Exploratory Mining Company in Salt Lake City, Utah. During his 30-year career, he has served in various roles of increasing responsibility in the Aerospace, Industrial, Consumer Products, and Mining industries with companies such as SPS Technologies and OC Tanner.

Butler holds a Bachelor of Science degree in Mechanical Engineering Technology from Spring Garden College and an MBA from Temple University in Philadelphia, PA. He has worked with the Shingijutsu Consulting Group in the past and, for over 20 years, has been a Senior Lead Examiner with the Shingo Institute in Utah and travels the world evaluating world-class facilities in manufacturing, medical devices, and consumer products that have been applicable for the Shingo Prize. In the past, he has served on the Board and as Vice President of Expansion for Guadalupe School in Salt Lake City, Utah. Mr. Butler resides in Salt Lake City, Utah with his wife Erika and they have four fabulous daughters! Mr. Butler is also a Muay Thai Blackbelt.

Dr. Gerhard Plenert, former Director of Executive Education at the Shingo Institute, has more than 25 years of professional experience in organizational transformations, helping companies and government agencies to strive for Enterprise Excellence by utilizing the Shingo model to drive cultural transformations. Dr. Plenert is an internationally recognized expert in supply chain management; Lean/Six Sigma; IT, quality, and productivity tools; and in working with leading-edge planning and scheduling methods. He has literally "written the book" on leading-edge supply chain management concepts, such as finite capacity scheduling (FCS), advanced planning and scheduling (APS), and world-class management (WCM).

His experience includes significant initiatives with Genentech, Johnson & Johnson, Aerojet Rocketdyne, Shell, Aramco, Sony, Cisco, Microsoft, Seagate, NCR Corporation, Ritz-Carlton, the US Air Force, and numerous other branches of the US Department of Defense. In addition, Dr. Plenert has consulted to major manufacturing and distribution companies such as Hewlett-Packard, Black & Decker, Raytheon, Motorola, Applied Magnetics, Toyota, AT&T, IBM, and Kraft Foods. He has also been considered a corporate "guru" on supply chain management for Wipro, AMS, and Infosys, and a Lean/Six Sigma "guru" for the US Air Force and various additional consulting companies.

With 14 years of academic experience, Dr. Plenert has published over 150 articles and 23 books on Lean, supply chain strategy, operations management, and planning. He has also written MBA textbooks and operations planning books for the United Nations. Dr. Plenert's ideas and publications have been endorsed by people like Steven Covey and companies such as Motorola, AT&T, Black & Decker, and FedEx. His publications are viewable at www.gerhardplenert.com.

Dr. Plenert previously served as a tenured Full Professor at California State University, Chico, CA; a Professor at BYU, BYU–Hawaii, University of Malaysia, University of San Diego; and has been a visiting Professor at numerous universities all over the world from Europe to Southeast Asia, Latin America, and Australia. He has earned degrees in math, physics, and German, and he holds an MBA and MA in international studies and PhD in resource economics (oil and gas) and operations management. Dr. Plenert continues to serve as a Shingo educator and examiner.

Black Dog
Institute

We are proud to support Black Dog Institute's work to improve the lives of people impacted by mental illness and suicide. One hundred percent of the authors' royalties goes toward Black Dog Institute's research and education programs to help raise awareness and create real-world solutions. One in five of us will experience symptoms of mental illness in any given year, and approximately 60 percent of these people will not seek help. As the only medical research institute in Australia investigating the importance of maintaining our mental health throughout our lifetime, Black Dog Institute aims to create a mentally healthier world for everyone. Black Dog Institute works to improve the lives of people impacted by mental illness through their pioneering research, high-quality clinical services, and national education programs.

These royalties will be directed toward education and awareness activities and supporting innovative research into new clinical solutions for all Australians. You are helping Black Dog Institute raise vital funds for:

- researching suicide prevention and clinical treatment;
- expanding education programs to reach more communities, schools, and health professionals; and
- developing apps and websites to serve as real-time mental health tools so that people can manage depression, anxiety, and stress at their own pace.

Chapter 1

Review of CI Program Challenges

A couple of years ago, one of the authors met with a General of the United States Air Force to discuss continuous improvement (CI). The General described the many programs that had been implemented over the years, including Lean programs like Value Stream Mapping, 5S, Standard Work, Six Sigma, and numerous more. He discussed how each of the programs had provided spot improvements and had demonstrated spot successes. Then he said,

> In spite of all these years of improvements, all of which were successful in their own realms, I can't see any improvements over-all. The organizations still trudges along at its slow, painful pace that sometimes seems to have no over-all direction. Many of these improvements have been discarded after just six months and organizations have reverted to their old processes. I don't think we're any better than we were ten years ago.

Many CI programs, including Six Sigma, Agile, and Transformation or Lean implementations, have been implemented over the last 30 years across most industry sectors in many countries around the world. Many companies have failed to build any sustainability level for these CI programs and have achieved only partial, short-term financial benefits for many reasons. Around 70 percent of these programs fail in the first 3 years of establishment (Miller, 2001). However, it is essential to note that we should not consider CI as a project or program but rather a long-term cultural strategy that is endless

DOI: 10.4324/9781003224747-1

for an organization. It applies across all departments, for example, the sales department, where it eliminates waste and increases earnings. Therefore, industries or companies should not consider CI as a project as it may lead to its failure in the future but should consider it a culture enabler through defining and building a clear set of CI behaviors.

Reasons for CI Failure

The benefits of implementing CI are undeniable. However, they have reported high failure rates (McLean, Antony, and Dahlgaard, 2017). Building a CI culture is the first step, followed by sustaining this culture (Burrill, Parker, and Fitzgerald, 2019). Sustaining is difficult, as it requires a fundamental change in the organizational culture and retaining this change, which is why most companies fail to build sustainable CI behavior and fail to achieve sustainable benefits (Shingo Institute, 2016).

The Shingo Institute has an excellent graphics on how traditional program approach focuses on tools and a second one on their model approach focuses on behaviors. Figure 1.1 shows the traditional approach of

Figure 1.1 Traditional CI approach focuses on tools and results.

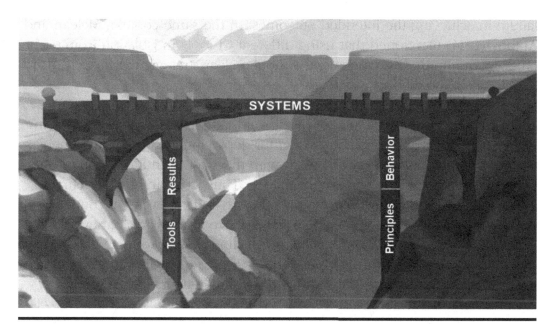

Figure 1.2 Shingo model bridge.

CI programs on results and tools, and Figure 1.2 shows the holistic Shingo model approach focusing on behaviors.

Implementing a Tool-Oriented Approach

The Shingo model of operational excellence defines successful organizations in terms of improvement. These organizations can transform their culture into a CI culture led by managers where everyone is engaged. However, focusing on the tools required for a CI program rather than building a culture may result in the success of a project but a failure to sustain this success (Shingo Institute, 2016). A tool-based change improves the performance of specific processes where these tools are used, but a tool-oriented culture cannot be a solution (Hines, Taylor, and Walsh, 2018). Tools can explain the "how," but they fail to explain the "why" (Shingo Institute, 2016), which means that the employees will not be able to relate to the strategic goals of the company.

When using the proper tools in the context of a strategic system, improvements will be more noticeable. However, behaviors guided by the same company's people are still disconnected (Hines, Taylor, and Walsh, 2018). Tools, systems, and principles that form the behavior, later on, are what constitutes a culture (Shingo Institute, 2016). The misalignment between these elements leads to variation in behaviors, which leads to failure in achieving the intended outcomes. In the same context, Mclean and Antony (2014) mentioned that using different CI tools in isolation from each other in an improper arrangement without a clear strategic roadmap leads to the failure of the whole CI process.

Most managers can hardly differentiate between building a CI system and a CI team (Burrill, Parker, and Fitzgerald, 2019). Theoretically, a system involves the tools and techniques used for deploying a CI program, whereas the team is the people who will work with these tools and techniques; their behavior, in this case, is part of the change. Thus, combining a system and a team able to work with this system is the key to improvement (Burrill, Parker, and Fitzgerald, 2019). Using a governance framework that everyone can relate to (M and Prashar, 2020) and selecting the appropriate tools under this framework (Antony and Gupta, 2019) can prevent a disconnect between the system and the team—the reasons for CI implementation failure.

Focus on Performance

Dewar et al. (2011) mentioned that companies fail to sustain their improvement as they only focus on performance. The overall performance is essential, but it is not the only indicator of success and failure. The organization's health is defined as the alignment, and execution of improvement and renewing itself continuously are key indicators of performance (Dewar et al., 2011). The vast majority of failure cases are because of reasons related to the health of the organization (Dewar et al., 2011), that is, organizations either fail to align all the efforts together, fail to execute an aspect or more of the program, or fail to follow up with the process. Although CI is not considered a single project or program, it should be continuously monitored and managed (Dewar et al., 2011). Reviewing each step and getting feedback using the suitable metrics to fix any errors that may emerge during the process are essential to guarantee sustainable CI behavior (Mclean and Antony, 2014).

Lack of Motivation

One of the authors worked with a company that had several factories and because of a turndown in business, one of the plants was slated for closure. The one selected for closure was the one with the worst quality record. The plant manager of the closing plant invited the author for a visit, wanting to know why their quality was so poor. He said, "We have a quality department. We have quality training for all the employees. We have banners throughout the facility reminding everyone about the importance of quality. Everyone knows that quality performance is critical. Why do we have such terrible quality?"

The author, being an outsider, could easily see the problem and asked, "What are the employees measured on?" The manager responded, "Units produced. We pay bonus pay based on units produced." The author asked, "What you're telling me is that you're paying them for speed, not for quality. Why would they be motivated to produce quality? They just assume that quality is the responsibility of the quality department, and their responsibility is to pump out parts."

The manager was stunned and said, "I get it! How sad!"

Lack of motivation or an inability to find the motive for change will encourage a task-oriented culture rather than a CI culture. Moreover, starting a CI program to cope with the behavior changes and doing the same as others lead to the same undesired culture (Mclean and Antony, 2014). In an attempt to learn from others, some organizations may take a CI program adopted by a successful company and copy the same practices to their organization to achieve the same results, but the fact is that they fail. CI is an integration of more than one element including the system, the tools, and the behaviors. While organizations may copy the tools and practices, they cannot copy the complete organizational culture, which is critical to a CI program (Burrill, Parker, and Fitzgerald, 2019).

When leaders are disappointed and lack the motivation to change, this disappointment will certainly pass to the employees, creating an unwillingness to change or improve. Successful change efforts are about understanding what needs to be changed, who will initiate the change, and how it will be implemented and monitored (Bird, Lichtenau, and Michels, 2016).

Poor Communication

Communication, which most often comes in the form of systems and metrics, can be a success and a failure factor in a CI transformation. The ability to convey accurate and useful information about the program and define the program's scope reduces the failure possibilities resulting from a misunderstanding (Antony and Gupta, 2019). In contrast, unclear and inadequate communication practices are reasons for failure (Antony et al., 2019). In many cases, the program's scope may change inconsistent communication. Reporting the changes results in a disharmonized performance leading to waste in the effort and resources allocated for the change.

Communication also plays a vital role in convincing people of the need to change behavior. Without effective communication and a shared understanding of the behavior changes required, employees can unintentionally be the reason for failure. They resist changing behavior because they do not understand the objectives or consequences of the change (Antony and Gupta, 2019).

Organizations that could not foster a change in the culture adopt a culture shift from a narrow scope culture focusing on the short-term financial benefits to a culture of CI. Where the employees are convinced of the importance of CI programs and are willing to contribute to the success of this change reported high failure rates (Antony et al., 2019). When acceptable communication means are maintained and employees have enough reason to follow the change, they become champions who drive the CI implementation process forward (Burrill, Parker, and Fitzgerald, 2019).

Inexperienced Manager

Another common reason that CI programs fail comes from the top managers and the company's maximum managerial levels (Albliwi et al., 2014). The inability to link the business objectives and strategic goals with the CI program efforts and the failure to convey this relationship to the employees can hinder the process (Antony et al., 2019). Moreover, managers who are not committed to the transformation and do not show support at different levels will accelerate the failure (Antony et al., 2019). It does not mean that managers are the only contributor to failure; management has a role in the team's performance, but the overall performance is a team result (Antony and Gupta, 2019). However, when opting for a transformation or a change, leaders are the catalysts for the difference (Dewar et al., 2011). Although management and leadership have different roles, they appear to be interrelated in this context; managers are the leaders who should initiate the change (Mclean and Antony, 2014).

Inexperienced Team Members

Since the overall performance results from the whole teamwork, less competent or inexperienced team members may face many difficulties in complying with a new CI program (Antony et al., 2019). Those are team members who fail to work harmoniously and transfer their knowledge and expertise seamlessly. Besides, the absence of experienced team members who can work closely with others to ensure the proper implementation of the chosen CI approach and this approach's sustainability can predict the inability to continue the CI program (Antony et al., 2019; Albaliwi et al., 2014).

Learning and training can be key solutions to this problem. By providing adequate training programs synchronized with the new changes in the organization and ensuring they satisfy the learning needs at the individual, team, and organizational levels (Antony and Gupta, 2019), the implementation and sustainability of a CI program are ensured. However, providing ad-hoc based training is ineffective in CI transformation (M and Prashar, 2020). CI is an ongoing process that needs structured and continuous training to achieve the desired outcomes (M and Prashar, 2020).

Many companies provide learning and training programs to the employees. They may also hire experienced members for the CI change, but this does not guarantee their success. The reason behind this takes us back to the point of "why" and "how." Training programs provide the "how," but they do not necessarily mention the "why" (Shingo Institute, 2016); in other words, the employees will know how to use the CI tools and techniques, but they will be left asking when and why to use them.

Inadequate Infrastructure

The absence of the infrastructure ready for adopting the CI projects and sharing information among managers and employees results in an unsuccessful CI transformation attempt (Burrill, Parker, and Fitzgerald, 2019). Organizations that wait for a problem to emerge and then try to figure out the solutions or tools to fix the problem usually face a problem with CI programs (Shingo Institute, 2016), as this is not the CI concept. CI is an inclusive framework that should be extended to all departments and entities (Ey, 2020). It is not a system to be adopted by the executives and frontline managers, leaving the middle- and lower-level managers unaware of the program and creating a gap between different managerial levels (Burrill, Parker, and Fitzgerald, 2019). On the other hand, organizations may attempt to deploy the CI program on all levels and departments without the necessary infrastructure needed for such transformation (M and Prashar, 2020).

The infrastructure includes the availability of the latest technologies and the ability to use them for the new change. However, when companies start using technology as a change driver, the improvement is seen in specific processes and performance, not as an overall organizational improvement (Burrill, Parker, and Fitzgerald, 2019). In this case, the use of technology is a complementing tool to aid the transformation, but not a transformation enabler. CI transformation starts with the culture, not the tools. Kortian and Harrison (2018) pointed to some of the technologies that can foster a CI culture as artificial intelligence and machine learning as an example of CI's digital technologies. Such technologies can enable a data-driven decision-making process, which may reduce the duration of implementing the CI culture but will not deploy this culture solely (Ey, 2020).

Contextual Reasons

CI failure cannot be separated from other contextual variables. The country of the organization, its size, the type of CI program and tools used, and the organization's maturity all contribute to the success or failure of CI (M and Prashar, 2020). Despite today's globalized world, regional culture still affects CI, as it is a culture-based concept that is influenced by the national culture (M and Prashar, 2020). Similarly, the organization's size can affect the CI implementation, as large organizations may have the needed capital and resources but lack the flexibility in managing changes (M and Prashar, 2020). Each organization has to choose a suitable CI program for its business while considering the maturity level. Starting a CI today is certainly different from an organization with an old CI practice record (M and Prashar, 2020).

Focus on Short-Term Results

While most organizations want to see immediate results from implementing a CI system reflected in business metrics like sales or profit, CI is not a way to provide this kind of change (Burrill, Parker, and Fitzgerald, 2019). CI is constant. It is not a tool used to fix emerging problems or to improve performance in certain areas. It may take 2–5 years to truly change a culture and enhance the improvement culture (Burrill, Parker, and Fitzgerald, 2019). CI should be regarded as a long-term investment in its resources and people rather than a short-term solution for financial results (Burrill, Parker, and Fitzgerald, 2019).

CI is essential to solving problems in processes at all levels of the organization, and most importantly, at the frontline where the work is done. Today's market in the global environment shows that it is essential to recognize organizations' critical factors or undesirable failure, including customer service, quality, and cost competitiveness. Service providers, manufacturers, and engineering firms share a drive to lower costs, offer a diverse product mix, maintain product or service quality, and reduce cycle time as they pursue increased market share and higher profits in a growing global market or environment.

The failure of any CI program can cost the company millions of dollars, particularly for large companies. In addition, lost resources, such as time, is another concern for managers who cannot build a sustainable CI culture (Antony et al., 2019). Thus, understanding the reasons of failure can help to develop a structural approach to mitigate such losses.

Previous Attempts at Continuous Improvement

CI approaches are not a new trend. Several companies have been trying to deploy different methods to achieve specific outcomes, all centered on continuous business improvements. While most CI attempts fail because of various reasons, others succeed and achieve impressive results. The legacy of these attempts cannot be ignored. Organizations willing to implement any CI strategy should learn from both success and failure and reflect on what should be done.

Amazon started as an online bookstore and implemented a six-sigma method in 1999 as part of its operational excellence program. The company achieved CI in customer experience, backed by productive and efficient operations within the entire company (Sharma, 2017). Amazon focused on hiring the best people, in addition to training existing employees to foster CI. It also decreased variance in business KPIs and eliminated unnecessary procedures by using Six Sigma, Lean, and other tools (Sharma, 2017). The results for Amazon were positive, despite the time and effort a six-sigma implementation may take.

Richard Hemsley, the COO of global transaction services at the Royal Bank of Scotland Group, emphasized the impact of lean management on the customer experience, engagement, productivity, and overall work performance (McKinsey and Company, 2011). For him, lean management was not about improvements only; it was about sustaining this improvement, which was done by engaging all employees (McKinsey and Company, 2011). Lean can deliver quick progress, but without focusing on training to stabilize the method, the attempt will not last, and the change will not stick.

Thomas de Rycke, the transformation leader in The Proximus Group in Belgium, also emphasized the importance of training CI skills and capabilities as a fundamental element when deploying any process excellence approach. During the Agile transformation deployment in the company, he found that people are different, where some may understand the Agile principles and embed them in everyday work, and others need time (KPMG, 2019). Organizations that previously implemented an Agile methodology reached different levels of success and failure according to their ability to handle the resistance to change and give adequate training tailored to everybody's needs.

Companies that choose to deploy a BPM (beats per minute) as a **tool** to drive change usually face the difficult task of convincing their employees that the new tool is an agent to help them make the change. On the other hand, when considering BPM as a **strategy** that involves a set of technologies, it starts to gain weight as a CI approach and influences the entire organization (Ward-Dutton, 2008). The Carphone Warehouse, for example, as a European telecommunication retailer and service provider, realized this point. The IT department is where the change started by using BPM tools and collaborating with other departments to expand the strategy instead of using ad-hoc business systems (Ward-Dutton, 2008).

Where functions are not aligned with purpose or goals and CI is not applied with an overall roadmap, it results in waste, defects, or cost shifted either up or downstream, which is not CI for the organization.

EXAMPLE

An iron ore mine had a program to remove AUD$55 million from the bottom line, and each department was tasked with coming up with and implementing cost savings to collectively reach the goal. The Drill and Blast Department decided that an excellent cost-saving initiative would be to use fewer explosives in the blasting process, thus resulting in significant savings. Unfortunately, the unintended results meant that blasting fragmentation yielded larger fragments which were oversize for the crusher, meaning blockages and significant downtime in the ore handling plant, which negatively impacted the number of tonnes produced and ultimately revenue.

Change Management

Every business aims to grow. However, this can only be achieved if the company invests in new products and services and looks for ways to improve the way it operates. Competition is real in today's business life, and to face it, a company should develop new products and good quality. True competitive advantage is achieved when organizations make CI part of the way they operate and have the skills, capability, and systems in place to quickly identify opportunities for improvement and manage these changes effectively.

Organizational change is an inevitable risk that should be mitigated to ensure a sustainable competitive advantage (Jung, Kang, and Choi, 2020). The risk behaviors and mindsets are factors to be considered in a CI change as they ultimately affect the process. Leaders need to foster risk-taking behavior as a factor having a positive impact on the commitment to organizational change and sustaining the improvement (Jung, Kang, and Choi, 2020). With a risk-aware mindset, employees are enabled and empowered to become decision-makers with more potential to accept fundamental changes.

Resistance to change is one of the main barriers to a thriving CI culture; change management can remove this barrier by seeking to understand how the change being introduced will influence individuals and enabling people to manage the change, by providing the right support and resources at the right points in time.

For change management to be effective, it should be initiated, not reactive (By, 2005). It means change management should be planned and proactive and commence early on, when designing the new strategy or approach, rather than once the change is ready to be rolled out. It should be embedded within the fabric of the organization and be seen as the way the business works, rather than an add-on or an activity completed at a singular point in time. Successful change management is dependent on creating a need for change within all organization departments, planning the change and getting everyone engaged, understanding the role of customers, and improving communication within the organization (Aljohani, 2016).

Change management is not an easy process, as it requires great effort from leaders to encourage people to try new ways of working, new products or services, which may not be seen as necessary by employees when they cannot see the need for change or have experienced negative impacts and outcomes from past changes. Often, people are not willing to change unless there is a defect in the old way of working (Aljohani, 2016). It is the role of change leaders to inspire individuals to challenge the status quo, consider better ways of working, and share an image of the potential future (Bird, Lichtenau, and Michels, 2016).

For employees to recognize the need for a change and their role in this, they should realize that their job is not only the day job they are employed to do; they have another job which is improving their original position. Focusing on improving every individual's performance is a way of improving organizational performance (Marchant, 1999). Implementing a CI culture means that every employee should continuously improve himself as part of the organization. Altering the focus of incentives and appraisals from a financial-reward-based strategy to a system that assesses the skills, the development of those skills, and deficiency areas, in addition to focusing on intrinsic motivations, (Marchant, 1999) are ways to ensure that the employees understand and execute their two main jobs within a CI organization.

Every business aims to grow. However, this can only be achieved if the company invests in new products and services. Competition is real in today's business life, and to succeed, a company should develop new products and good quality. Therefore, every business's responsibility is to know what is in the market, create new products, or add a new feature to an existing product. Project management is required to properly plan, control, and organize these growth projects. Further, putting in place a project team well equipped with the necessary information about what they are supposed to do is what a company needs.

This book will explore a number of core lenses aligned to a clearly defined set of behaviors. Figure 1.3 shows the flow of the book as we walk through each potential lens with the defined behavioral frameworks as the center of this book, viewed specifically through each lens.

Figure 1.3   The book's structure of lens and definitions of ideal behaviors.

Summary

Overall, numerous CI programs have been developed over the years to enhance the efficiency of organizations. However, throughout the years, most companies have failed to develop a level of sustainability through which these programs can operate effectively. In this chapter, we have reviewed some of the reasons that lead to the failure of CI programs such as lack of motivation from the employees, poor communication, lack of experience from the team members and the manager, inadequate infrastructure, and so forth. From these failures, a need for CI of culture and the need to sustain it appear to be the first steps in promoting organizational efficiency.

Although numerous failures have been reported during the implementation of CI programs, it only shows that organizations have attempted to achieve particular outcomes that can promote success. Some of the attempts have failed while others have borne fruits. As a result, it becomes essential for organizations willing to try CI programs to learn from the failures and successes affiliated with them. Most significantly, the process would lead to a change, which makes it necessary for both leaders and employees to learn how to embrace and manage the transition process to achieve the goals of the organization. However, before this change is achieved, it would be essential to look at the desired behaviors that should be embraced for ideal results. The next chapter looks at these behaviors including how they can be integrated into the system with efficient leadership to accomplish the anticipated transformation.

Chapter 2

Introduction to Desired Behaviors

One of the authors was hired on by a luminescent printer manufacturer to improve quality. Their current failure rate was 13 percent, which caused them to overbuild everything by 20 percent. This seriously damaged capacity and resulted in a large, excessive, and often unusable finished goods inventory. Behaviors in the plant were fear-based. Floor employees were not comfortable with making changes on their own. All problems, even minor ones, were directed to supervisors and above to solve. Supervisors and managers were considered the harbingers of all knowledge. Employees' only function was to pump out parts. When the author was brought into the facility, the company was on the verge of being shut down. The author started by requiring an off-site conference of all leadership. During this meeting, he focused on the need to have a cultural and behavioral shift throughout the organization. He stressed that the only way to get this shift is by respecting the knowledge of the employees and by showing humility. Management needed to realize that the employees knew more about their functional roles than did management, and this understanding needed to be demonstrated to the employees via a change in management behavior.

Once the message of a change in management behavior was understood, the next step was to establish an organizational vision. They needed a set of goals that the organization could focus on. They needed a mission statement that the employees could relate to and understand. Something that would show how each individual fits into the big picture.

DOI: 10.4324/9781003224747-2

The next requirement of the author was that the leadership allowed him to train the employees on some of the basic concepts of lean including value stream mapping, 5S, Standard Work, quality at the source, and more. This process would take about 6 months. Then, the author wanted the company to shut down for 1 week during which time the employees would be allowed to make any changes throughout the production floor, including moving equipment, modifying equipment, modifying processes, etc. This week would be called Quality Week, and the only requirement would be that anything that was produced had to have zero defects.

The training proceeded as planned and Quality Week started. In the first 2 days of the week, nothing was produced. However, the employees went crazy, changing everything. They felt free. Their behavior changed from one of fear to one of empowered. They felt trusted, and they were committed to living up to the trust that they had been given. The look of the production floor changed dramatically.

By the third day, parts were slowly starting to be produced. By the fifth day, they were back into full production. The result of this shift in behaviors was a 2 percent defect rate (down from the original 13 percent), a 20 percent increase in capacity (no more overbuilds and time wasted on repairs), and finished good inventory eventually went to near zero. The author left the company, considering his job completed, but the improvements continued. After another 6 months, by maintaining this transformation in culture, this shift in behavior, and by maintaining this level of trust, the failure rate went down to one-half percent.

One may ask what behavior is and whether it differs from one company to the other. For us, behavior is what we say and do. Behavior is specific actions and reactions that occur in a pattern. It may come from a group of people, known as group behavior. It may also come from inanimate objects—the change or movement of this object (Lazzeri, 2014).

Behaviors are actions or reactions. People's behaviors inside an organization are their actions and responses to others' actions in relation to this organization. Karahanna, Evaristo, and Srite (2005) indicate that an organization's culture influences behavior. The Shingo Institute (2016) states that the behavior, including the principals, values, and system forming this behavior, defines the culture. From both approaches, we can note that behaviors and culture are interconnected concepts that influence each other.

Organizational culture is the real personality of the organization (Morcos, 2018). It is a result of how work is done (processes) and how people do the work (behaviors) (Morcos, 2018). In other words, the organization's culture is the set of behaviors and systems that determine the different interactions inside and outside the company about its business.

Often, a company's culture is implied, not expressly defined. It is fluid and needs time to grow (Morcos, 2018); it develops organically over time from people's cumulative behavior inside the company.

Organization's Core Behaviors

For organizations willing to continuously improve their performance and thus embrace a continuous improvement (CI) culture, they should be able to define and determine their ideal core behaviors. They need to keep behavior focused on the previously described principles and values and control it when needed (Morcos, 2018). The organization's core behaviors are determined through three levels: an individual's core behaviors, group behavior, and overall organization behavior (Bauer and Erdogan, 2012).

Although each level can be studied alone, they cannot be separated (George, 2014). It is because each of the three levels influences the other levels in one way or another. For example, an individual's behavior inside an organization is influenced by how the organization responds to their behavior. The behavior of the top managers and leaders determines organizational behavior as a whole.

Now that we know how culture affects behavior and how cumulative behavior contributes to forming a culture, it is essential to know why organizations should define their ideal core behaviors and how they can do this in a way that reflects their identity.

Why Define Core Behaviors?

Organizations have recognized the importance of determining their core values and principles as guides to behavior. Research shows that healthier organizations that perform better have strong organizational behavior characteristics (Bauer and Erdogan, 2012).

Whether they are commercial, nonprofit, or public sector, every organization has in common that it operates to get results. The difference is that results may represent profit, a return to shareholders, offering support to specific groups, or affecting people's lives in a certain way. In the past, managers have focused on technical performance and delivering results without much care for the human aspect until they understood the influence of human behavior on the outcome (Amah and Ahiauzu, 2013).

No matter what the results are, all of them require people to deliver them. Even though we see ever-increasing automation, there remains a significant dependency upon people in most organizations. Suppose we accept that results are the outcome of accumulated actions and behaviors of people. In that case, any leadership team's focus needs to drive its people to deliver the best results.

Research on how to drive people to do certain actions to produce specific results is vast. Different strategies and tactics can be employed to encourage result-driven behavior. Several approaches can be tried here. The first one is to use a controlled approach where a process is documented in such a level of detail that everyone can do something the same way, every time. This approach is more of an automated work process using human capital instead of machines. In this extreme, people do not need to think or make decisions. They have a set of rules and guidelines to follow and need to be told what to do in every new situation.

At the other extreme, another approach involves people as much as possible and gives them total freedom to do what they must do. This higher level of involvement gives employees more control over decision-making and the outcomes (Amah and Ahiauzu, 2013). It might sound fine and may well work in some environments, but it is likely to lead to many inefficiencies and an increased risk of something going wrong.

In between these two extremes is where people have a level of involvement and control in decision-making and directing their performance to achieve results. Setting general guidelines is a way to both control the outcomes and, at the same time, allow people to impose their way of doing things without going beyond those guidelines. Therefore, organizations need to define their ideal core behaviors for employees to follow as general guidelines in their everyday work.

The Ideal Core Behaviors

The Shingo Institute (2016) defined three insights for organizational excellence. These insights are summarized as:

- Ideal results of an organization are delivered by embedding "ideal behaviors."
- Behaviors are driven by systems and their purposes.
- Principles and values only guide the behaviors of people.

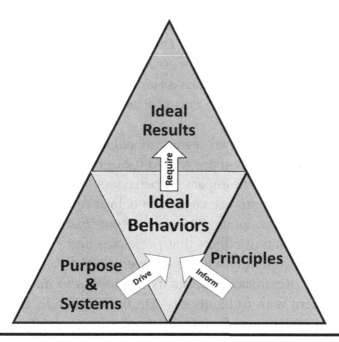

Figure 2.1   Three insights' interconnectedness.

Figure 2.1 illustrates the interconnectedness of these three insights with the behaviors as the core.

It is obvious now that for organizations to get ideal results, they need ideal behaviors. People's behavior can extend from small behaviors such as an employee deciding to show up to work on time to more extensive and effective behaviors such as forming a new partnership. To achieve ideal results, leaders must create a culture that embraces perfect behaviors. They act as role models of these required ideal behaviors and expect employees to behave in the same way (Shingo Institute, 2020).

A dictionary definition of principles is the fundamental foundations of a system, and values are the fundamental beliefs that determine a thing's importance. Both principles and values are foundational rules that are integrated into the company's personality (Gorenak and Košir, 2012). Thus, they not only guide but also direct people's behaviors. Consequently, they can influence an employee's performance and influence their relationships inside and outside the organization (Gorenak and Košir, 2012).

To understand an organization's ideal core behaviors, people working within the organization should deeply understand its values and principles. However, principles and values only cannot drive the behavior; they are guidance to the desired behavior. A well-defined organizational system and purpose are the real drivers (Shingo Institute, 2020).

An organizational system is a tool used to implement the strategy and achieve the organization's objectives (The RBL Group and Dave Hanna, 2013). These systems include the processes, the structure, hierarchy, rewards, and people (The RBL Group and Dave Hanna, 2013). Strategies that drive the behaviors here are the end-to-end processes, including all the previous elements.

According to system theory, an organizational system is how different elements inside the organization are related (Glaser and Halliday, 1980). Systems can have a significant impact on behaviors. Although they may be underestimated, most systems are created to deliver results without considering the behaviors they can encourage (Shingo Institute, 2020).

To illustrate the different effects that principles and systems have on a behavior, consider a company with "empowerment" as a core value. By empowerment, the organization wants its employees to make decisions and implement them with full authority. On the other side, the company has a risk-control system and financial power is in a specific department's hands. Therefore, in this case, employees are empowered according to the company's principles, but at the same time, the system will not let them act upon these principles. Thus, the behaviors here are driven by the system, not the values or principles.

In brief, having a set of defined corporate values informs behaviors, while systems designed for specific purposes drive the behaviors.

Now that we have discovered that an organization's ideal results are delivered by embedding "ideal behaviors," let us explore this first insight.

Ideal Results Require Ideal Behaviors

First, what are the ideal results? Results, as mentioned before, vary from one organization to another. Each organization can define its intended results in terms of economic profit or other indicators. However, the ideal results are different. While it is possible to get short-term financial results without exemplary behavior, excellent results are long-term achievements in various social, economic, and personal aspects.

According to the Shingo Institute model of excellence, results are among the four dimensions of operational excellence. Companies that wish to get sustainable results should link their behaviors, which will drive the results, to creating value for customers (Shingo Institute, 2020).

KPIs and KBIs

The quote is usually attributed to Peter Drucker, the brilliant management theorist: "What gets measured gets managed—even when it's pointless to measure and manage it, and even if it harms the purpose of the organization to do so." A bit of digging reveals, however, two surprising things.

A question that might arise here is how an organization can make sure it delivers the intended results. Traditionally, results are measured using key performance indicators (KPIs). KPIs are closely related to organizational performance (Bhatti, Awan, and Razaq, 2013) as they give insights about what has already happened and what needs to be changed. Organizations need to identify their KPIs to determine if they are going in the right direction toward achieving the organizational goals and objectives or not.

Different researchers study KPIs. Most of the studies tackling this area divided KPIs into financial-based and non-financial-based KPIs (Bhatti, Awan, and Razaq, 2013). These indicators measure customer satisfaction, quality, reliability, and other tangible results regarded before as sustainable results.

However, KPIs are not the only way to measure the achievement of ideal results. Since we are talking about behaviors and their impact on driving results, it is worth mentioning the key behavior indicators (KBIs). KBIs are indicators that measure employees' behaviors, such as motivation to work, commitment, proper communication, cooperation, and other characteristics that affect the work process (Cox, Issa, and Koblegard, 2005).

Therefore, both KPIs and KBIs are essential in measuring results, either financial or nonfinancial, for organizations that want to get the best outcomes and sustain their achievements over time.

One way of thinking about this is that using only KPIs is like trying to drive a car while only looking in the rear-view mirror (Hines and Butterworth, 2019). The concept of KBIs is not new, but they are often harder to define and measure than KPIs, as they tend to have a qualitative nature rather than a quantitative one. For example, how effective was the top managers' meeting rather than how many times they meet?

Leaders tend to focus a lot of their managerial effort on the outputs (what were the results today, this week, this month). Employees, by extension, focus more on these outputs as they are measured and assessed upon. For this, organizations may focus their improvement efforts on the systems to get better results. For example, reduce downtime in equipment, implement the improved flow of information or product, etc. These improvements are critical to driving continuous performance improvement, but they will be limited in success and sustainability if they are not grounded in ideal behaviors.

While KPIs are the outputs of the process, KBIs are the inputs. Using KBIs, organizations can manage the behaviors, provide a qualitative assessment of KPIs, and determine potential issues that may drive undesired behaviors (Hines and Butterworth, 2019).

Other measurement indicators are the key activity indicators (KAIs). These indicators are derived from the KPIs and KBIs; they are used to measure the activities performed to achieve the goals (Murata and Katayama, 2009). While KPIs measure the results of project improvement, KAIs are measurements used to accomplish the purpose of project improvement. Examples of KAIs are the number of training sessions and workshops on a specific tool or system for employees who will be using this tool and the number of employees who passed a particular training program.

Habit Formation

Habits are the automatic repeated behaviors in response to specific cues (Verplanken and Aarts, 2011). Past behaviors of people that were in response to a particular situation are not habits. For behaviors to become habits, they must be repeated numerous times and occur automatically (Verplanken and Aarts, 2011). As sustainable results are the outcomes of ideal behaviors, managers may be interested in creating sustainable behaviors or habits.

Understanding the science behind the brain, habits, and behaviors and how they are developed is essential to create the desired behaviors that develop into habits later on to achieve the desired ideal results.

According to Northwestern Medicine (2019), the brain is formed of billions of neurons. It develops from the backside to the frontal lobes. These frontal lobes are responsible for reasoning and planning. The full development of the brain is usually completed by the age of 25. The neurons of the brain can store unlimited information. Neurologists suggest that the number of neurons in a typical human brain is 86 billion neurons. These neurons form connections with each other leading to trillions of connections with a huge storage capacity.

Jones, Butterworth, and Harder (2018) mentioned in their book *4+1 Embedding a Culture of Continuous Improvement in Financial Services* the following five essential principles around the neuroscience of habit formation:

- A brain is a connection machine
- No two human brains are alike
- Constrained conscious processing capability
- The brain does not unlearn
- Stressed brains don't learn or listen

The human brain makes connections between things and situations influenced by each one's unique experiences and environment. The brain then creates reference frames where information is categorized. There is no natural way to remove or delete these categories. Each new data is processed in the brain's prefrontal cortex, and if repeated for a long time, the information takes its place in the preformed categories. People facing stressful situations cannot perform this process, so their ability to think or act upon their prior experience is reduced (Jones, Butterworth, and Harder, 2018).

It may now seem very easy for people to form habits. They repeatedly do the desired behavior, and the brain will automatically convert it into a routine. So why do people struggle to change bad behavior to a desired one to be a habit?

In addition to being responsible for habit formation and changing behaviors, the brain is also responsible for resisting the change. It is because our brains' first mission is to keep us safe (Jones, Butterworth, and Harder, 2018). Any changes may threaten the safety status the brain has created, so many people who are unaware of how the brain works may fall into this comfort zone and resist any changes.

Khera (2018) talks about the habit loop and how to break the loop using the 3 R's of forming a habit:

- Reminder: The trigger motivates a behavior or habit.
- Routine: We do the actual behavior in response to the trigger.
- Reward: What we get after we perform the behavior.

To form any new habit or get rid of a bad habit, one must break the loop (Khera, 2018). For example, when at work and a notification from Facebook or any social media app pops up, this is a reminder to check our social media accounts. We follow our routine of browsing the news feed and postpone the work we were doing. We are then rewarded with the sense of happiness and enjoyment we got from leaving our work and doing something more comfortable.

To change this habit, one must break the loop by avoiding using social media apps while working. The same thing applies when forming new habits; once we get a reminder to do our work, we should follow it, develop a routine, and are rewarded with the results.

Similarly, Gutierrez (2016) referred to the same habit cycles for forming new habits, but reminders do not always work the way we want. Gutierrez (2016) mentions another way of following reminders by tying the new practice with already developed procedures. For example, a team leader may link a new method of conducting a 10-minute meeting with his team every workday with an already developed habit of checking his e-mail every morning. This way, the new routine will follow the old one and goes into the loop.

Forbes (2018) mentioned some reasons for failing to form new habits despite following the 3 R's habit cycle. One of the reasons is forgetting to reward ourselves. Although work-related good habits may have a delayed ROI (return on investment), our brains need an immediate reward for positive deeds. A 10-minute break after an intense hour of work may be enough for our brains to move on with the new habit.

Building on the above principles and habit cycle, managers willing to induce desired behaviors and change them to habits can start by applying simple tools and setting applicable instructions with suitable rewards for implementing the new behavior until it becomes a habit for all the employees.

To sum up, if leaders require ideal results, they need to define and proactively manage ideal behaviors measured by KBIs. Behaviors can be transformed into habits and habits that reinforce behaviors (Jones, Butterworth, and Harder, 2018). Thus, creating a working environment that encourages and rewards desired behaviors and practices is crucial for getting the intended results. To do this, they need to ensure that the organization's purpose and systems directly drive and reinforce the ideal behaviors.

It leads us to the second insight of "Purpose and Systems drive behaviors."

Purpose and System Drive Behavior

The defined purpose of the system or team is the reason behind implementing a particular system and performing its processes. All too often, processes evolve in response to day-to-day tactical issues. So, how could a purpose and a network drive the behavior?

The Shingo Institute (2021) regards a system as "a collection of tools or tasks that are highly integrated to accomplish an outcome." Such a system:

■ Has a structure
■ Contains parts that are directly or indirectly related to each other
■ Have behaviors defined
■ Contains processes that fulfill their purpose
■ Has interconnectivity in terms of structure and behavior

Therefore, systems should have purposes. If a goal is defined, a system could be designed to fulfill this purpose. For example, in a call center, people's activities were managed every minute of the day, right down to how long they spent on toilet breaks. Deviations above the expected standard resulted in corrective conversations with their immediate supervisor. This system aimed to drive efficiency and increase output by controlling how people spent their time. However, it resulted in resentment, high staff turnover, and low morale as people felt they were not being respected and became disengaged. In this example, the system drove the wrong behaviors and led to the opposite result than that intended.

While this is an extreme example, it is quite common that the system unintentionally drives the wrong behavior. A personal example from one of the authors is given to illustrate this.

A large pub chain in the UK was offering a free pint of beer with every pie purchased. It seemed like too good a deal to miss, so I decided to take advantage of this as I worked away from home. I ordered my vegetarian pie and pint of beer to be told when my order was input to the system that vegetarian pies were out of stock. Declining the offer of beef or chicken pie, I asked what the vegetarian options on the menu were.

There was an excellent pasta dish that was 2 pounds more expensive than the pie, but I agreed to have that instead, as I was hungry. However, much to my surprise and the server's embarrassment, this meant I could not have a free pint of beer because that only came with pies!

The server called over the manager and asked him to override the system to have my free pie. His response was, "I'm sorry, but I'm not allowed to do that. I want to, but the system monitors our stock levels and matches pies' sales to free pints. If we give you a free pint without selling you a pie, we will have to explain the stock discrepancy to the area manager, and that's never a pleasant experience."

Realizing this was an example of a system driving behavior that people knew was wrong, but they could do nothing about (and feeling hungry and thirsty), I said "no worries" and paid for the pint and the pasta! After all, it was not their fault, and no one had deliberately designed the system to deliver a low customer and staff experience.

Designing a System

Systems can drive wrong behavior and things may go wrong, resulting in unintended consequences. If a process is poorly designed, it does not consider the purpose it was intended for. To solve this problem, people may try to find a way to work around the system instead of creating a new system. In this case, the system hinders and does not drive the ideal behavior. Another way to solve the problem is to redesign the system. Unless the newly redesigned system has a clear purpose and aim of reinforcing the ideal behaviors, the cycle will start all over again.

■ Designing an organizational system that works requires the following:
  – **Aligning the system with the strategies and objectives**

The organizational systems are developed to achieve the goals of the organization. Therefore, strategies and plans should be defined first, and methods are then derived from the process (The RBL Group and Dave Hanna, 2013).

Internal and External Relationships for a Well-Designed System

External relationships here include relations with customers, suppliers, and other stakeholders. These should be integrated into the system (Brethower, 2004). Going back to the RBL group definition of a system, internal relationships include the people of the organization who are a part of the system, and their interactions should be defined (The RBL Group and Dave Hanna, 2013).

Structures and Hierarchies

Organizational systems should have a way to operate. One organization may have different correlated systems. Therefore, the clearly defined structures of those systems allow them to work as a whole (Dominici, 2013). In this essence, redundancy (i.e., unused resources) is not a waste of resources commonly understood (Dominici, 2013). Organizational systems may need redundant processes and an established routine to speed up the processes and reduce errors (Edgeman, 2018) while creating internal resonance and integration among system parts (Dominici, 2013).

Defining a Purpose for the System

One of the most common reasons that systems do not deliver the intended outcomes is a failure to clearly define the purpose of that system. Even for a very well-designed system that does not have a clear sense, it may drive the intended results for some time, but it will fail eventually.

We recommend that every system should have a clearly defined purpose; otherwise, how can its effectiveness be assessed? Hines and Butterworth (2019) detailed four core systems necessary for organizations to sustain a culture of CI in the essence of excellence. An example of a purpose statement for one of these systems (learning and development) is given below.

Learning and development is a system that:

The what	Develops a learning culture and continuously develops its people aligned to the needs of the organization
The how	Identifying learning and development opportunities at all levels Focusing on the improvement of work competences, improvement competencies, and culture change competences Undertaking pull-based coaching to improve competence, performance, and culture Ensuring that learning and development competencies are embedded and lead to changes in behavior and tangible results Recognizing people for their learning achievements
The why	The whole organization maximizes its human potential, with the members taking the initiative

Integrating Behaviors into Systems

By now, we know that comprehensive systems drive desired behaviors. So, how can organizations integrate their ideal behaviors into their plans?

The first step is undoubtedly to set and define the ideal behaviors. Each organization should have its list of the perfect behavior clearly defined for all the organization's people.

Once these have been established, the following approaches can be used to integrate systems and behaviors.

Step 1: Identify Critical Business Systems

As mentioned before, organizations may have different systems for different business processes. Each process is composed of activities performed to respond to a particular event and add a specific value to one or more of the stakeholders (Kaniški and Vincek, 2018; Edgeman, 2018). All of the organizational systems with the processes, activities, and people involved should be identified.

Step 2: Prioritize Which System(s) Need to Be Addressed First

In some cases, it is impossible to start implementing all the systems at the same time. Therefore, it is advisable to choose the ones that will have the most significant impact on strategic goals or the ones that need immediate solutions.

Step 3: Agree on a Purpose Statement for Priority Systems

As systems perform multiple processes that may be aligned or work at cross-purposes (Edgeman, 2018), it is essential to solely define the purpose of each course.

Step 4: Agree on a High-Level System Map

A system's map defines how it should work. Their importance lies in unifying the approaches to implementing procedures and avoiding any misalignment resulting from different perspectives.

Step 5: Agree on KPIs and Targets for Each System

Once systems are established and how they should be implemented is defined, there must be a way to measure their success. KPIs and KAIs can help to determine whether the system is working well or not.

Step 6: Use Value Stream Mapping (VSM) If Applicable

If useful at this stage, a VSM activity is undertaken on the system. A VSM is used to analyze the material and information flow to eliminate waste and improve the workflow (Muniyappa et al., 2014). It is not about collecting data, as data alone is useless unless it is transformed into insightful information (Brethower, 2004). For newly implemented systems, this step may not be of importance now.

Step 7: Use the Behavioral Deployment Process

In this step, people already know the expected behaviors and have a system that encourages this behavior. Now, they just need to use the system to define how they will behave at a local level to ensure that the system is driving the predetermined ideal behaviors.

Step 8: Get Feedback

As KPIs and KAIs give insights about the system, KBIs can provide feedback and assess the behaviors (Hines and Butterworth, 2019). Setting a structured way of measuring KBIs and getting feedback is necessary to know if the system supports all the ideal behaviors or a particular behavior the system is not helping.

Step 9: Refine the System

Finally, it is essential to use the feedback received in the previous step by ensuring that there is a corrective action process to refine the system driven by the input continually.

In summary, systems and behaviors can be seen as two sides of the same coin. Methods alone cannot lead to ideal results. They may give short-term results, but they will decay over time. On the other hand, good behaviors with low systems will waste resources, energy, and time. Thus, good behaviors driven by well-designed systems lead to a mutually reinforcing feedback loop where systems and behavior support each other and enable further improvement.

To clearly understand the ideal core behaviors, there must be guidance or informant to better understanding. It leads us to the third insight, "principles inform ideal behavior."

Principles Inform Ideal Behavior

Defining the ideal behaviors and creating a system that drives these behaviors are essential for superior results. However, there must be a base to start from, a common ground that managers and leaders of the organization agree on to move toward defining their ideal behaviors. Many organizations already have company values. These, along with principles, can act as the foundations for describing the ideal behaviors to be tangible and observed.

The Shingo Institute model has developed a set of guiding principles to inform and guide the ideal behaviors (Shingo Institute, 2021). These principles are categorized into three dimensions: cultural enablers, continuous improvement, and enterprise alignment.

Cultural Enablers

Cultural enablers consist of two principles that focus on the people of the organization.

Respect Every Individual

The principle of respect for every individual is a broad one that includes several meanings. The Shingo Institute's definition of respect for every individual shows respect to all stakeholders, starting from the employees to the customers, suppliers, and the community as a whole.

Respect is usually the first and top value employees seek from their jobs (Quaquebeke, Zenker, and Eckloff, 2009). It is not about being nice to each other and creating a cozy, working environment where there are no challenges or work pressure. Respect is about providing adequate tools and a suitable working environment for people.

Rogers and Ashforth (2014) defined two types of respect in organizations: general respect, which means that "we" are respected and valued inside the organization, and individual respect, which is the sense that "me" is respected and valued for the particular efforts and achievements.

The two dimensions of respect—general and individual respect— are related to one another. Creating a general respect climate within the organization encourages sending and receiving respect between individuals (Rogers and Ashforth, 2014). Furthermore, respect reinforces the sense of belonging to the organizations, which leads to positive outcomes and increases the collaboration between the employees (Edmondson, 2003).

Examples of behaviors associated with the respective principle are given below:

Respect every individual	Example behavior
Leader	Leads by personally demonstrating respect in all interactions
Manager	Actively listens to all team members and acts on their input
Associate	Ensures that any safety concerns are highlighted immediately

Lead with Humility

Leading with humility means the willingness to listen and acknowledge the vulnerabilities to learn from others. Karmes (2014), lead with humility, emphasized the importance of leading with humility as the first lesson learned from Pope Francis. He mentioned that leadership is not about perfection, it is about inclusion, communication, listening, and counseling to spot mistakes and get everyone involved in learning and developing themselves from these mistakes.

Prime and Salib (2014) also mentioned that employees who perceived their leaders to show acts of humility, such as admitting their mistakes and learning from them, had more space to create and innovate. They showed more engagement and willingness to contribute.

Leading with humility required leaders to admit mistakes and share them with their employees as lessons to learn from. This will encourage the employees to learn and develop from their own mistakes (Prime and Salib, 2014).

Examples of behaviors associated with the lead with humility principle are given below:

Lead with humility	Example behavior
Leader	Publicly recognizes leaders and managers who act with humility
Manager	Actively seeks knowledge and suggestions from their team
Associate	Actively seeks opportunities to learn from colleagues and associates

Continuous Improvement

The second dimension of Shingo's principles is the CI principles. They include the following five constituting principles.

Focus on Process

The business process in an organization is the process or processes by which the organization deploys, monitors, reviews, develops, and redevelops its strategy over time (Acur and Bititci, 1999). This definition indicates that the business process is ever dynamic, one of the CI features.

All business activities and their outcomes are the result of a process or more. In any organization, changes may occur that require a difference in the process. It is a natural thing, but more often, organizations respond to these individual changes without addressing the process from the beginning. Thus, repeated issues occur every time.

A vital aspect of the focus on process principle is to focus on the "how" not the "who." It will result in structured processes that everyone can follow, and chances of making mistakes are minimized.

By focusing on the process, organizations can make the required changes to the processes whenever necessary. The focus here is on the process itself, not on people. In other words, it does not matter who is responsible for performing certain business operations or procedures. As long as they acquire the needed knowledge, they can follow the process.

Examples of behaviors associated with the focus on process principle are given below:

Focus on process	Example behavior
Leader	Encourage and ensure that there is an open and honest dialogue about mistakes
Manager	Publicly thank people for highlighting when a process allows a mistake to occur
Associate	Highlight any mistakes immediately

Embrace Scientific Thinking

Scientific thinking is about reasoning. The reasoning is to draw inductions, deductions, causal relationships, testing, and experimenting from concepts (Dunbar and Klahr, 2012). Scientific thinking is applied to almost every situation in our life at different levels. People practice scientific thinking in their everyday life (Dunbar and Klahr, 2012).

Applying this principle to organizations, managers and leaders should manage with facts, not opinions. Organizations should embrace scientific thinking by encouraging a behavior of finding the reasons behind everything before jumping directly to the solutions.

Another aspect of scientific thinking is generalizing this principle to all organizational levels, not only managers and leaders. All principles should be generalized, but scientific thinking, in particular, is closely related to risk-taking behavior. With scientific thinking, employees can think appropriately in work-related problems and consequently develop a risk-taking behavior.

Examples of behaviors associated with the embrace of scientific thinking principle are given below:

Focus on process	Example behavior
Leader	Frequently celebrate successes around the application of problem-solving tools
Manager	Lead by example and coach in the application of structured problem solving
Associate	Understand and deepen their knowledge of structured problem-solving tools through frequent application

Pull and Flow Value

Pull and push are terms used to describe the flow of services and products in the market. Pull means offering products, goods, and services based on the customers' demand (Minculete and Olar, 2016). Pull systems are effective in reducing waste as much as possible because they supply the demand only.

Flow and pull value is usually seen as applicable in the manufacturing industry only, but actually, it can be applied in different ways. Flow and pull value as a CI principle means creating value for customers based on their demands and understanding the flow of this value until it reaches customers.

Examples of behaviors associated with the pull and flow value principle are given below:

Pull and flow value	Example behavior
Leader	Engage in frequent conversation with people at all levels to understand what might be interrupting the flow of customer value
Manager	Demonstrate a deep understanding of flow and pull and how they can be applied in their area
Associate	Always look for ways to reduce waste in their process

Assure Quality at the Source

Many business procedures have errors. They may be errors in the process, transportation or storage of goods, data collecting and analysis, and decisions based on these elements. The importance of quality assurance is to determine a framework to minimize these errors as much as possible (Ambrus and Suszter, 2019).

Quality assurance is different from quality inspection. Quality inspection compares products to the predetermined framework and requirements (Kurniatia, Yehb, and Linc, 2015), while quality assurance is ensuring that every need is met in every step. Therefore, ensuring quality at the source is the principle to be followed here to reduce waste and improve the business instead of inspection, which does not add any value. Quality at source means assuring every step and every process from the beginning is of the highest quality standards. Doing this prevents errors and minimizes mistakes at every step.

Examples of behaviors associated with the assure quality at source principle are given below:

Assure quality at the source	Example behavior
Leader	Through everyday conversations, actively encourage the use of prevention rather than inspection
Manager	Ensure that systems are in place and operating well to highlight problems and resolve them promptly
Associate	Never knowingly accept, make, or pass on a defect

Seek Perfection

While perfection is impossible in every life aspect, the keyword here is "seek." Organizations should always strive to be perfect. This principle gives a sense of continuity, as trying to be perfect is a never-ending process. However, seeking perfection may hinder the improvement process in some cases. Organizations may prefer to wait for the perfect moment and ideal situations to start their CI. This perfect moment will never come.

The same thing applies on the individual level. Managers and employees who are seeking perfectionism may work hard and strive to find better ways for improving their performance, or they might fall into the "dark side" of perfectionism as no one will be able to reach the ultimate perfect state ever (Beheshtifar, Mazrae-Sefidi, and Moghadam, 2011).

Perfection is about challenging the status quo and having the courage to try new ways of doing things. The key here is to accept the fact that there is no ultimate perfect solution. There will always be room for refining. Therefore, we preferably say countermeasures, not solutions, as solutions imply no improvement is needed again.

Examples of behaviors associated with the seek perfection principle are given below:

Seek perfection	Example behavior
Leader	Proactively encourage people to challenge the status quo and publicly celebrate when they do
Manager	Ensure that systems are in place and effectively used that encourage new ideas and manage them in a timely and effective manner
Associate	Always challenge if there is a better way (more straightforward, faster, safer) to carry out their tasks

Enterprise Alignment

The last dimension of Shingo's principles is the enterprise alignment dimension, which includes three principles.

Create Value for the Customer

Most businesses have a goal of creating a customer and keeping them (Singh, 2011). Customers tend to deal with those whom they feel offer added value for them. Therefore, a deep understanding of what the customer values and how to create a benefit is critical to organizational excellence.

Value creation is done through several steps. The first is choosing the value based on a deep understanding of the customers' needs and then providing this value through developing and improving the offered goods and services. Finally, this value should be communicated to the customer through advertising and promotion methods (Singh, 2011).

Customers are now more educated and can understand whether a particular business provider offers a real value for them (Singh, 2011). Organizations that try to improve their products and services without understanding what the customers need are at risk of making the wrong changes. They may either add a value that customers do not need or remove something that customers valued.

The table below gives some examples of behaviors associated with creating value for the customer principle.

Create value for the customer	Example behavior
Leader	Ensures that what the customer values is embedded in all decision making
Manager	Always ensures that their team understands how their actions relate to what the customer values
Associate	Uses what the customer values to inform decisions and priorities

Create Constancy of Purpose

Systems should have purposes. Keeping these purposes constant is the challenge here. Creating constancy of purpose is about communicating a clear intent to all involved parties and keeping everyone and every operation aligned to this purpose. The endurance of purpose helps allocate resources and work on the long-term results rather than short-term profits (Deming, 2000).

The principle of creating constancy of purpose in an organization resembles rowing a boat to a specific destination. All the crew of the boat is looking forward to the same goal. If any of the crew decided to row in the opposite direction, he might not change the boat's direction, but he will undoubtedly make it more difficult for the other members to reach the goal.

However, constancy does not mean priorities will never change. The principle is here to avoid confusion between employees. Purposes remain constant, but priorities and objectives vary from time to time.

The table below gives some examples of behaviors associated with the create constancy of purpose principle.

Create constancy of purpose	Example behavior
Leader	Frequently communicate and reinforce a clear and common purpose
Manager	Demonstrate actions that ensure that the purpose is understood and deployed to all team members
Associate	Always discuss the purpose at the start of team meetings

Think Systemically

While constancy of purpose focuses on the organization's vertical alignment, the principle of thinking systemically focuses more on the horizontal alignment. Think systemically means thinking about the whole system instead of thinking about individual departments or focusing on certain performances.

Daryani, Ali, and Asli-zadeh (2012) mentioned the following three steps to think systemically when solving a problem:

■ Identifying the whole system that has the problem and detecting this problem.
■ Investigating the behaviors and features of the whole system to find out the reason for the problem.
■ Analyzing the system's behaviors or features that cause the problem with other parts or functions of the system.

An example to clarify the above three steps is to change KPIs and bonuses from rewarding individual or departmental performance to rewarding the whole business performance and collaboration. This way, all people of the organization will work together and function as a connected system.

The table below gives some examples of behaviors associated with the think systemically principle.

Think systemically	Example behavior
Leader	Proactively encourage collaboration across departmental boundaries
Manager	Always focus on optimizing the end-to-end process, not their department
Associate	Understand how their role contributes to the end-to-end process and seek to optimize the whole

To sum up, values and principles are the foundation of and guidance to ideal behaviors, while systems drive these behaviors. The Shingo Institute developed a behavioral-based approach toward enterprise excellence. The process is based on all the above-discussed elements:

■ Ten guiding principles
■ Systems with clear purposes

■ Set of tools to implement the systems
■ Culture is influenced by behaviors informed by principles and driven by systems
■ All these elements will give sustainable results

Risk-Taking Mindset and Behavior

Operational excellence and organizational improvement require an ideal risk-taking behavior. Risk-taking behavior can take a potential risk decision and accept challenges for possible positive consequences in a situation where adverse effects are expected (Jung, Kang, and Choi, 2020).

The ideal risk-taking behavior is different from one organization to the other, but different results are obtained according to the risk-taking mindset in all organizations. An organization that encourages risk-taking behavior has more committed employees than organizations with a fear culture mindset (Jung, Kang, and Choi, 2020). Furthermore, risk-taking behavior encourages organizational changes and improvements. Thus, it is critical to a CI culture (Jung, Kang, and Choi, 2020).

Giulioni (2015) talks about the following four steps to foster ideal risk-taking behaviors between the employees:

Modeling: Give employees a model for ideal risk-taking behavior. This should not be a hypothetical model, but leaders and managers should apply this model themselves first. Besides, managers should be transparent about the outcomes of any implemented risk-taking behavior.

Enabling giving examples is not enough. Employees should have adequate tools and authority needed to undertake risk-taking behaviors. An authority without the necessary information will lead to wrong decisions. Enabling provides employees with the required information, authority, and tools to practice ideal behavior.

Support: New behaviors need support. In an organization where risk taking is a new behavior, support is required from all managerial levels. There will be times that the behavior will not result in the intended outcomes, but the more that behavior is driven to ideal practices, the more it will drive superior results.

Consistency: Consistency is required from leaders and managers to support ideal behavior. They cannot encourage the behavior in one situation and refuse or prevent it in another situation. As long as the behavior is practiced in the ideal way guided by the related principles and driven by the system, it should be encouraged all the time.

Organizations need risk-taking mindsets to get ideal results. Risk takers believe in the unlimited possibilities and are ready for the challenge (Richmond, 2020). Organizations that truly look forward to CI and change will support those kinds of mindsets to achieve remarkable outcomes.

Anatomy of Key Indicators (KPIs, KBIs, and KAIs)

Here is a simple anatomy guide for building up key indicators

$$\{\mathbf{Unit}\} + \{\mathbf{Behavior}\} + \{\mathbf{Population}\} + \{\mathbf{Timing}\}$$

Applying this for key indicators for an example of recruiting employees

KPI	% of first offer accepted from all offers per month
	{%} + {first offer accepted} from { all offers} {per month}
KBI$_1$	% of questions answered/or clarified leading to first offer acceptance within 3 days
	{%} + {questions answered/clarified} leading to {first offer acceptance} {within 3 days}
KBI$_2$	% of positive experience/treated with respect responses during the recruitment process to first offer acceptance per month
	{%} + {positive experience/treated with respect} during the {recruitment process to first offer acceptance} {per month}
KAI	% of planned offers issued today on plan
	{%} + {of planned offers} + {issued today on plan}

Summary

Every organization requires its employees to behave in a particular way the management thinks is the best for organizational success. This chapter brings out the concept of organizational culture by explaining the core behaviors of a company. It is deduced that in order for an organization to succeed, it must base its operations on ideal set of behaviors that define its culture. This is measured through KPI and KBI. Both the indicators are essential to an organization aiming to achieve positive results from a successful implementation of change. In other words, a good behavior is likely to show that employees are committed to their work and motivated, thereby leading to high organizational performance.

Apart from KPIs and KBIs, this chapter highlights KAIs as a measure of behavioral transition. From the employees' activities, it can be easy to know whether they would welcome a behavioral change or not. As a result, it is significant for organizations to develop systems that would lead to a successful implementation of organizational behavior. This system should have a layout that effectively integrates the required organizational behavior. As this happens, leaders are also advised on the path they should follow to ensure that they have appropriate principles that inform ideal behavior. Most ideally, it should be noted that a new culture in an organization comes with numerous challenges. In such a context, both the leaders and employees should have a risk-taking mindset and behavior as these make it possible to achieve remarkable outcomes. The next chapter presents a case study of CI in financial services using Suncorp Group from the perspective of a business improvement program the management adopted. The need for a particular set of behavior and culture seems imminent in this chapter in relation to achieving ideal results.

Chapter 3

Change Management

It has been said that there are two types of companies:

1. Those that are trying to achieve excellence.
2. Those that are too busy fighting fires to be bothered with excellence.

The question that each company needs to ask themselves is, which one are they.

The importance of holistic change management approach tools is fundamental to maintaining a sustainable improvement program. One of the authors was invited to a plant in Malaysia where they rebuilt alternators and starters for the United States auto market. The plant manager was struggling. He explained, "My competition, just down the street, has about the same number of employees, doing the same type of work, but they have about three times the output that we have in this plant. My employees work just as hard as theirs. Can you help me understand the difference?"

The author answered, "Let's go out on the production floor and observe what is happening." He took the plant manager out on the production floor where they performed a Gemba or "go and observe" exercise. They stopped at one workstation and the author advised, "Let us watch this person work. Let us pay attention to what they do and how they do it. And as we watch, let us time how much time they spend actually working on the product in proportion to how much time they spend moving the product around, doing setup, doing cleanup, etc." What the author was doing was teaching the principle of value-added vs. non-value-added time and the concept of waste, basic tools of change management.

DOI: 10.4324/9781003224747-3

After about 30 minutes of observation, the plant manager excitedly stated, "I get it. These people are working hard, but they are doing busywork. They are not creating value. I need to reorganize their work so they spend more time creating value and less time on non-value-added activities."

"Exactly," responded the author. "And who do you think would be the best at helping reorganize the work?"

The plant manager thought for a few seconds and then stated, "Why the employees, of course. I need to get them thinking about how best to improve their work. I need them to understand what you just taught me. They can fix the problem themselves if they know what to watch out for."

In this example, the plant was so inefficient that a basic understanding of tools was critical. This shop needed to understand and implement tools like 5S, Standard work, Gemba, etc., even before it was ready to work on higher-level concepts like the Shingo Principles. This plant needed to literally "get off the ground" before it could successfully achieve a cultural transformation. However, understanding that the employees were the best source of information about how to make these improvements was also a critical insight and is a start down the road toward a change management transformation.

In recent years, most organizations have started to adopt one of the continuous improvement programs such as Lean, Six Sigma, or Agile in an effort to build their ability to rapidly respond to change and build competitive advantage. Each of these programs has its strengths and proves its success in one or more business areas. However, they did not deliver the overall desired outcome, which is continuous improvement. Agile and lean programs deliver positive results, but they fail to reach the end goal of operational excellence.

Although these programs can deliver financial outcomes and an initial uplift in performance, two significant problems exist when applying these programs. The first is the tool approach these programs advocate, and the second is focusing on the performance more than focusing on people. These two problems are described by Hines and Jekiel (2021) as the disconnected bridge.

The Disconnected Bridge

Assume that a whole organizational department and their attempts to improve these departments lie on two opposite sides of a bridge. The left-handed side has the companies' traditional department quality, engineering, information technology, and others. In contrast, the right-handed side has the human resource management, health and safety, and organizational development departments. Most attempts to improve the bridge's left side are known as continuous improvement programs such as lean, sigma, and agile. Simultaneously, attempts to improve the other side of the bridge are employee development, culture initiatives, and leadership improvement.

The problem is that both attempts are separated from each other. While lean and similar programs work very well on improving quality or IT departments, the right side of the bridge is often working separately from the goals of lean and other continuous improvement attempts. Thus, the result is a program with short-term effects without a change in the culture, which is the critical lever to sustain the improvement over time. It is what Hines and Jekiel (2021) described as the disconnected bridge. A detailed look at this issue is given in the following.

Systematic Approach Rather Than Tool-Based Approach

Organizations that wish to achieve a sustainable continuous improvement strategy should move from a tool-based approach to a systematic approach. A tool-based approach is that adopted by many organizations, such as lean, sigma, and agile. The problem is not with the tool itself. It is with how the tool is applied. Organizations take the same tool and apply it at several levels by developing a whole system to work with different tools in different conditions. Developing a system will be discussed later in this chapter.

The same is true for the people's side! Often change management is confused with communication. A varied and situational communications plan is a critically important component of any change management strategy, but it is only one suite of tools in the change manager's toolkit. Sponsorship, active listening, measurement and analysis, collaboration and facilitation, training, coaching and mentoring, and rewards and recognition are some of the other critical components for sustainable change. Each of these then has multiple tools and techniques that should be selected to align to the technical framework and to the level of the organization being targeted.

Emphasis on People and Culture

Caring too much about the tools and system without considering people is a technical approach to solve problems. George Eckes (2007) put forward the relative importance of the technical and people sides in his equation:

$$\textbf{Success} = \textbf{Quality} \times \textbf{Acceptance}$$

This simple equation highlights that, without people accepting (and being proficient in) the new way of working, even the best planned and highest quality deployment of tools and systems will fail to deliver a successful and sustainable outcome. A change management practitioner colleague once asked a senior leadership team, who were debating the merits and cost of change management, to quantify the expected financial return for their lean deployment. On receiving the dollar value, he then asked what % of this was dependent on people adopting and using the new ways of working (the outcomes of effective change management). The amount dependent on adoption and usage far exceeded the investment required for change management—this is true of most high-value organizational-wide transformation projects.

Organizations should move from this technical approach to a cultural one where people are the main improvement component, and the tools they apply are secondary to the desire to improve and the general "know how." Engaging and improving people should be aligned with the organizational improvement approaches. Every "hard" technical tool used must be accompanied by "softer" engagement and development tools if we are to be successful in developing the desired behaviors, and thereby, delivering the right results at all levels of the organization.

Change Management Methodologies

Change is not a one-step process that occurs once the decision is made. For businesses to change, they must follow a change management methodology. Different change management models have been executed by organizations, all of them sharing the same goal of improving the organization's outcomes.

Without a consistent and effective change management methodology, organizations are unable to guide priorities, decision-making, and performance management or effectively mitigate impacts on their people. Lack of a common language, inconsistent approaches, and limited measurement and tracking of outcomes have a detrimental effect on change initiatives. Research by Prosci (2022b) demonstrates that organizations that use a disciplined approach to change management are 6× more successful in their deployment. A poorly executed change strategy can also impact overall organizational change capacity in the long term because learning and experience are not easily shared. Reoccurring inappropriate behaviors or negative outcomes can undermine an organization's confidence in its ability to implement new initiatives while building a legacy of failed changes in the organization. High levels of cynicism arise, which are then difficult to dispel (Change Synergy, 2016).

ADKAR Model

Jeffery Hiatt, the founder of Prosci, created the ADKAR model. This model provides five building blocks that each individual, impacted by the change, needs to navigate, in sequence, for a change initiative to be successful:

- Awareness (of the organizational reasons to change the current situation)
- Desire (to personally participate in the change)
- Knowledge (of how to work in the future state)
- Ability (becoming proficient in the new ways of working)
- Reinforcement (to sustain the new ways of working)

The ADKAR model focuses on successfully changing the individuals of the organization leading to cumulative change in the organization. The model assumes that organizations are not capable of change but that people are (Hiatt, 2006).

The 2022 Prosci Change Framework is divided into three phases.

Stage 1: Prepare Approach

Through the use of proprietary tools and assessments, this phase focuses on assessing the current state and developing a change strategy that will bring each individual, impacted by the change, successfully through the ADKAR model.

Stage 2: Transition

To move from the current situation to a desirable future one, the organization must pass through a transition phase. This is where the change efforts are applied and their effect will be assessed in the next stage. Elements of this stage are knowledge and ability.

Knowledge

Desire is not enough to implement a real change. People must have knowledge of how to implement this change. Knowledge here is generalized to apply to all sponsors of change and other people who will be supporting the change.

Ability

This is the ability to practically use this knowledge to undertake the required change. The change can be behavioral or a simple change in the system or tools. In both cases, people in the organization should have the ability, supported by their knowledge, to undertake the change.

Stage 3: Future

This is the final stage of change, which is always overlooked (Prosci, 2021a). This stage involves sustaining the change. The future stage has only one element, which is reinforcing the change.

Reinforcement

Reinforcing is undertaken by measuring the effectiveness of the implemented change and assessing its success on different levels. Then, organizations have to act accordingly and decide to either reinforce the current efforts or apply corrective plans.

The successful application of the above five elements on the individual level first determines the ability of the organization to change. Therefore, this model is actually a link between individual change management and organizational change management (Hiatt, 2006).

Mckinsey 7-S Model

This model is based on the seven aspects of an organization that should be considered for any change. Mckinsey's model looks at the interrelated factors that affect the change efforts of any organization. The elements of the framework as described by Mckinsey (2008) are the following.

Style

Style is sometimes interchanged with culture. It is simply about how the organization is managed and what leadership styles are used. Style is the pipeline through which communication and processes flow from the top-level managers to the employees.

Skills

This refers to the skills of the employees and what they can do for the organization. The skills of the current employees should be assessed and compared to the skills needed to implement the strategy. Skills are also both the individual skills and the collective skills of different teams and how they work together.

Systems

Systems are the overall processes of the organization including, for example, the HR processes and the finance and management systems. The level of integration between these systems should be assessed as well.

Structure

How is the organization structured? What are the authority relationships underlying each system? How do different managers manage their teams in the structure of the organization? These are all questions that need answers when analyzing the organization for change using the 7-S framework.

Staff

Staff is the most important part of the organization. They are the people who will do the change. This is the talent and the skill that they bring to the organization. The number of staff in the organization is important to consider, but more important is whether they fulfill the needed skill sets.

Strategy

The strategy of any organization starts with the objectives that the organization is striving to achieve and then moves to the efforts being exerted to reach those objectives. Further, the strategy of the organization includes what it does to stand out from its peers and stay competitive.

Shared Values

What is the organization trying to achieve as general goals? What are the general values that the organization is always adhering to? These do not usually change much over time. However, any change in the organization should always be linked to the organization's values so that the change is relatable to everyone working in the organization.

Mckinsey's framework for change management can be implemented in four steps (Kocaoglu and Demir, 2019).

First, analyze and identify the above seven elements, answer all the related questions, and then clearly identify the deficiencies of each element.

Second, define the change needed for each of the elements and what the organization aims to achieve. The relationship between each of the seven elements and how they affect each other should also be considered when identifying desirable outcomes.

Third, create an action plan to move from the first step to the second one in relation to the desired outcomes. Action plans should be realistic and suit the desired outcomes.

Fourth, restructure the organization according to the created action plan. Here, restructuring does not mean changing hierarchies or changing leaders (although this may be needed as part of the change). It means a whole restructuring of the process, the system, the staff, and whatever other elements that need restructuring to achieve the change.

Kotter's Theory (Including Accelerate)

Kotter's theory of change comprises eight elements. The primary benefit of this theory is that it focuses on people as the main drivers of change. The eight elements of the model are (Kotterinc, 2021) the following.

Create a Sense of Urgency

Similarly to the ADKAR model of change, Kotter's theory starts by making people aware of the need for change. The theory not only focuses on the necessity of the change but also on its immediacy.

Build a Guiding Coalition

These are the initiators of the change. The group of people who will lead the change and urge others to change as well. These people need to have leadership skills and be able to communicate the change to other organizational members.

Form a Strategic Vision and Initiatives

The vision should be clear from the beginning to all participants in the change. Everyone who will support and act for the change should know where they are going and why they are doing this. Thus, every change action should be related to the vision of the company.

Enlist a Volunteer Army

After the vision is clear for all, everyone should be engaged in the change. This step is about creating communication channels between managers, leaders, and employees to promote the change and receive feedback about this change.

Enable Action by Removing Barriers

Barriers can be communication barriers, deficiencies in the systems or staff, inefficient tools, or any other defects in the process. Those barriers should be analyzed and reduced as much as possible to eliminate anything that could hinder the change process.

Generate Short-Term Wins

Change is an on-going process that usually takes a very long time. The motivation for change that employees may show at the beginning will not last forever. Therefore, there must be some kind of motivator every now and then along the journey. These are the short-term wins.

Sustain Acceleration

Sudden major changes that do not last are not something to celebrate. The idea is to sustain the change and not just achieve it for the first time and that is it. Sustaining acceleration is achieved through the continuous assessment and improvement of each effort. Thus, change becomes a habit for people.

Institute Change

Finally, if we want the change to become a habit, connections between the changed behaviors and organizational success should be established.

Change is not made for the sake of change; it is implemented because it leads to real success.

The current change management methodologies, whether ADKAR, Kotter's theory, or the Mckinsey 7-S model, focus on one thing, that is, how to apply and later comply with the methodology itself. Although these frameworks consider people in their application, they do not focus on behavior. For example, ADKAR methodology focuses on creating the desire needed for change. It further insists on having the proper knowledge and ability to implement the change. However, a sustainable change is not guaranteed, as people's behavior is not addressed.

Similarly, Mckinsey's 7-S model includes restructuring the people of the organization but in a manner that suits the newly adopted system. Permanent behavior change is not necessary to adopt this method. One can tailor it sufficiently to suit the new system to drive short-term results. In addition, for Kotter's theory, the focus is on people, but again change is connected to the systems and tools implemented not to change the behaviors of people.

Thus, having a change management model that addresses both the tool and behaviors at the same time is the key. The proposed model should focus on not only changing people's behaviors but also sustaining this change. It should be able to define the behaviors needed when the change methodology is already implemented.

TFSD Model

According to Rudd (2020), the TFSD model is a map divided into four parts: think, feel, say, and do. These maps can help managers or leaders capture the employees' behaviors and discover how they think, feel, say, and do.

Think

Think is about describing what is in the minds of the employees. What do they think of the work environment; what are their ideas about development? What are their goals, and what do they need from the job?

Knowing the thoughts of employees can help find ways to change their behaviors and thoughts to suit the continuous improvement strategies of the organization. Moreover, their thoughts will give ideas for improving the business as well.

Feel

Feelings are the emotions that employees have for the organization. What do they like and dislike? What do they feel about work? In addition, what motivates them more?

Knowing how employees feel will allow organizations to make the changes and adjustments needed to motivate employees more and manage the changes made for improvement.

Say

Say is the reflection of thinking and feeling. What employees say is usually what they feel or think. However, sometimes there might be employees who say something different from what they feel or think. However, this is not the case most of the time. When employees feel they have the space to say whatever they feel or think, this will allow the leaders and managers to know exactly what needs changing.

Do

Finally, do is the result of feeling, thinking, and doing. What are the employees doing every day at work? What are they excelling at? What are they capable of doing and what are they not? How do their actions affect the organization?

The TFSD model can be the initial step toward change and change management. The TFSD model helps to perfect the situation in the organization and, more importantly, focuses on people rather than performance (Stormboard, 2021).

The TF part (think and feel) drives the behavior. Knowing how others think and feel can determine their future behavior. In contrast, the SD part (say and do) is the actual behavior. Therefore, the TFSD model is a comprehensive model to adopt for successful and, more importantly, sustainable change management.

For successful implementation of change management, one should consider having models of principles and tools that are technically suitable for the organization but culturally strong. Organizations should focus on and utilize people's abilities. This is an excellent opportunity to deliver the required results. Thus, there must be a certain department or section within the organization to regulate this. This is usually known as the human resource management (HRM) department. HRM has a significant role in this essence.

HRM Role in Continuous Improvement

The human resources department should be regarded as a business partner whose job is to help other departments develop and improve continuously (Benders, 2011). To do this, HRM should work together with other organizational efforts toward the same business goals.

HRM's role in continuous improvement, as mentioned by Hines and Jekiel (2021), is to drive employees and people in the organization to be able to:

Know the organization's strategies and tools and align their efforts with the organization's objectives and goals.

Know how the continuous organizational programs provide value for the customers and themselves as well.

Detect the waste that can be avoided, identify the problems that need solutions, and implement the required solutions.

Finally, HRM is also responsible for the hiring process. They have to hire suitable leaders and managers who can model the change and drive other employees to this needed change toward a continuous improvement culture.

As the TFSD model points to the importance of knowing what people think and feel, these are some of the important roles of HRM. As Jørgensen, Laugen, and Boer (2007) mentioned, HRM can encourage learning from experiences and share what is being learned, thus encouraging speaking about what employees feel and think. On the same side, HRM enhances the alignment of implemented activities with the goals of the organization (Jørgensen, Laugen, and Boer, 2007). Thus, what is said and done is always related to the change methodologies adopted.

Another function of HRM is to measure the success of the process. How would organizations know they are on the right track without measuring the results of the change management framework of the methodology adopted?

KPIs and KBIs

Organizations usually measure their programs' results using traditional measuring tools such as KPIs. These indicators do not truly measure the success or failure of continuous improvement initiatives of any company. On the contrary, they measure the applied tools' performance, not the organization's overall performance toward constant improvement.

Consider the following activities:

- The team leader has a good idea of who is doing an excellent job in the team
- The team leader knows how and when to recognize people within the team
- The team leader recognizes the appropriate people in the team

While the first two activities are good and required from a successful leader, only the last one is considered a behavior and can encourage the employee to deliver more outcomes. So a question that might come to mind here is what needs to be measured? Is it the performance of the leaders and employees or their behaviors?

According to Jørgensen, Laugen, and Boer (2007), three performance measurements should be considered. These performance measurements are the following.

Production

It includes the cost of the production process, the speed of the process, the lead time for getting a customer, and all other KPIs related to the productivity and end products or services.

Relationship

The relationship includes three different levels: The relationship between the employees themselves (i.e., the relationship between various departments), the relationship between leaders and employees, and the relationship between them and the customers. Each of these levels has its own KPIs.

Organizational Performance

These performances are related to the people of the organization. For example, the employees' commitment, attitudes toward work, and overall behaviors in the work processes.

Whereas all the three performance measures are necessary, the first one is always emphasized more than the other two. Most organizations use lag and lead KPIs to measure the production and miss relationship and behavior measurement.

Lag KPIs

Lag KPIs are the indicators that measure a particular process's outcomes and results (Ngucha, 2019)—for example, measuring the sales at the end of the month and comparing it with the previous month's sales to detect the improvement. The problem with this kind of indicator is that they measure the process after it is already done (Middlesworth, 2018). Organizations that want to improve cannot rely on these indicators to determine the improvement but do not help to improve.

Lead KPIs

Lead KPIs are the opposite of lag KPIs. They are used to predict what can cause an improvement (Ngucha, 2019). Taking the same example of sales, a lead KPI can be the number of marketing campaigns needed to drive more sales. Lead KPIs are more beneficial for improvement as they help define the activities required for progress to occur (Mohamed et al., 2020).

However, both lag and lead KPIs are not enough for a continuous improvement strategy. Those indicators lack measuring the behavior itself. There are different challenges associated with measuring the performance only using KPIs without measuring the behavior as those mentioned by Delatoura et al. (2014):

Focusing on Results Only

Using KPIs shifts the focus from the process itself to the results of the process. It means that there will be no change in the behavior. Instead, employees will deliver the results that show an improvement in sales, production, etc.

Decision-Making

KPIs rarely add to the decision-making process. Although lead KPIs can predict the activities needed to deliver the intended results, they do not help with decision-making at the managerial level. Changes rarely occur in an organization because of an indicator.

Variability of Measurement

Continuous improvement needs continuous change for the better. KPIs need a standard or benchmark to compare the results of today to the previous results.

Using behavioral measures, known as KBIs, can help overcome those challenges as measured here are people themselves. Organizations then should strive to change the behaviors as discussed earlier and manage and measure this change instead of focusing on the performance only.

To illustrate the difference between using KPIs and KBIs, let us look at the below example:

An organization wants to improve its performance on different levels. The manager decided to undergo a transformation in the whole organization. Before any changes are introduced, the organization should first measure the current performance. Thus, lag KPIs were used to measure things like the number of units produced per person daily.

In this first step, lag KPIs are not enough to implement the transformation. They are used to determine what needs to be changed. In order to improve the performance, lead KBIs should be used to predict what specific performances are needed. Some of these lead KBIs could be the number of ideas that each team member should develop.

Still, the transformation cannot be sustained using both KBIs only. Change management needs a kind of measurement that assesses the change in behaviors. KBIs, in this case, will measure the behaviors that need changing to improve the lead KPIs. For example, leaders will need the behavior of spending more time coaching their team members to develop new ideas.

At this point, the organization is using a set of indicators to measure the performance and the behaviors behind this performance. Only then, the transformation efforts can be assessed and change management could be implemented.

Developing a Whole System

In this approach, eight simple steps are discussed in order to execute a change management strategy. The approach is divided into two parts, the first four steps cover the behavioral formation and the last four steps cover behavioral deployment drawn from Hines and Butterworth (2019):

Step 1—Set the Principles

First, organizations should start with a set of guiding principles, as mentioned by the Shingo institute (Shingo Institute, 2021). Organizations usually have a defined set of values and principles that everyone in the organization should adhere to.

Step 2—Why Those Principles?

Defining the principles is important for further defining the behaviors connected to those principles. Many organizations can create perfect change strategies; however, employees do not adhere to those strategies. This is because they have deployed the HEAD (the logical strategy) and the HANDS (the deployment and tools) but have missed the HEART.

People in the organization should have a clear idea of what they are doing and a belief in this before they are asked to change. As Shigeo Shingo often said, "We have to grasp not only the 'Know-How' but also 'Know-Why' if we want to master the Toyota Production System." Hence, if organizations want the principles to be truly cultivated within people, they have to discuss what these principles mean and why people should believe in them.

Step 3—Understand the Principles

The Shingo Principles are quite a high level as are many company value statements. In some cases, this can mean that people cannot grasp them as easily as they would like to. However, there are supporting concepts with each of the main principles to aid in understanding them (Shingo Institute, 2021). For example:

Assure a safe environment—"there is no greater measure of respect for the individual than creating a work environment that promotes both the health and safety of employees and protection of the environment and community."

Develop people—"Through people development, the organization creates the "new scientists" that will drive future improvement. People development includes hands-on experiences where people experience new ideas in a way that creates personal insight and a shift in mindsets and behaviors."

Empower and involve everyone—"For an organization to be competitive, the full potential of every single individual must be realized. People are the only organizational asset that has an infinite capacity to appreciate in value."

Therefore, in this step, organizations should have a clear and deep understanding of what each principle really means.

Step 4—Set the Behaviors

Now that an organization has its principles, it can start defining the behaviors behind these principles. Each principle should be accompanied by a behavior or set of behaviors reflecting this principle. Yet, there are two difficult areas:

What is and what is not a behavior?
How do you make these behaviors as close to ideal as possible?

Step 5—Deploy the Behaviors

In this step, organizations try to deploy the behaviors across all the departments. This can be done at a role or a team-based level. In addition, behaviors should be deployed to new recruits. There are three types of behavioral deployment that might be considered:

- Individual behavioral deployment
- Team-based behavioral deployment
- Behavioral-based recruitment

The role of HRM, as discussed before, is to ensure the behaviors are deployed and understood by all the employees and managers. Over time, HRM may undertake each of these deployments. However, HRM may opt to start with one type of deployment—probably the first or second type— and later use the third type. Eventually, solely focus on, as you have already said, "later on" at the end of the previous sentence. It reads as if you are introducing a fourth option instead of expanding on the third one.

Step 6—Assess the Behaviors

Here, the previous step is assessed on being correctly implemented or not. Are we regularly deploying these types of behaviors in a local environment? This can be done in a number of ways. The most effective way of doing so is using the KBIs as discussed before. However, the most important thing to consider is the conversation that ensues as well as any appropriate recognition or corrective action.

Step 7—Diagnose

The seventh step is to diagnose the capability of the individual or team concerned. This is assessing performance. KPIs are the best measuring tool to use here (both lag and lead KPIs).

Step 8—Implement

From this collection of data and diagnosis, it will be possible to then start working on the capability of the individual or team concerned. Several methods can be used here, such as education, coaching, or observation of other individuals who might be role models.

Effective Communication for Change Management

Major changes in any organization need a whole transformation in the culture and identity of the organization (Cherim, 2002). This process includes two steps:

Disidentification: In this process, all the employees and leaders should put to one side their old behaviors and attitudes in the working environment.

Reidentification: The process follows the previous one where the employees are introduced to the new behaviors.

For the two processes to occur, all organizational departments should take part in the transformation. Cherim (2002) pointed out that the public relations department, in particular, has an important role to play in communicating the change. Effective communication is known to be an important element in change management (Myers-Briggs et al., 2012). For communication to be effective, Myers-Briggs et al. (2012) mentioned two main strategies that organizations should implement either one or both of them. Sheikh (2013) further explained the two strategies, as follows:

Programmatic Communication

In this approach, communication flows from top to bottom, that is, from the manager down to the employees. The manager is responsible for disseminating information and directing employees toward the desired behavior. Managers and leaders adopt this strategy believing that this is the best way to convey the change. When the information is communicated through defined channels, the chances that employees will be misinformed are minimized. Another benefit is that everyone, on the same employee level, receives the same information.

However, this approach is not as perfect as it may seem. The problem with such an approach is that, sometimes, managers believe that they are delivering the message effectively. They assume that all employees receive information in the same way. Yet, some people will perceive the message differently, according to their underlying culture, principles, and norms.

Participatory Communication

In this approach, communication flows from bottom to top, that is, from the employees up to the manager. In the participatory approach, employees are not passive receivers of information. It requires employees and all organizational people to take part in the process, therefore stimulating two-way communication. Organizations that prefer to adopt this approach provide employees with the opportunity to contribute to the change, thereby giving them a sense of control over the transformation process. Further, employees are less resistant to the change if they are a part of it.

However, one limitation to this approach is that too much involvement by employees may sidetrack the original transformational efforts. In an attempt by organizational managers to listen to employees, the intent behind the change may get lost.

A comprehensive framework for effective change management through communication is presented in Table 3.1.

To return briefly to the TFSD model, understanding what employees think and feel effective communication is the key. For higher-level managers, they must first use a communication strategy that involves all employees and stakeholders. They must also ensure that the messages they are sending are delivered in an effective way. On the other hand, it is their responsibility to ensure that all employees are engaged; implementing the TF part of the model will not occur without managers taking the initial steps of encouraging employees to speak about their thoughts and feelings.

Table 3.1 Communication Behavoral Framework

	Change Management/Effective Communication—*Communicating Clearly and with Impact to Ensure Understanding, Engagement, and Commitment to Action*					
	Team Member	*Team Leader/ Manager*	*Executive Manager*	*General Manager*	*Executive General Manager*	*Group Executive/CEO*
Plans and understands communication	Identifies who needs to be communicated with and determines the most appropriate approach.	Identifies stakeholders and determines the most appropriate approach.	Conducts stakeholder analysis and plans best-fit approach.	Leverages and appropriately links knowledge of the business and key stakeholders to develop communication plans and impactful key messages.	Leverages and appropriately links knowledge of the business and key internal and external stakeholders to develop strategies and compelling key messages.	Leverages and appropriately links knowledge of the organization and key internal and external stakeholders to develop strategies and compelling key messages.
	Actively reads and questions communications to ensure understanding of the impact on self and others.			Anticipates reactions and prepares potential responses.	Anticipates reactions and prepares potential responses.	Anticipates reactions and prepares potential responses.

Table 3.1 (Continued)   Communication Behavoral Framework

	Change Management/Effective Communication—*Communicating Clearly and with Impact to Ensure Understanding, Engagement, and Commitment to Action*					
	Team Member	*Team Leader/ Manager*	*Executive Manager*	*General Manager*	*Executive General Manager*	*Group Executive/CEO*
Delivers clear and impactful messages	Outlines the purpose and key messages, following a logical sequence.	Outlines the purpose and key messages, following a logical sequence.	Outlines the purpose and key messages, following a logical sequence.		Takes command of a message to convey logically and succinctly.	Takes command of a message to convey logically and succinctly.
	Engages customers and other stakeholders through appropriate communication channels.	Engages team, customers, and other stakeholders through considered use of different communication styles and tools.	Utilizes existing and emerging communication channels.	Utilizes existing and emerging communication channels to create impact and elicit action.	Utilizes multiple communication styles and tools to create impact and elicit action across the business/ division.	Utilizes multiple communication styles and tools to create impact and elicit action across the organization.
		Simplifies complex messages to ensure fit for the audience.	Exhibits a presence that demonstrates personal impact and commitment.	Exhibits a presence that demonstrates personal impact and credibility and commitment	Exhibits a presence that demonstrates credibility and commitment.	Exhibits a presence that demonstrates credibility and commitment.
			Applies simple and compelling language and stories to inspire commitment.	Applies simple and compelling language and stories to inspire commitment.	Applies simple and compelling language and stories to inspire commitment.	Applies simple and compelling language and stories to inspire commitment.

(Continued)

Table 3.1 (Continued) Communication Behavioral Framework

	Change Management/Effective Communication—*Communicating Clearly and with Impact to Ensure Understanding, Engagement, and Commitment to Action*					
	Team Member	*Team Leader/ Manager*	*Executive Manager*	*General Manager*	*Executive General Manager*	*Group Executive/CEO*
Ensures understanding	Seeks input from recipients and listens actively.	Seeks input from recipients and listens actively.	Invites input from others and constantly assesses reactions, adjusting messages accordingly.	Invites input from others and constantly assesses reactions, adjusting messages accordingly.	Encourages input from a diverse range of stakeholders.	Encourages input from a diverse range of stakeholders.
	Checks for understanding and clarifies points, adjusting style and language as required.	Comprehends and responds appropriately to input from others.	Comprehends and responds appropriately to input from others.	Navigates complex discussions to successful outcomes.	Constantly assesses reactions and adjusts messages accordingly.	Navigates complex discussions to successful outcomes.
	Responds appropriately to input from others.	Reinforces key messages and checks for understanding, adjusting style and language as required.			Navigates complex discussions to successful outcomes.	

Table 3.1 (Continued)   Communication Behavioral Framework

Change Management/Effective Communication — *Communicating Clearly and with Impact to Ensure Understanding, Engagement, and Commitment to Action*

	Team Member	Team Leader/Manager	Executive Manager	General Manager	Executive General Manager	Group Executive/CEO
Influences others	Conveys own perspective in a positive and compelling manner.	Conveys own perspective in a positive and compelling manner to gain agreement from others.	Determines appropriate influencing strategies to gain genuine agreement.	Develops an influencing strategy to favorably position own agenda.	Develops an influencing strategy to favorably position the business/division.	Develops an influencing strategy to favorably position the organization.
		Determines appropriate influencing strategies to gain genuine agreement.	Adjusts approach to overcome objections.	Translates and advocates business decisions, balancing with stakeholder interests.	Translates and advocates business decisions, balancing with stakeholder interests.	Translates and advocates organizational decisions, balancing with stakeholder interests.
		Adjusts approach to overcome objections.	Steps up to conflicts and sees them as opportunities.	Utilizes appropriate negotiation techniques.	Utilizes appropriate negotiation techniques.	Utilizes appropriate negotiation techniques.
				Can hammer out tough agreements and settle disputes equitably.	Coaches and guides others through difficult conflicts.	Sets the tone for tackling tough conflicts that lead to organizational improvement.

(Continued)

Table 3.1 (Continued) Communication Behavioral Framework

Change Management/Effective Communication—*Communicating Clearly and with Impact to Ensure Understanding, Engagement, and Commitment to Action*

	Team Member	Team Leader/ Manager	Executive Manager	General Manager	Executive General Manager	Group Executive/CEO
Engagement through communication	Seeks and listens to the views of others.	Proactively seeks the ideas, input, and feedback of others.	Actively seeks to include views from a wide variety of people in their circle of advisors.	Actively seeks to include views from a wide variety of people in their circle of advisors.	Actively seeks to include views from a wide variety of people in their circle of advisors.	Actively seeks to include views from a wide variety of people in their circle of advisors.
		Creates an environment where people are safe and encouraged to speak up.	Encourages two-way communication from their stakeholders and team.	Creatively encourages two-way communication from their stakeholders and team.	Creatively encourages two-way communication from every corner of the organization.	Creatively encourages two-way communication from every corner of the organization.
			Creates an environment where people are safe and encouraged to speak up.	Creates an environment where people are safe and encouraged to speak up.	Creates an environment where people are safe and encouraged to speak up.	Creates an environment where people are safe and encouraged to speak up.

Furthermore, team members also have a role in this effective communication strategy. Their role lies in conveying their perspectives in a compelling way. They have to actively listen to managers and other team members and then react (say and do) after having analyzed the received messages.

Barriers to Effective Change Management

Applying the previous strategies and approaches will foster change in the organization. Yet, there exist a set of barriers that managers should be aware of when implementing a change. Some of these barriers as mentioned by Neill (2018) are the following.

Lack of a Plan

Change management for improvement should be combined with a detailed plan of each aspect of the organization that needs changing. General goals and undetermined objectives will not add to the organizational transformation process. In addition, plans should be consistent. Managers who tend to change their plans every now and then are just confusing their employees and demotivating them as they cannot see any results of their work.

Lack of a Leader

A leader should initiate organizational change. Leaders here are not necessarily the managers. They are any people in the organization who can influence and model the behavior and lead the change. Moreover, leaders of the same organization should be aligned with the same goals and objectives of the organization. Similar to changing plans, different leaders with different visions may confuse the employees too.

Change Fatigue

The continuous change is definitely time-consuming. Employees may get fatigued from the new requirements and tasks in addition to the new skills and behaviors they have to learn for the change. For this, gradual change is recommended to give some rest time to the employees. In addition, celebrating short-term wins is essential to always motivate them to exert more effort.

Technology Issues

These problems are common in many organizations especially those working in IT and similar sectors. Sometimes technology issues are related to the resources and the inability to get adequate technology equipment. In other times, it is related to the personnel who are not used to the new technology required by the organization.

Existence of Multiple Cultures

As always mentioned, changing the culture is necessary and the first step for any change in the organization. The organizational culture should be unified and every member of the team should be engaged in this culture.

Let us conclude with a story that one of the authors experienced during an overseas assignment with the largest company in the world. The project was focused on reducing bureaucracy and one example of a system failure occurred in the purchase order approval process. When a purchase order was created, it needed 16 signatures in order for the purchase order to move forward, and the approval process would take 6–8 months. The question that everyone needed to ask immediately was where did the 16 required signatures come from and the answer is "tradition." Informal tradition within the company caused every process failure to be corrected by adding another checkpoint. Whenever there was a failure in the purchase order process, the traditional solution was to add another signature to the purchase order procedure in the hope that this additional signature would prevent the failure from reoccurring in the future. Another checkpoint was added. These additional checkpoints caused the process to take longer, and the result was 16 signatures and a 6–8-month lead time.

In the team's effort to reduce the bureaucracy of this process, possibly by automation, they decided to interview each of the 16 individuals and ask them what that individual looked at to see if the purchase order should be approved and each one of the 16 individuals said something to the effect that they just checked to see if a certain other individual had approved the purchase order, then they were sure it would be correct. The net effect was that no one actually looked at the purchase order and its approval progressed as if no one would have signed anything. However, it took 6–8 months to accomplish this failure.

Here, we have a system, driven by traditional corrective action procedures that had created an enormous bureaucracy, and had still failed to achieve

Table 3.2 Change Management Behavior Framework

Change Management/Effective Training and Coaching — Training and Coaching to Ensure Understanding, Engagement, and Commitment to Actions that Build Proficiency in New Skills and Behaviors

	Team Member	Team Leader/ Manager	Executive Manager	General Manager	Executive General Manager	Group Executive/ CEO
Analyzes and closes knowledge gaps through training	Identifies who needs to be trained and determines the most appropriate approach.	Identifies capability gaps and determines the most appropriate approach to training.	Conducts capability (skills and behaviors) analysis and plans, with HRM/L&D best-fit approach to training.	Leverages and appropriately links the purpose and values of the organization to develop, with HRM, the key competencies and behaviors.	Leverages and appropriately links the purpose and values of the organization to develop, with HRM, the key competencies and behaviors.	Leverages and appropriately links the purpose and values of the organization, with HRM support, to the desired skills and behaviors.
	Actively participates in the training to ensure understanding of new ways of working and desired behaviors on self and others.	Actively supports and participates in the training.	Organizes the training and participates in the leadership training.	Actively sponsors the training and participates in the leadership training.	Actively sponsors the training and participates in the leadership training.	Actively sponsors the training and participates in the leadership training.

(Continued)

Table 3.2 (Continued)   Change Management Behavior Framework

Change Management/Effective Training and Coaching—*Training and Coaching to Ensure Understanding, Engagement, and Commitment to Actions that Build Proficiency in New Skills and Behaviors*

	Team Member	Team Leader/ Manager	Executive Manager	General Manager	Executive General Manager	Group Executive/ CEO
Confirms understanding of training	Seeks feedback from peers and listens actively.	Seeks feedback from team and peers and listens actively.	Invites feedback from others and constantly assesses knowledge and reacts accordingly to fill gaps.	Invites feedback from others and constantly assesses knowledge and reacts accordingly to fill gaps.	Encourages feedback from a diverse range of stakeholders.	Encourages input from a diverse range of stakeholders.
	Responds appropriately to input from others.	Comprehends and responds appropriately to input from others.	Comprehends and responds appropriately to input from others.	Navigates complex discussions to successful outcomes of the training.	Constantly assesses reactions and adjusts training and delivery methods accordingly.	Constantly assesses reactions and adjusts training and delivery methods accordingly.
	Checks for understanding and closes gaps as required.	Reinforces key messages of the training and checks for understanding and comprehension.			Navigates complex discussions to successful outcomes.	

Table 3.2 (Continued) Change Management Behavior Framework

Change Management/Effective Training and Coaching—Training and Coaching to Ensure Understanding, Engagement, and Commitment to Actions that Build Proficiency in New Skills and Behaviors

	Team Member	Team Leader/ Manager	Executive Manager	General Manager	Executive General Manager	Group Executive/ CEO
Builds proficiency in the new skills and behaviors	Accepts assignments that build capabilities in new skills and behaviors.	Coaches others to proficiency using the appropriate leadership styles and coaching models.	Determines appropriate coaching and feedback models to develop measurable ability in the desired skills and behaviors.	Develops a learning strategy to favorably position own agenda.	Develops and maintains learning and support channels, enabling capacity for learning, building general skills, and setting standards.	Provides and maintains organization-wide standards, partnerships, policies, and channels for learning and support.
	Actively seeks feedback, coaching and mentoring from those skilled and proficient in the desired skills and behaviors.	Actively seeks feedback, coaching and mentoring from those skilled and proficient in the desired skills and behaviors.	Adjusts approach to overcome objections while establishing the desired skill and behaviors.	Translates and advocates learning decisions, balancing with stakeholder interests.	Translates and advocates business decisions, balancing with stakeholder interests.	Incorporates, with HRM, the desired competencies in the performance and development systems.
	Takes time to reflect and continuously improve.	Takes time to reflect and continuously improve.	Steps up to conflicts and sees them as opportunities.	Utilizes appropriate negotiation techniques.	Utilizes appropriate negotiation techniques.	Utilizes appropriate negotiation techniques.
				Can hammer out tough agreements and settle disputes equitably.	Coaches and guides others through difficult conflicts.	Sets the tone for tackling tough conflicts that lead to organizational improvement.

(Continued)

Table 3.2 (Continued)   Change Management Behavior Framework

	Team Member	Team Leader/ Manager	Executive Manager	General Manager	Executive General Manager	Group Executive/ CEO
Change Management/Effective Training and Coaching—*Training and Coaching to Ensure Understanding, Engagement, and Commitment to Actions that Build Proficiency in New Skills and Behaviors*						
	Visibly models the desired behaviors.	Visibly models the desired behaviors.	Communicates the culture, policies, frameworks, and processes to support sustainable change across the organization.	Monitors the culture, policies, frameworks, and processes to support sustainable change.	Monitors the culture, policies, frameworks, and processes to support sustainable change.	Provides the culture, policies, frameworks, and processes to support sustainable change across the organization.
		Uses KBIs to visibly measure and improve the desired leadership behaviors in team members.	Visibly models the desired behaviors.	Visibly models the desired behaviors.	Visibly models the desired behaviors.	Visibly models the desired behaviors.
			Communicates the agreed KBIs to hold the organization accountable to the desired leadership behaviors.	Uses appropriate KBIs to hold managers accountable to the desired leadership behaviors.	Uses appropriate KBIs to hold the organization accountable to the desired leadership behaviors.	Uses appropriate KBIs to hold the organization accountable to the desired leadership behaviors.
Reinforces the skills and behaviors through rewards and recognition						

the goals and objectives of the organization. The entire system was a waste. One auditor who had a checklist of things to check on the purchase order replaced it, and then he could give approval for the purchase order to move it forward. A 6–8-month process had been reduced to 2 weeks.

This example seems obscenely stupid; however, it took an outsider to see how stupid it really was. And before you laugh too loudly, you may want to look at a couple of the processes within your own enterprise where the solution to any system failure was to incorporate another checkpoint, thereby adding additional complication to the process, causing the process to take longer, and adding an additional point where failure could occur.

A bad system will beat a good person every time.

We are being ruined by the best efforts of people who are doing the wrong thing.

It is not enough to do your best; you must know what to do, and then do your best.

Best efforts will not substitute for knowledge.

W. Edwards Deming

Summary

Change management is essential to an organization in terms of maintaining a sustainable improvement program. This chapter reveals that the process of change must integrate two sides of the work environment, namely, the one where CI programs are implemented and the one where improvement of leadership and cultural enhancement need to be done. This calls for a systematic approach to change management in the organization rather than using a tool-based approach.

Various methodologies and theories have been applied in the change management arena. As a result, it is essential for the organizational management to choose the model that appears suitable to them in terms of leading to a strong cultural ground. This is where the human resource management comes in. The human resource management can measure the success of any change policy and analyze whether the behavior of the employees is leading to the required outcome or not. This would require having the whole team onboard using suitable techniques such as efficient communication. It is a process that would take time to be achieved with many challenges along the way but the benefits to bring the organization to a new level of performance. As this happens, increasing the level of customer satisfaction by improving the customer experience is essential to the success of the organization as well. In such a context, the next chapter presents a discussion of customer experience in terms of challenges organizations face in maintaining a good customer experience and the critical steps that need to be followed in satisfying the customers.

Measuring Success

Traditional KPIs for change management initiatives or programs are the following:

a. Efforts to bridge the gap of enforcing change in the organization (bridging the CI programs and leadership and cultural improvement plans).
b. Number of issues added prior to implementation.
c. Percent of communications completed on time.
d. Analyze the success of the strategies enforced.

Suggested KBIs for change management initiatives or programs are the following:

a. Number of enquiries/question to understand change
b. Assess the behavior of employees in relation to change
c. Request for support prior/during implementation
d. Note the behaviors that need to be changed to improve KPIs
e. People following the change as designed post implementation

Suggested KAIs for change management are the following:

a. How many questions/requests for actions to clarify change have we received today/this shift on our improvement idea/initiative?
b. How many improvements have been generated to improve the change have we received today/this shift on our improvement idea/initiative?

Reference—Making Six Sigma Last: Managing the Balance between Cultural and Technical Change (George Eckes, 2007)

Chapter 4

Agile and Patterns

Agile was first termed in the business improvement/project management format; we know it as part of the Agile Manifesto in 2001. The Agile manifesto was created by a team of leading software/technician innovation delivery experts looking to help the IT world improve its project management systems and leadership behaviors/practices. The noughties for those that can remember it was not a good time for innovation development and releases. Software bugs, long lead times to fix them, late releases, and poor customer service were a standard. The team of 17 individuals who formulated the Agile Manifesto wanted to change this and boy did they ever.

Two business partners who had been working on a high-performance team and project delivery approach called Scrum were at this meeting. Jeff Sutherland and Ken Schwarber had both dedicated much of their career to studying, experimenting with, and creating approaches in forming, sustaining, and improving high-performance teams focused on project delivery and continuous improvement. They were both operating in the fields of software and technology. Scrum was not new; it had been in circulation as a brand since 1993 and had its origins through work Jeff was doing far before this. Following the Agile Manifesto formation, Scrum became the backbone to everything relating to Agile. Jeff and Ken had already down the work, years of experimentation and learning, to crack the challenge the team was facing. This is not to say that Agile and Scrum have not been continuously improved and enhanced in the years since 2001. The technology world embraced Scrum and Agile and the rest is history, and the results have been amazing! New technologies enter our market rapidly; companies continuously improve and evolve their products

DOI: 10.4324/9781003224747-4

in a highly customer-centric manner. We have seen the rise of a new set of leading organizations globally; many of the more traditional "world's largest organisations" have been reformed by these more Agile, fast-moving, and innovating companies.

Jeff and Ken drew on many elements of research in the formation of Scrum, including the works of Taiichi Ohno (Toyota Production Systems—TPS) and authors of Lean such as Jeff Liker and others. Jeff openly states that Scrum has its background in Toyota Production Systems and Lean. We will now explore what Agile and Scrum is?

What Is Agile and Scrum

Agile and its skeletal framework of Scrum is a highly systemized approach. There is a process, roles, forms, and tools you can be trained in. You can become a Scrum Master, Product Owners, and Scrum@Scale Practitioner. Ultimately, the system of Scrum creates a highly customer-focused, collaborative, learning, continuously improving, and innovating team and organization. Jeff Sutherland once said to me that the system of Scrum can create a culture of Agility and innovation. It is a definite case of systems and leadership impacting culture and behavior.

In its simplest explanation, Scrum and Agile move away from the traditional Gantt chart time planned step-by-step project management approach to an iterative experimental approach built on scientific thinking/PDCA (plan do check act). It provides techniques to break large challenges and projects down to small items and then execute and experiment on these in a focused time blocked approach (Figure 4.1).

I need to emphasize that this is only a high-level overview provided as part of this book. I recommend reading the book "Scrum – Doing twice the work in half the time" by Jeff Sutherland for a more detailed outline.

In short, small teams of five to eight people are formed with the knowledge and skills to deliver the goal and vision they need to achieve. This could result in a cross-functional team rather than the traditional siloed-based role and responsibilities within organizations. Each small Scrum team has a meaningful goal and vision they are moving toward that is aligned to the organization strategy and customers.

There are three roles within a Scrum team, a product owner, Scrum master, and Developers. The role of the product owner is to align strategically with the top line organizational plan and customers of focus.

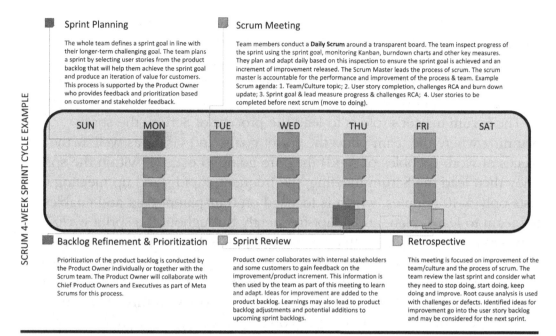

Sprint Planning

The whole team defines a sprint goal in line with their longer-term challenging goal. The team plans a sprint by selecting user stories from the product backlog that will help them achieve the sprint goal and produce an iteration of value for customers. This process is supported by the Product Owner who provides feedback and prioritization based on customer and stakeholder feedback.

Scrum Meeting

Team members conduct a **Daily Scrum** around a transparent board. The team inspect progress of the sprint using the sprint goal, monitoring Kanban, burndown charts and other key measures. They plan and adapt daily based on this inspection to ensure the sprint goal is achieved and an increment of improvement released. The Scrum Master leads the process of scrum. The scrum master is accountable for the performance and improvement of the process & team. Example Scrum agenda: 1. Team/Culture topic; 2. User story completion, challenges RCA and burn down update; 3. Sprint goal & lead measure progress & challenges RCA; 4. User stories to be completed before next scrum (move to doing).

SCRUM 4-WEEK SPRINT CYCLE EXAMPLE

| SUN | MON | TUE | WED | THU | FRI | SAT |

Backlog Refinement & Prioritization

Prioritization of the product backlog is conducted by the Product Owner individually or together with the Scrum team. The Product Owner will collaborate with Chief Product Owners and Executives as part of Meta Scrums for this process.

Sprint Review

Product owner collaborates with internal stakeholders and some customers to gain feedback on the improvement/product increment. This information is then used by the team as part of this meeting to learn and adapt. Ideas for improvement are added to the product backlog. Learnings may also lead to product backlog adjustments and potential additions to upcoming sprint backlogs.

Retrospective

This meeting is focused on improvement of the team/culture and the process of scrum. The team review the last sprint and consider what they need to stop doing, start doing, keep doing and improve. Root cause analysis is used with challenges or defects. Identified ideas for improvement go into the user story backlog and may be considered for the next sprint.

Figure 4.1   Scrum sprint cycle (4-week example).

Their job is to lead the team in breaking down the overall project into small prioritized, executionable items. The best way I find to describe this is to think of a strategic project or objective for a team as being a mountain it needs to be tackled/broken down. The job of the product owner is to lead the breaking of the mountain down into boulders, rocks, pebbles, and sand. This technique is called large-scale planning. Scrum is not about planning out project steps and placing them in predicted flows of work (Gantt chart). Alternatively, it is about breaking the project down into small executionable items and then working on them a few items at a time, releasing iterative versions of a product, project, or improvement, gaining feedback from customers and stakeholders, learning and adapting along the way. The reason for this is that no one has truly figured out how to predict the future yet. When they do traditional Gantt chart project approaches may become viable and successful. In a world where the future is not predictable, Scrum is a great approach to gradually work toward a project or organization/team objective, learning, and adapting at each step.

There is another key part the product owner plays in this step-by-step, learning and adapting approach. They are also responsible for gaining feedback from customers and stakeholders at each step, after each time blocked sprint. To do this, a version of the product or project change is released at the end of each time blocked cycle (Sprint). The release may be to the market, part of the market, or an internal organizational customer/stakeholder. It may be to a select group of customers either internal or external to the organization. The crucial part is that as part of the sprint review the product owner is able to report back to the team on feedback from customers and stakeholders, enabling them to learn and adapt every sprint cycle.

The Scrum master's role is to lead the process of Scrum, the sprint planning where the team plans the sprint goals, and vision as well as the pieces of work (pebbles of sand) they are going to execute within the sprint. They then lead the Scrum meeting, the frequent, rapid stand up meeting that lasts only 5–10 minutes, which is focused on transparent data and enables the team to learn, plan, and adapt frequently throughout the sprint cycle. You will note in Figure 4.1 that the sprint cycle is 1 month and the team is conducting a Scrum meeting every day. There is a process to conducting a Scrum meeting, simply define the team members' start by discussing culture and teamwork (potentially there is a measure of focus on this). They then look to the sprint goal and vision to confirm that they are on track; they then outline if they achieved the work they committed to in the last Scrum meeting and what they will commit to achieving before the next Scrum meeting. During each Scrum meeting, they will monitor the measurable goal and vision of the sprint (that aligns with the project goals) and other measures of importance.

At the end of the sprint cycled, the Scrum master leads a very important meeting that produces amazing results. It is called a retrospective or retro for short. During this meeting, the Scrum team gathers together to review their performance throughout the sprint and capture potential improvements to backlog for the future or take into the next sprint. The team typically asks three simple questions:

1. What went well, what do we need to keep doing?
2. What do we need to just stop doing, what are we doing that is wasteful, not valuable to customers and we can simply stop?
3. What do we need to start doing? Is there anything we are not doing that we should be doing?

This system pattern is extremely powerful; it results in teams improving their culture, enhancing their performance, and overcoming potential cultural or systemic problems quickly. A key outcome of the retrospective meeting is a prioritized improvement to go into the next sprint. We will explore some additional patterns of success in the next section.

Developers are team members that develop value for customers along with the product owner and Scrum master as part of the team. Agile/Scrum is a very flat structural approach. All team members develop value, they also focus on cross-training and developing each other. You will often find scrum teams that include cross-functional or multi-skilled Developers/team members. Teams are often formed based on customers and strategic requirements rather than traditional skill set silos in traditional organisations. This makes the opportunity for Developers to develop each other's skills as well as develop value for customers.

It is important for me to stress that this is only a high level in Scrum. Please conduct further studies and research to learn more. Some great books and resources are referenced as part of this chapter.

Leadership and Agile/Scrum

As previously mentioned an important point when considering leadership and Scrum is that the product owner and Scrum masters are not leaders of the team. They have a role, a function that needs to be respected, but they are not the leaders of the team. A Scrum team is an autonomous small team, each team member with their own skills, capabilities, and functions they bring to the team. The great Scrum teams cross-train each other on skills and competencies. This builds resilience in the team, adaptability, greater flexibility, and speed in executing work. I don't know if Jeff and Ken drew on the approaches taken by special forces globally when developing Scrum. I see a lot of the structures of Scrum in these teams. A special force team is typically a small autonomous team when in action that has within it the skills and capabilities needed to survive and complete the mission within the environment they are deployed. They may have a demolition specialist, medic, and sniper as part of the team. They will all know how to shoot and perform other key functions as soldiers. The team will work to cross-train and develop each other, i.e., the medic will train the others in core medical skills. It is integral in this industry; should a team be in country fighting and the medic gets injured or killed someone needs to be able to take over. They may not be able to take over to the same level as the medic, but they will have the ability to support the team throughout the rest of the mission.

Senior leadership in organizations running Scrum/Agile play an important role. They set strategic and cultural direction and help teams form their own plans relating to these. Aside from this obvious function, there are two others that are critical:

1. Continue to help teams prioritize backlogs of work and coordinate efforts across the organization. (Often separate meeting called an Executive Meta Scrum—EMS.)
2. Help teams overcome large issues and challenges that they are unable to handle themselves. (Often, a team called the Executive Action Team—EAT is formed to eat large problems and impediments. They may be supported by specialist improvement teams in this process.)

It is these two functions that enable autonomous teams to align, stay focused, and keep moving forward. Without the executive playing these important roles, Scrum teams could easily start to diverge, and even work against each other. Scrum teams could also find themselves road blocked with challenges and issues that stop them from moving forward toward their goals.

In smaller organizations or Agile deployments, there may be five to eight Scrum teams reporting to a leadership team that is helping them to coordinate and overcome challenges. This is a simple structure and relatively simple to implement. One of the amazing outcomes with organizations that successfully implement Scrum as a startup and grow is that they lose little of the agility they experience as a startup. Typically, an organization will start in an Agile fashion with a founder and a few team members achieving amazing outcomes in an Agile fast manner. As they grow, however, they start to place people in functions, build silos, and the whole thing slows down.

Jeff Sutherland has codified/developed the ways in which organizations can retain their start-up agility and speed as they scale. This approach is called Scrum@Scale. The roles of the executive and front-line teams are as previously described in this chapter. The difference comes with how information from hundreds if not thousands of Scrum teams is coordinated, and issues escalated to higher levels if needed. The way this is achieved is through small Scrum style meetings that occur above the front-line Scrums, which are called scaled daily Scrums (SDSs) with the team called the Scrum of Scrums (Figure 4.2). The SDS is a meeting where representatives from five to eight related front-line Scrum teams go (Figure 4.2). During this meeting, they focus on the sprint goal and vision for the combined team's work. They report their progress and raise any issues that they are having challenges with. These may be handled in this meeting but alternatively may need to escalate to a higher-level Scrum of Scrums team or the executive action team. There is typically

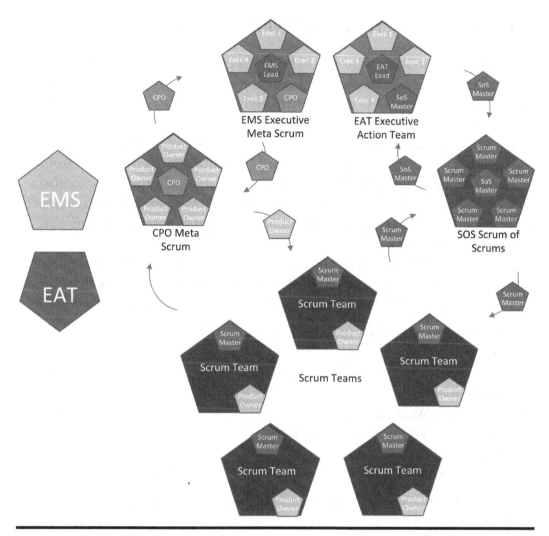

Figure 4.2 Simple Scrum@Scale example.

a Scrum of Scrums master (SoS Master) as part of this meeting whose role is to facilitate the meeting and escalate issues and challenges. The other higher-level meeting is called a Meta Scrum. This is a meeting of product owners and key executives. The purpose of this meeting is to coordinate backlogs of work and support each other. This meeting is typically facilitated by a chief product owner (CPO) who then escalates from there (Figure 4.2). It is through these meeting rhythms that middle management becomes defunct. Large organizations remain flat, autonomy and focus is strong at the front line with more people delivering value and less performing bureaucratic roles.

This is a high-level overview of the Scrum@Scale approach. Please research and learn further to enhance your knowledge if this system is of interest to you.

Agile/Scrum Patterns of Behaviors and Systems

At the heart of the Agile system are behavioral and systematic patterns that passionate Agile practitioners have been working for years to decipher. Jeff Sutherland and James O Coplien documented these in their book *A Scrum Book: The Spirit of the Game.*

The Agile world chose the use of the word patterns as they saw these key behaviors and systems as being like beautiful patterns in architecture. Architectural beauty has been defined as repeatable patterns that can also be seen in nature. The Agile community has borrowed from this to define patterns of success in high-performance, continuously improving, innovating teams and organizations.

There are literally hundreds of patterns that have been defined; a Scrum Book outlines many of these. Some of the core capstone patterns that by themselves will lead to many other great behaviors of success are as follows:

1. Small teams and cross-functional team
2. Autonomous teams
3. Small items
4. Sprint goal
5. Yesterday's Weather
6. Swarming: one-piece continuous flow
7. Regular product increment
8. Happiness metric

Let's explore these, their associated systems, behaviors, and potential key behavior indicators (KBIs).

Small Teams and Cross-Functional Team

The knowledge that small teams will outperform larger teams is not new. Maximilien Ringelmann outlined the findings of his research in 1913 that showed as a team grows the contribution of team members to performance reduces (Figure 4.3). Rigelmann conducted a study of people performing in a tug of war. He found consistently that the contribution to performance was reduced in the manner shown in Figure 4.3. Many researchers over the years have studied this phenomenon and provided theories as to why this occurs. Some of the theories are as follows:

1. As a team grows, team members feel their contribution matters less, and they lose motivation.

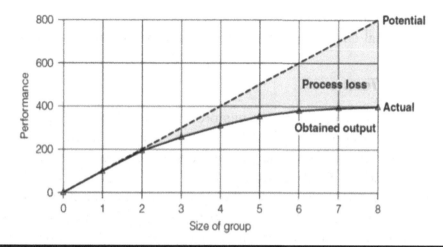

Figure 4.3   Ringelmann effect.

2. Communication breaks down as teams grow. There is less connectedness and performance reduces.
3. Additional team members in teams bring with it additional distractions and impacts. Each person you add amplifies this level of wasteful noise.

The small team Scrum pattern is a blend of system and behavior. The system of creating large teams creates a behavior in humans that reduces overall individual performance.

Cross-functional team is a Scrum pattern that has found that higher performance is achieved when the skills and capabilities are included within small teams needed to deliver improvement for customers and strategic outcomes for an organization. To define who should be in a small team, starts with the team's customer. Ask yourself who is my team's customers and what skills, capabilities, and traits do they need in the team to create amazing outcomes and experiences for them? This question will help you plan if these capabilities can be trained and developed within a team as a whole or if you need to bring specialist cross-functional knowledge and skills into the team to deliver the results. The pattern of cross-functional teams has found that performance increases dramatically when a team has the cross-functional team members/skills, capabilities, and traits in the team. The reason for this is the rapid conversations, learning, and adapting that can be achieved when the knowledge and capability is present within the team rather than outsourced from others. This creates an internal learning and sharing environment where team members naturally develop each other and share knowledge. It eliminates the negative behaviors we all know can originate between divisional silos within organizations such as delays, lack of trust, conflicting goals, and poor service for internal customers, which ultimately impacts external customers.

Autonomous Teams

Autonomous team is a pattern that has proven to create greater results in Scrum teams. Autonomy within Scrum teams leads to many positive behavioral outcomes such as engagement, energy, constant learning/ development, and ultimately performance. In most cultures around the world, autonomy is very important. We want to be masters of our own destiny, have control over our life, and play a part in achieving something greater than ourselves. The autonomous team's pattern plays to this human desire, producing great results. There are many other Scrum patterns that work with the autonomous team's pattern to help avoid negative elements that could arise with purely autonomous teams.

Small Items

The small-item Scrum pattern links with the large-scale planning system defined earlier in this chapter. A key pattern of Scrum is breaking large items into smaller ready to execute items (mountains to boulders to rocks and sand). The reason this pattern is powerful is that humans like to see movement. Especially in the today's environment, our attention spans seem to be getting shorter and shorter. If we don't see movement in a project or improvement effort, we will often lose interest, put in less effort, and in the worst case forget about it and go back to the way we previously did things. Breaking a large project into small executionable items enables team members to execute small items/steps every day/week toward their project goal. The team sees movement; they can also pick up on challenges rapidly that invariably are not as big as they would have been if the project was being handled in traditional ways. The pattern of small items enables team members to enact behaviors of rapid simple execution and receive the dopamine hit of achieving something that many of us experience. This creates many small wins and dopamine hits toward the larger goal.

Sprint Goal

The Scrum pattern of sprint goal is a very important systematized pattern. The sprint goal needs to align with the project/strategic goals for the team and organization. If this is in place including a purposeful vision, a team is in a strong place to execute and improve rapidly and autonomously. Again, humans typically find it hard to stay focused on a longer-term goal way off in the distance. Breaking the project/strategic goal down into smaller short-term sprint goals aligns with the "Small Items" Scrum pattern. Team members can sprint/move quickly together on the short-term goal, celebrate and receive the associated dopamine hit, and then set the next sprint goal. This is another motivational pattern that leads to many positive behaviors, which results in a greater performance of the team and organization. Mount Everest is a great analogy to think about when considering this pattern. I have many friends who see reaching an Everest base camp as one of their life's achievements. I also have friends who have made it to camp 3 and will go back one day to make it to 4 and ultimately the summit. The base camps up Mount Everest allow climbers to break the large challenging meaningful goal into smaller steps. They have been able to build process, recognition, and celebration around these steps to keep climbers as safe and motivated as possible on a journey that is extremely challenging. This is the power of the sprint goal pattern.

Yesterday's Weather and Teams That Finish Early Accelerate

Yesterday's Weather Scrum pattern relates highly to another pattern that winning teams keep winning. Teams that are motivated with high morale have more chance of nailing the next sprint goal than a team that did not achieve their last sprint goal. Yesterday's Weather is a Scrum pattern focused on only bringing into a sprint the average amount of work delivered from the last three sprints. The reason for this is that the past is the best predictor of the future. This results in teams having a good chance of winning, achieving the sprint goal, and sustaining motivation. This pattern works well with another known pattern of success—teams that finish early accelerate. A team that uses Yesterday's Weather to plan the workload in a sprint can still execute quickly and efficiently and work to finish the work early. When they finish the work early, they can then bring in additional work from the backlog of small items and execute more, ultimately completing more work in the sprint and accelerating over time. These two patterns working together create motivation and a winning culture that fuels greater performance. An analogy for this can be found in the way many long-distance runners train. An individual training for a marathon does not go out and run 40 km straight away in a world record time. They often start their training at shorter distances, increasing their speed at that distance, and then gradually going further. Many will have an initial set run time, similar to a sprint. They will look to run a set distance in that time, and if they achieve the distance prior to the time completion, they will keep running. This sets a new personal best, and they will expand on this from there. The key to it all is that winning with a challenging goal still out ahead of you fuels motivation and morale, which ultimately helps in delivering results.

Swarming—One-Piece Continuous Flow

The Scrum pattern of Swarming—one piece continuous flow is the pattern seen in high-performance Scrum meetings. The term Scrum was derived from a Harvard report titled "The New New Product Development Game" (Takeuchi and Nonaka 1986). Takuechi and Nonaka studied the most innovative companies back in the mid-80s. They were trying to understand how these companies could release new products and innovations so much faster than their competitors. What they found in these companies was development teams acting a lot like rugby teams. They all had a challenging goal at the end of the field; they worked in small cross-functional teams rather than silos of skills. They would regularly come together in a short meeting which they called a Scrum (I think it should have been called a Maul), and then they would split and sprint toward the next step/short-term goal (Sprint goal). You can see how this article influenced a lot of the language of Scrum and Agile; it was pivotal. One of the key patterns of this process was the cross-functional/skilled small team swarming together in a rapid meeting (Scrum), taking stock of where they are at, committing to additional pieces of work, often only one, and then splitting to execute. The swarming part of the pattern relates to this regular, rapid Scrum to review work, learn, and adapt. The one-piece continuous flow relates to teams/team members working on minimal small items at a time, focusing on these, executing them and then drawing on more work during the next Scrum. This pattern creates positive behaviors of teamwork, recognition, support, challenge resolution, etc. It is one of the pivotal patterns to the success of Agile.

Regular Product Increment

The regular product increment is at the core of the scientific iterative learning and adapting approach of Agile. This pattern is focused on the release of a product/project increment every sprint to internal or external customers to enable learning based on the most important people to any project. This learning enables rapid adaption (often called a pivot) in line with the most important people in any organization—internal and external customers. The problem with traditional large project management approaches is that a lot of work needed to be executed before anything is released to customers. Learning in this environment is not regular, and there is a real risk that a lot of the work is waste (not valued by internal or external customers). There has been a lot of wasted human effort in projects over the years. The Scrum pattern of regular product increments mitigates this risk and amplifies performance through the frequency of learning and adaptation. This is not new to our work; think of the moon shot effort of NASA in the 60s; they didn't work for years to build the best rocket and take a last-ditch effort to put a person on the moon. They ran 11 experiments, each with a differing sprint goal, with the final sprint putting a person on the moon. Their iterations were longer than they are now. If you look up SpaceX, you will see how rapid sprint iterations are in the space race today. Most organizations starting out with Agile/Scrum iterate every month and run monthly sprint cycles with a concluding sprint review to learn from the increment. Some organizations are down to product increments twice a day. The more frequent the increment, the more frequent the learning. The trick is to win and then get faster from there as the team's capability and patterns of success improve.

Happiness Metric

I love this pattern because it isn't what it seems. For years, we have been reading books and having researchers talking about the secret of success being employee happiness. The experts in Scrum and Agile have found this to not be the full story. It has been found that a happy team is not necessarily a performing team. A happy team can find themselves in a happy bubble, feeling great but not increasing performance for their customers. There is a Scrum pattern called "Pop the happy bubble" if this occurs and move to the happiness metric. The key to the happiness metric has been found to be morale not purely happiness. A motivated team that is engaged and fired up toward a challenging meaningful goal they believe in is a performing team. They are focused, motivated, and delivering improvement and results for internal and external customers. The happiness metric is about finding the metrics and measurement of morale and motivation for your team. It can be different between Scrum teams within the same organization. The importance is to be aligned strategically, relevant and motivational for the team and delivering morale and results.

Chapter Conclusion

This chapter has explored Agile and its core backbone Scrum at a high level. We have reviewed the history, systems, and some of the key patterns of success in achieving great outcomes with Agile. Many of our world's leading organizations have achieved amazing things with Agile; it is important to note that they did not achieve this overnight. Agile like any excellence system and journey requires a focus on the behaviors and systems (patterns) of success. It requires us to systematically run experiments, learn, and adapt our excellence journey the same way we do in Agile. The Scrum patterns provide a great measurement system for an Agile excellence journey. They allow you to make your journey transparent, inspect it regularly, and adapt based on your findings. If you are on an Agile excellence journey or planning to start one, consider how you can work with the most senior leaders possible in your organization to engage them and set up a system to make the journey transparent using the Scrum patterns, inspect it regularly, and adapt based on your findings. The system and behavioral elements of transparency, inspection, and adaption are critical to any excellence journey. The behaviors people display in relation to these will determine your success or failure. Jeff, Ken, and all the contributors to Scrum and Agile have developed some amazing systems and behavioral approaches, which are defined as patterns. You can find a set of pattern cards together with additional Agile/Scrum resources and a podcast episode with Jeff Sutherland himself at www.enterpriseexcellencepodcast. com/downloads (Table 4.1).

Summary

This chapter reviews Agile management as an innovation technique that can improve organizational outcomes. Although it has been used in IT sectors and automobile companies, the technique has been widely applied in other industries to bring about innovation and efficiency, particularly where product development and testing methods are involved. As a result, it can be used in various business operations.

Table 4.1   Agile Behavior Framework

	Agile—Delivering Projects, Products, Services, and Organizational Improvement in a Calm Accelerating Way					
	Team Member	*Scrum Master*	*Product Owner*	*Scrum of Scrums Master*	*Chief Product Owner*	*Executive*
Fosters a culture of speed, calmness, and agility	Sharing culture moment at the start of a Scrum.	Supporting and coaching team members on Scrum systems.	Participating as a team member to deliver sprint goal.	Supporting Scrum masters with cultural and system challenges the team cannot handle.	Supporting a culture of Meta Scrum team.	Reviewing team performance and cultural measures. Supporting teams to improve.
	Discussing their work in relation to the sprint goal and vision. Adapting if needed to achieve goal.	Supporting and coaching team on ideal behaviors and patterns to enhance team culture and performance.	Supporting team members with insights on customer and stakeholder feedback.	Reviewing with Scrum masters their cultural performance and providing coaching.	Supporting product owners to actively prioritize based on customer value, ease, and returns to the business.	Spending time with teams where they work to learn and gain insights to improve.

(Continued)

Table 4.1 (Continued) Agile Behavior Framework

Agile—Delivering Projects, Products, Services, and Organizational Improvement in a Calm Accelerating Way

	Team Member	Scrum Master	Product Owner	Scrum of Scrums Master	Chief Product Owner	Executive
Accelerates improvement speed and agility of organization at all levels	Committing to small actions and delivering these between Scrums.	Using Yesterday's Weather to help the team sprint plan.	Ensure backlog is prioritized, clean, and ready to execute with a clear definition of done.	Supports the overcoming of escalated issues and roadblocks.	Analyzing backlog priorities and helping product owners align.	Supports the overcoming of escalated issues and roadblocks.
	Being able to describe how the work they are performing will help achieve sprint goal and vision.	Supports teams toward finishing the sprint backlog early and then drawing more backlog.	Provides quality feedback from customers and stakeholders during sprint reviews to help team members learn, focus, and improve.		Helping product owners keep focus on customer and stakeholder feedback.	Actively working with Agile practice/specialists to learn and improve their leadership for an Agile organization.
	Actively handling interrupts to the product owner to analyze.	Effectively runs sprint retrospectives, generating ideas from the team to improve.				

Table 4.1 (Continued) Agile Behavior Framework

Agile—Delivering Projects, Products, Services, and Organizational Improvement in a Calm Accelerating Way

	Team Member	Scrum Master	Product Owner	Scrum of Scrums Master	Chief Product Owner	Executive
Customer centricity and iterative innovation to deliver greater value and delight	Focus on customers with every bit of work performed.	Referring to customers, sprint goals, and vision during every meeting.	Collaborate with customers to gain feedback and learnings from every product release every sprint.	Referring to customers when supporting the overcoming of challenges and other decision-making efforts	Coordinate and share customer learnings from different product owners.	Coordinate and share customer learnings form different product owners.
		Using customer data as a point of decision-making.	Share from customers in a way that resonates and connects with the Scrum team.		Maintain absolute focus on the customer, fostering learning, and adaptation from reviews.	Maintain absolute focus on the customer, fostering learning, and adaptation from reviews.

(Continued)

Table 4.1 (Continued)   Agile Behavior Framework

Agile—Delivering Projects, Products, Services, and Organizational Improvement in a Calm Accelerating Way

	Team Member	Scrum Master	Product Owner	Scrum of Scrums Master	Chief Product Owner	Executive
Team morale and performance improvement	Lead culture as part of the Scrum team.	Asking Scrum team members their view on a challenge, helping them get to the root cause, and coaching to help them define a path forward.	Asking what our stakeholders and customers would want us to do when a challenge or question arises in a team.	Monitor culture across different Scrum teams and support sharing and learning amongst teams.	Develop team culture within the product owners associated with them.	Focus on culture and teamwork as the primary driver it is. Constantly communicate and support organization focus on teamwork and culture.
	Support teammates and help them develop and grow by sharing your knowledge and skills.	Bring culture and teamwork into sprint reviews as a key topic for reflection, learning, and adaptation.				Visit Scrum teams where they operate daily to learn and adapt as a leader.

Nonetheless, the chapter reveals some challenges and hurdles associated with embracing Agile management. Despite the hurdles, this technique appears advantageous in terms of saving production time, minimizing waste, increasing attention on particular needs of the client, and so forth. There are common methods for implementing Agile, although literature shows that it has not been able to reach its potential. Nevertheless, there is a possibility that in future, it might help numerous organizations in creating a business mindset. While achieving all the progress, the notion of fostering a safety behavior comes to play, as discussed in the next chapter.

Measuring Success

Traditional KPIs for Agile management initiatives or programs are the following:

   a. Team velocity (Points/Sprint executed)
   b. Happiness Metric—Team Morale
   c. Technical debt—# defects or open defects.

   Suggested KBIs for Agile management initiatives or programs are the following:

   a. The response exhibited in relation to change
   b. The kind of interaction shown between employees put in the project and other fellows involved
   c. Assessment of the flexibility exhibited by the employees involved in the project
   d. Assess the engagement and satisfaction of the employees in using the program

   Suggested KAIs for Agile management initiatives or programs are the following:

   a. Number of net promoter surveys conducted
   b. Number of customer surveys at the end of each interaction

Chapter 5

Case Study of CI in Financial Services

Organizations have used various CI programs for years. Typically, companies start with tools, then implement systems and finally embed behaviors toward a continuous improvement (CI) culture. However, organizations that started this way and followed the same approach did not reach the desired sustainable results as expected. They realized that instead of starting with tools, they needed to go the opposite way. Organizations that strive for CI should begin with culture and ideal behaviors, design the system that reinforces these behaviors, and finally select the appropriate tools that people can use to implement the system and foster the culture, this is the approach of the Shingo model, which creates a Culture for sustainable change.

Suncorp Case Study

Suncorp Group is an Australian corporation working in the finance and banking industry as well as general insurance. In 2017, the Suncorp CFO decided to start a business improvement program (BIP) that would last for 3 years. The intention of the BIP was to improve the work processes, improve the customer's experience, and, above all, enhance the financial performance of Suncorp. The goal was $1 billion gross profit in three years.

The BIP had seven work streams. They all worked toward cultivating a CI culture with desired behaviors and sustainable results. A benefit realization

DOI: 10.4324/9781003224747-5

framework (BRF) was created to measure the success of the program. The program was governed throughout the 3 years of implementation, and data was collected to give insights into the improvements.

Suncorp's Previous Transformation Attempts

For Suncorp, it was not their first attempt to implement such a program. Suncorp had a history of transformations and improvement programs that yielded results but needed a CI program that delivered sustainable outcomes.

A quick look at Suncorp's previous programs starts from 2009 when they began the building block program. The goal was to simplify their processes, especially those related to the insurance sector. The program included a new software for a faster claiming process and a general ledger system to consolidate all the financial data for a quicker and more simplified work process. Other projects were also included in this transformation phase, which lasted until 2015.

The two following years, 2016 and 2017, witnessed a transformation based on the customer's needs. Suncorp focused more on the customers' experience and the solutions they could provide to enhance this experience. They also started digitizing parts of their processes and redesigning the organizational structure.

Coming to the year 2018, when the BIP was launched, the goal was to optimize the processes and improve the way of working to produce cost-effective results. Furthermore, the aim was to deliver long-term sustainable results, something that had not happened with the previously implemented programs.

Each of the previous programs included its tools and desired behaviors. These tools and behaviors were not aligned and resulted in inconsistent practices. Thus, they failed in producing sustainable benefits, even though they might have produced results at the time of implementation.

BIP Achievements

The BIP was intended for long-term benefits, but the results showed the opposite. Results were positive in many areas, but it could not shift the culture of Suncorp to a CI culture driven by the desired behaviors. The program also introduced several business frameworks and initiatives that added to the delivered results. On the other hand, the program could not provide sustainable results, and a change in behaviors was not seen. The achievements of the BIP were as follows:

- Initiatives and frameworks
- Financial outcomes
- Process and performance optimization
- Improved business performance and services
- Enhanced customer experience and removal of pain-points

Initiatives and Frameworks

Benefit Realization Framework

The BIP introduced a BRF, and with the use of this framework, Suncorp was able to:

- Create protocols that define the finance department's collaboration opportunities, the project management people, and the organization leaders.
- Classify benefits into financial benefits (including the tangible and nontangible benefits according to whether they affected the budget) and nonfinancial benefits.
- Achieve a consolidated benefit-reporting process using comprehensive benefit-tracking tools.
- Provide more reliable and truthful numbers. Thus, the focus shifted from discussing the reliability of numbers to questioning what was next.
- Enable leaders to make decisions regarding the benefits based on facts and numbers.
- Include financial and nonfinancial benefits derived from the BRF in the prioritization and planning process.

Governance Program

Another framework initiated by the BIP was the governance program. The governance framework was designed with the assistance of the A.T. Kearney (ATK) consulting firm. The framework was intended to govern all activities and improvements related to the BIP and build on the results. ATK governed the program in the first year until a central team was trained and provided with the adequate tools to govern the process in the following years. The governance program led to the following:

- Leaders became more accountable for delivering the benefits and the required outcomes.
- Discussion and conversation between employees and team leaders was emphasized for any business-related consultations to ensure the expected outcomes.

Claims Benefit Framework

The framework was designed to set several guidelines and principles for any initiatives related to the claim sector. The framework assessed the viability of these proposed initiatives according to the guidelines it determined and the expected outcomes these initiatives would deliver.

Initiatives regarding the insurance and claims sector were developed to reduce the costs and mitigate possible risks. They also focused on customer satisfaction as one of the main objectives.

Financial Outcomes

The BIP had a goal of delivering $1 billion gross profits in the 3 years of implementation. The financial outcomes of the project were encouraging. Some of these results were as follows:

- Improved relationships between the finance department and procurement team resulting in better financial outcomes in all spend categories.
- The resulting financial benefits were added to the budget instead of spending such savings on budgetary shortfalls.
- The benefits delivered from the deployment of BIP in the insurance sector were $347 million.
- The insourced legal team initiative delivered $3.3 million in gross benefits.
- The Live Flow model in home & motor insurance resulted in $20 million yearly savings.
- For the banking sector, the same model resulted in financial benefits of $4.4 million yearly.

■ $7 million cost reduction per year was delivered in the home loan sector and $1.7 million cost reduction for the same sector services.

Process and Performance Optimization

The business processes were optimized to produce the maximum results possible with the least resources. The notable achievements were as follows:

■ All resources (human and financial) were used and optimized to deliver cost-effective outcomes.
■ A central program for claims processing was developed to optimize the business workflow.
■ Digital interactions with customers were increased to lower the pressure on the customer call center. An estimated 1.46 million calls were redirected to the digital channels.
■ Increased communication with customers through digital channels instead of other communication methods led to a 6.5 million reduction in hard mail packs.
■ Digital communication also reduced the cost of print mail, saving 280 tons of A4 paper sheets.
■ Removing unnecessary bank letters and shifting to electronic notice delivery (END), where bank customers were encouraged to opt for such service. The opt-in to END has seen tremendous success. For example, the opt-in for Suncorp has increased by 12 percent since 2018.
■ Insourcing a team of legal professionals instead of depending on the external legal panel reduced the costs needed for his external panel. The insourced team resulted in a 2 percent reduction in the hourly rates charged by external firms.
■ Cutting discretionary discounts to 5 percent. The previously used 10 percent discounts (especially at the renewal dates of insurances) were found to be useless and did not obtain results.
■ Removing most of the unnecessary outbound calls with customers and using SMS instead.
■ Creating a dynamic customer request platform for home loans. This form eliminated the need for ten forms, five mailboxes, and five workflow queues.

Improved Business Performance and Services

The BIP improved most of the services offered by the organization in its different sectors. Time and resources were more considered than before when planning for any changes in the organization. Some of the changes made were as follows:

■ Working with a Live Flow model, which included a team to analyze the customers' pain points, develop solutions, and test these solutions before implementation.

Brainstorming and developing ideas were emphasized while considering customers' pain points and employees' opinions.

■ Data and insights were used for future planning.
■ Improved lines of communication across all organizational levels.
■ Stakeholders were engaged in the decision-making process, and all decisions were aligned with the organizational strategic goals and objectives.
■ Establishing a Business Planning Steering Committee to which all initiatives and projects were submitted for approval. The committee also had the responsibility of determining the priorities of any project.
■ An enterprise project governance (EPG) subcommittee was established to deeply review projects and cases before final submission to the higher-level EPG committee.
■ Introducing technology in most business fields and building a roadmap for the loan lending sector improved its process toward determined benchmarks.

Enhanced Customer Experience and Removal of Pain Points

The project considered the customers' needs and their pain points in every process. Some of these pain points were already known, while others needed further investigation and analysis to develop the best solutions. Some of the achieved results were as follows:

■ Digitization of the claims process to speed up the process and make it easier for the customers.
■ Addressing the bank's key customers' needs, such as PIN set and reset, obtaining digital bank statements, and solving missing and lost card blocks.

- Same day approval for new loan applications using the Live Flow model. Virtual teams were created to cover the whole lending process according to a set of conditions.
- Sending an SMS with a link to renewal before its due date.
- Improve the processes via digital tools such as intelligent virtual assistance, self-service enhancements, and manual password reset.
- Designing the Suncorp mobile app to deliver more comfortable and seamless services.

BIP Shortfalls

A quick look at the results of the BIP may indicate that the program was successful in most areas. However, there were many shortfalls in the same areas where the program was successful. Some of the documented shortfalls were as follows:

- No change was seen in the accepted behaviors and norms regarding benefit management. There is a risk of not achieving the expected benefits in the future despite the presence of the BRF.
- Leaders focused on delivering the results, but they lacked the willingness to change the behaviors toward sustainable accountability.
- Compliance was driven by the governance program only. The behavior defined by the BIP will change as per the business needs because they are governance driven, not from an underlying cultural belief.
- The implementation of a system named Bright flag to control the invoices. The system was not successful because Suncorp needed short-term outcomes, but the Bright flag system was designed for long-term results.
- A wasted effort was noticed in some business areas because of the multilayered process.
- A loss in technical expertise resulting from optimization goal and attempting to decrease unnecessary costs (from the BIP point of view). Although an increased reduction in costs was achieved, it was further compensated with the loss of professionals and experienced staff.
- Functional finance leaders and teams were not educated on the BFR. Consequently, the results of BFR were limited to the project management team and were not sustained after the completion of the BIP.

In short, the BIP was set to deliver long-term outcomes, but the focus of the program shifted toward immediate or short-term results. The program succeeded in implementing several initiatives that could reduce costs and increase benefits. However, such a shift made the leaders and managers focus on the "in-year outcomes"; they did not focus on building a sustainable culture driven by the changed ideal behaviors. The case of BIP was not a successful CI case for these reasons.

Using Tools and Systems Only

The BIP, just like most of the improvement programs adopted by Suncorp, relied on external consultants (ATK firm) to deploy the project. The consultancy firm did its job of creating frameworks and governing the project in its first phase. The internal team members were also trained on most of the tools and systems. Despite the expensive external consultancy, the project was not a success. The reason is that all the focus was given to the tools, frameworks, and systems developed by the external firm. In contrast, no focus was given to the underlying desired behaviors and culture.

Focusing on the Benefits and Profits Only

The biggest goal of the consultancy firm was to increase the capabilities of Suncorp to achieve the intended results. For example, the BRF focused on gaining as many benefits as possible. Although the goal was achieved at some point, the sustainability of this goal is questioned. Thus, the BIP took the same track as previous transformation projects of delivering results in a short-term period only.

Leaders Did Not Show a CI Behavior

Although the leaders of Suncorp wanted the change, they did not present a role model for this change. Perhaps the reason is that the change conveyed to them was increased benefits and financial profit. By extension, leaders communicated a profit-based transformation to their employees. Managers and leaders then did not care about presenting a role model of ideal behaviors informed by principles to sustain a CI culture in the organization.

Absences of Guiding Principles and Behavioral Framework

Since the outcomes were the only goals of the BIP, there were no guiding principles in most cases. Systems and tools were developed to address pain points and optimize the business process. Employees were trained to use these systems and tools, but there was no general behavioral framework. Systems like the Bright flag system, which did not result in financial outcomes, were terminated. Some technical expertise professionals were made redundant in the so-called optimization process. Such changes were led by the intention of achieving the goal (short-term effects) without looking forward to building a future improvement framework.

Lessons Learned from the BIP

The BIP experience was not a complete failure, as some might think. The main lesson Suncorp learned is that focusing on the outcomes only and forgetting about the behaviors will not yield sustainable results. If the desired behaviors are not defined before implementing any upcoming improvement projects, Suncorp will continue to revolve in the loop of improvement projects with short-term returns.

To start a CI project, leaders and managers must initiate the process. Suncorp's leaders concentrated their efforts on what the transformation is and what the outcomes are. They completely neglected to identify why this transformation was needed. This great focus on the outcomes changed the way the transformation was done. For example, when introducing the new BRF, one goal was to reinvest the benefits and reflect them in the budgets. Failing to identify the "why" of this new framework led to great confusion. An action designed to improve workflow and increase profit was met with resistance and much debate. An agreed "why" between all people involved in this framework would have established a foundational base for accepting the change.

Another example was the governance program that was intended to demonstrate the transparency of the organization. This program's lack of underlying behaviors resulted in a costly attempt with no sustainable accountability or transparency behavior. Leaders could not present a model of consistent behaviors required from employees. Furthermore, they did not commit to the targets determined in some cases.

The contact center of Suncorp was a vital sector where changes were required. Several initiatives were conducted, such as automation and partnering. However, the results were below expectation. This particular part of the BIP was seen as a cost-intensive program with minimum results. The decision was finally made to terminate the initiatives and give up on the targets. Disappointingly, leaders and employees were part of the failure. They lacked the willingness to improve and see a real change.

Suncorp learned that leaders should be incentivized first to role model the desired behaviors for their employees. Leadership behaviors are to be identified to eliminate negative behaviors that promote resistance to change. One of these negative behaviors that led to negative results was the "budget preservation behavior."

The budget was frequently preserved as intended in the first half of the year. However, the second half forecast showed the opposite, indicating full budget expense. In attempting to "preserve the budget," employees tended to either unnecessarily expend the budget or keep it to reach an equivalent budget for the following year. This behavior is initially driven by a focus on outcomes and reaching the targets for rewards. If the rewarding criteria are shifted to measure the CI behaviors and results, this will incentivize the leaders first to demonstrate the desired behaviors. By extension, these behaviors will be transmitted to the employees.

Cultural change was overlooked despite its importance in any transformational program. People assumed that the change would come all together. In other words, when system change and new tools are introduced, then behaviors will be tailored to suit this change. In reality, the opposite occurs. Behaviors should be role modeled by leaders first. Principles and systems come next.

BIP Competencies Behavioral Framework

Suncorp realized that they should have defined these ideal behaviors from the beginning. The guiding principles should also have been determined to cultivate the culture needed for change. The process works by addressing the "what"— which is the transformation being adopted—followed by "why" implement a transformation, considering the sustainable results as the essential part of the answer. Finally, the "how" to implement this transformation, through using a behavioral framework generalized to all organizational members.

The BIP behavioral framework is divided into two sections. The first is related to business improvement, where each member has a role in this improvement. In contrast, the second part is about decision-making and whether leaders or employees follow these decisions (Table 5.1).

Table 5.1 Example BIP Behavior Framework

	Business Improvement—Continuously Improving and Innovating What We Do to Make Things Simple and Easy for Our Customers and Each Other			
	Team Member	*First Line Leader*	*Business Leader*	*Strategic Leader*
Fosters a culture of continuous improvement	Explores new ways of doing things. Contributes and supports team initiatives that drive continuous improvement.	Proactively and constructively challenges the status quo and encourages others to do the same. Visibly supports strategic initiatives and recognizes the efforts of others.	Invites others to challenge the status quo and envision possibilities to find better ways to achieve results. Visibly supports strategic initiatives and recognizes the efforts of others.	Encourages others to research new approaches that will deliver on strategic goals. Ensures that the business delivers upon funded strategic initiatives and positive results.
Develops and implements solutions	Identifies opportunities to eliminate waste, improve and/or simplify processes, and raises with Leader/Manager as appropriate.	Translates ideas into actions, considering both the downstream and upstream impact. Ensures improvement initiatives will deliver value before developing solutions.	Guides team to implement simpler ways of working considering the downstream and upstream impact. Ensures improvement initiatives will deliver value before developing solutions. Makes decisions about which improvement initiatives to resource. Measures results and modifies solutions as required to ensure the positive and sustainable impact.	Measures progress to ensure improvement efforts lead to the positive and sustainable impact.

(Continued)

Table 5.1 (*Continued*) Example BIP Behavior Framework

Business Improvement—Continuously Improving and Innovating What We Do to Make Things Simple and Easy for Our Customers and Each Other

	Team Member	First Line Leader	Business Leader	Strategic Leader
Leads change	Considers change and new situations as an opportunity for learning and growth. Adaptive to new ways of doing things. Understands the benefits and speak positively about change.	Accepts change and encourages the team to actively participate in change initiatives. Addresses people's concerns about change. Effectively leads and coaches others through periods of change/transition.	Leads their team through change by communicating the rationale and proactively addresses concerns. Includes others in the change process to leverage opinions and ensure commitment. Effectively leads and coaches others through periods of change/transition.	Champions change initiatives across the function and support organizational change. Leverages relationships across the function and organization to gain commitment. Proactively removes roadblocks that inhibit change.
Lives BIP and continuous improvement	Understands Group values and applies them frequently.	Understands Group values and applies them frequently.	Understands Group values and applies them frequently. Actively monitors performance and output across the team and reduces variation. Continually looks for ways to be more productive.	Understands Group values and applies them regularly. Continually looks for ways the function and organization can be more productive.

Cultivating the organization's desired behaviors will eventually lead to habit formation and creating a culture that promotes these behaviors. Leaders should start adopting these behaviors as guided by a set of principles for their respective leading positions. Whenever employees see opposing behaviors, they should be motivated by their leaders to eliminate such behaviors. Examples of the behaviors and principles associated with the behavioral framework are discussed below.

Fosters a Culture of Continuous Improvement

Suncorp's leaders must demonstrate a somewhat unusual behavior, where they are open to innovations and new ideas. They must be open to change and challenge the status quo whenever needed. A culture that does not foster CI is where a leader builds an empire to protect their position. Leaders seek to obtain wealth, power, and authority by controlling people and directing their way of work. Team members are not recognized unless they bring more returns to leaders.

Develops and Implements Solutions

Strategic leaders should link progress with the goals of Suncorp. Business leaders are responsible for identifying and trying to understand the pain points in every process and business area. They should convey this behavior to lower-level leaders and team members to improve the deficiencies. The BRF and governance programs, for example, should not be terminated as a whole. Instead, leaders and team members should work closely together to identify problems and solve them.

Leads Change

One of the most critical behaviors that managers and leaders should role model is willingness to change. Suncorp's leaders should initiate the change by accepting failures and promoting a culture of learning from mistakes. The required actions need to be driven by a real need for change, not by a need for achieving results and securing the targets.

Lives BIP and Continuous Improvement

Leaders are responsible for making the goals and objectives of the organizations clear to everyone. Moreover, they have to tie the BIP's goals with Suncorp's strategic goals. They should promote a culture of teamwork toward these intended goals. It can be done by showing support and trust to all members in their daily job. In this essence, team members have to abide by the rules and principles of the organization and speak up on any behaviors they believe are not meant for CI.

Understands Suncorp

Just as goals and objectives should be defined clearly, each member's role should also be defined. The first line leader's primary role is to communicate each team member's responsibilities in addition to how each one's role can contribute to the achievement of the goals. Business and strategic leaders to reflect the intended CI results should define business metrics and indicators.

Understands the Industry

Suncorp operates in several fields, although they might be related in one way or another. Even if they are working in a particular area, leaders should have an overall understanding of the whole industry. A deep understanding of industry trends and what competitors are doing can help make better decisions and improve performance. For example, knowing that most call centers operate using artificial intelligence (AI) technology to optimize the resources can encourage the organization to invest in an advanced AI system to take it a step further.

Reaches Measured Decisions

Decision-making should be associated with transparent behavior. Clear communication with teams is required and being open and honest when speaking about results and outcomes. Leaders cannot lie about the results of the previous BIP to their employees. If adopted by the whole organization, such behavior will leave the program continuing to deliver minimal results.

Upper-level managers will not be able to make decisions if no members are transparent.

Enhances Brand Reputation

Suncorp is not working separately from the external environment. Reputation is essential to consider. When making any change, it is important to assess how change can affect reputation. In most cases, managers are representatives of organizations, so they bear the most significant part of conveying a good reputation. However, managers should never conceal facts from the employees in an attempt to convey a good reputation. Following their leaders' behavior, employees will put their organization's reputation in front of mind when acting inside or outside the organization.

Applies Good Judgment

Finally, judgment and decision-making should be based on facts, not perceptions. For example, Suncorp's BIP created the BRF to provide reliable numbers to be reflected in the yearly budget. This action should be derived from an accountability behavior that is guided by taking ownership of the behavior. In this case, when the framework goes wrong, it is immediately judged and amended to deliver what is intended to be delivered continuously.

Comprehensive CI Competency Framework

Each organization can define its own set of behaviors to lead to a CI culture. However, general competencies apply in all organizations and can be tailored according to the situation. A comprehensive CI competency framework can be as follows:

	Team Member	Team Leader/ Manager	Department/ Executive Manager	Vice President/ Head of/General Manager	Group President/ Executive General Manager	Group Executive/CEO
Fosters a culture of continuous improvement	Contributes and supports team initiatives that drive continuous improvement.	Proactively and constructively challenges the status quo and encourages others to do the same. Visibly supports productivity initiatives and recognizes the efforts of others.	Proactively and constructively challenges the status quo and encourages others to do the same. Visibly supports productivity initiatives and recognizes the efforts of others.	Invites others to challenge the status quo and envision possibilities to find better ways to achieve results. Ensures that the business recognizes productivity initiatives and positive results.	Encourages others to research new approaches that will optimize results for the business/division. Ensures that the business/division recognizes productivity initiatives and positive results.	Encourages others to research new approaches that will optimize results for the organization. Ensures that the organization recognizes productivity initiatives and positive results.

	Team Member	Team Leader/Manager	Department/Executive Manager	Vice President/Head of/General Manager	Group President/Executive General Manager	Group Executive/CEO
Develops & implements solutions	Identifies opportunities to eliminate waste, improve and simplify processes, and raise with Leader/Manager as appropriate.	Translates ideas into actions, considering both the downstream and upstream impact. Ensures improvement initiatives will deliver value before developing solutions. Measures results and modifies solutions as required to ensure the positive impact.	Guides team to implement more straightforward ways of working considering the downstream and upstream impact. Ensures improvement initiatives will deliver value before developing solutions. Measures results and modifies solutions as required to ensure the positive and sustainable impact.	Guides the team on where to focus productivity initiatives. Measures progress to ensure improvement efforts lead to positive and sustainable impact.	Makes decisions about which improvement initiatives to resource. Measures progress to ensure improvement efforts lead to the positive and sustainable impact.	Makes decisions about which improvement initiatives to resource.

(Continued)

	Team Member	Team Leader/ Manager	Department/ Executive Manager	Vice President/ Head of/General Manager	Group President/ Executive General Manager	Group Executive/CEO
Leads change	Considers change and new situations as an opportunity for learning and growth. Adaptive to new ways of doing things. Understands the benefits and speak positively about change.	Accepts change and encourages the team to participate in change initiatives actively. Addresses people's concerns about change. Effectively leads and coaches others through periods of change/ transition.	Leads their team through change by communicating the rationale and proactively addresses concerns. Includes others in the change process to leverage opinions and ensure commitment.	Leads their teams through change by communicating the rationale and proactively addresses concerns. Includes others in the change process to leverage opinions and ensure commitment. Proactively removes roadblocks that inhibit change.	Champions change initiatives across the business/ division. Leverages relationships across the business/ division to gain commitment. Proactively removes roadblocks that inhibit change.	Champions organization-wide change initiatives. Leverages relationships across the organization to gain commitment.

	Team Member	Team Leader/Manager	Department/Executive Manager	Vice President/Head of/General Manager	Group President/Executive General Manager	Group Executive/CEO
Lives Productivity and Continuous Improvement	Understands the Organizations Group's productivity standards and applies them frequently. Where applicable, follows current Standard Operating Procedures.	Understands Organization Group's productivity standards and applies them regularly. Invests time in monitoring the adherence of team members to agreed Standard Operating Procedures.	Understands Organization Group's productivity standards and applies them regularly. Actively monitors performance and output across the team and reduces variation. Continually looks for ways to be more productive.	Champions Organization Group's productivity standards; reinforces the need to review and optimize the business continually. Continually looks for ways the business can be more productive.	Advocates the productivity standards to the business/division and productivity as an organizational capability. Continually looks for ways the business/division can be more productive.	Advocates the productivity standards to the organization and productivity as an organizational capability.

Or

Table 5.2 framework can be applied to any business. Examples of using this framework to reach the desired behaviors are shown below.

Fosters a Culture of Continuous Improvement

A CI culture is about challenging the status quo and encouraging new ideas and new ways of thinking. A manager who thinks that everything is perfect and does not need changing will hinder any employee's improvement trials. Continuous improvement is also about admitting the shortfalls within oneself and learning from the mistakes.

When a manager was asked why an ongoing improvement project did not get results and how he dealt with that matter, he answered by saying it was a lesson, not a failure case. In successful projects, the organization celebrates the success without reflecting on how they achieved this success. On the other side, failures are always analyzed to determine the reasons and avoid mistakes next time. It is an example of how a manager reinforces the CI culture.

Oppositely, a manager who fails to foster this culture hates challenges. He is always seeking to maintain the status quo instead of striving for perfection. For example, this kind of manager will refuse an initiative to digitalize a specific process as long as it works and delivers minimum results. The investment that would be made to transform the process will be seen as unnecessary extra costs.

Develops and Implements Solutions

Such behavior is implemented by confronting problems and finding solutions instead of searching for excuses for failure. One case to show how different behaviors can come up with different results for the same problem is the following.

The CEO of an organization decided to monitor the performance of different teams. He reviewed one team's target achievement and found that they were far below the targets in several areas. To solve this problem, he met the team leader and started shouting about the poor performance and that this leader is accountable for achieving different results next month.

This solution will probably yield positive results in the next month. However, these results are not sustainable, as an underlying behavior did not drive them. In the longer term, the team leader's focus will be shifted from achieving real success to only achieving targets and showing positive results to the CEO and covering up the negative ones.

Table 5.2 Generic CI Behavior Framework

***Continuous Improvement**—Continuously Improving and Innovating What We Do to Make Things Simple and Easy for Our Customers and Each Other*

	Team Member	Team Leader/ Supervisor	Manager	General Manager	Director/ Executive GM	Group Executive/CEO
Develops and implements solutions	Identifies opportunities to eliminate waste, improve and or simplify processes, and raises with Leader/ Manager as appropriate.	Translates ideas into actions, considering both the downstream and upstream impact.	Guides team to implement simpler ways of working considering the downstream and upstream impact.	Provides guidance to the team on where to focus CI initiatives.	Makes decisions about which improvement initiatives to resource.	Makes decisions about which improvement initiatives to resource.
		Ensures improvement initiatives will deliver value before developing solutions.	Ensures improvement initiatives will deliver value before developing solutions.	Measures progress to ensure improvement efforts lead to the positive and sustainable impact.	Measures progress to ensure improvement efforts lead to the positive and sustainable impact.	
		Measures results and modifies solutions as required to ensure the positive impact.	Measures results and modifies solutions as required to ensure the positive and sustainable impact.			

(Continued)

Table 5.2 (Continued)   Generic CI Behavior Framework

	Team Member	Team Leader/ Supervisor	Manager	General Manager	Director/ Executive GM	Group Executive/CEO
	Continuous Improvement—Continuously Improving and Innovating What We Do to Make Things Simple and Easy for Our Customers and Each Other					
Leads change	Considers change and new situations as an opportunity for learning and growth.	Accepts change and encourages the team to actively participate in change initiatives.	Leads their team through change by communicating the rationale and proactively addresses concerns.	Leads their teams through change by communicating the rationale and proactively addresses concerns.	Champions change initiatives across the business/ division.	Champions organization-wide change initiatives.
	Adaptive to new ways of doing things.	Addresses people's concerns about change.	Includes others in the change process to leverage opinions and ensure commitment.	Includes others in the change process to leverage opinions and ensure commitment.	Leverages relationships across the business/ division to gain commitment.	Leverages relationships across the organization to gain commitment.
	Understands the benefits and speaks positively about change.	Effectively leads and coaches others through periods of change/transition.		Proactively removes roadblocks that inhibit change.	Proactively removes roadblocks that inhibit change.	

Table 5.2 (Continued)   Generic CI Behavior Framework

	Team Member	Team Leader/ Supervisor	Manager	General Manager	Director/ Executive GM	Group Executive/CEO
Continuous Improvement—*Continuously Improving and Innovating What We Do to Make Things Simple and Easy for Our Customers and Each Other*						
Lives continuous improvement	Understands organization Group's CI standards and applies them constantly.	Understands organization Group's CI standards and applies them constantly.	Understands organization Group's CI standards and applies them constantly.	Champions organization Group's CI standards; reinforces the need to constantly review and optimize the business.	Advocates the CI standards to the business/ division and CI as an organizational capability.	Advocates the CI standards to the organization and CI as an organizational capability.
	Where applicable, follows current standard operating procedures.	Invests time in monitoring the adherence of team members to agreed standard operating procedures.	Actively monitors performance and output across the team and reduces variation.	Constantly looks for ways the business can be more productive.	Constantly looks for ways the business/ division can be more productive.	
			Constantly looks for ways to be more productive.			

Another solution would be to meet the team leader and hold him accountable for the performance but giving instructions on what should be done to change these results. The CEO, in this case, talked about the problem and came up with the solution. The results will be mostly positive but will not sustain either. It is because the CEO did not encourage the behavior of taking accountability for solving problems. The leader and employees are not taught problem-solving skills. The solution is neither the team nor the team leader's idea. It may not address their issue, and even if they come up with a solution, the CEO may refuse it because he does not trust others' solutions. The results are again short-term, unsustainable outcomes.

A better solution is that the CEO decided to conduct a meeting with the team leaders and members to discuss the issue. Members were allowed to address the problem and were asked to suggest solutions. The CEO then takes on the solutions and expands. At the end of the meeting, all team members have an agreed-on plan where everyone has a role. The team may then conduct another meeting with his or her leader or the executive manager to discuss further details, but generally, everyone has an idea about what should be done. In this scenario, every member endorsed ownership and accountability behaviors. Solutions are to be developed and implemented by every member, not just the CEO or the higher manager.

Leads Change

Leading the change requires encouraging a set of other ideal behaviors and eliminating the undesired behaviors. Although leaders must kick off the first step, this behavior is shared among all organizational members. All members should define the acceptable behaviors that will lead the change and define the unacceptable behaviors that will not be tolerated.

For example, when attempting to introduce a new project in an organization, the manager who focuses on self-interest only regardless of what it takes to achieve is not a change leader. Similarly, a manager who gives up on ideas or plans when they show the inability to achieve results at some point will not lead to any change.

On the other side, the manager who wants to embrace a change in leading behavior will engage other leaders and teams in the change. He will share his thoughts about the success and failure scenarios of the new project he is willing to introduce. Concerns will be considered to come up with the best way to implement the project or find an alternative.

Lives Productivity and Continuous Improvement

Leaders living productivity will share their experiences and contribute to educating other team members. They care about teaching new skills to every team member instead of thinking about targets and achieving results only. Managers who care about productivity invest in their employees. They allow team members to explore new tools and find new skills in themselves.

An organization decided to adopt new technology in its processes and use automation in several business areas to optimize time, cost, and effort. The general manager decided to rely on external professionals to implement this new system, as it requires a high level of technical expertise. The project was to be implemented in 6 months; the cost was divided between the system's cost and the costs of the external professionals who will implement this system. The manager did not allocate part of the budget for teaching the employees the new system.

Such behavior left the team members confused about operating the system after the 6 months duration ended. Results showed the success of the new system, but the inability to handle this system because of lack of knowledge could not sustain these results.

Embedding a CI behavioral framework in the organization's DNA will ensure the sustainability of the outcomes. Leaders should embrace the transformation and role model the desired change. This way, CI programs are not just projects implemented in a certain period to show outcomes for this particular period. They are then lifetime changes.

Summary

Organizations have unique ways of enforcing CI programs, which are mostly based on the Shingo model. The case study of Suncorp discussed in this chapter reveals all the processes of implementing a CI program including the challenges involved and the chances of success. Since the achievements are supposed to be long term, it is important to have a framework that would be followed to ensure that the outcome is sustainable and the behavioral change is achieved as required. The framework is for business improvement, and therefore, it should contain among other aspects collaboration segment between the government and the organizations and most significantly optimization of the processes and performance.

Nonetheless, the case of Suncorp presents the main lesson that every organization aiming to transform its operations for a competitive advantage must adhere to—merging strategical choices with behavior. Leaders must be able to define the behaviors of employees and help to channel them in the direction required for better outcomes. Considerably, there is a framework that would help them achieve that from the dimension of business improvement and decision-making process. It is all about fostering a culture of improvement and living by it for the success of the organization. On the other hand, it is worth noting that this would come with numerous risks due to occasional presence of risky situations. The chapter that follows presents the discourses of risk behaviors and their importance in risky situations facing organizations.

Measuring Success

In the pursuit of achieving desired behavior in an organization, key performance indicators (KPIs) and key behavior indicators (KBIs) can be used to measure the level of success in achieving the same. For this chapter, the following KPIs and KBIs can be derived.

Traditional KPIs for CI in financial services are as follows:

a. Improved work process
b. Optimized processes that are cost effective
c. Improved leadership
d. Enhanced financial performance

Suggested KBIs for CI in financial services are as follows:

a. Embracing culture and ideal behavior for CI improvement
b. Show interest in the changes being advocated for
c. Adopt a behavioral framework that would lead to an efficient following of the guiding principles
d. Show synchrony in actions from upstream to downstream management

Suggested key activity indicators (KAIs) for CI initiatives or programs are as follows:

a. How many actions have we completed today/this shift on our improvement idea/initiative?
b. How many ideas do we have waiting to be priorities?

Chapter 6

Risk Behaviors

What Is Behavioral Risk?

Behavioral risk can be viewed as a process encompassing the identification, analysis, and management of risk factors in an organization. Management of behavioral risk favors workplace-related risk factors management process pertinent to employees and organizational behavior, which may negatively impact company productivity and performance. Financial service institution faces various risk types, including systematic, operational, financial, legal or compliance, and counterparty.

One of the book's authors relocated a transmission production plant from Jackson, Michigan, to Queretaro, Mexico. The objective was to take advantage of the labor cost reduction that they expected to get from the cheaper Mexican labor. Looking at the KPIs (key performance indicators), the relocation was successful. The plant's operational cost was significantly less than in Michigan. However, some KPI considerations were not accounted for as they were ignored. Sometimes, the most significant risk in our behaviors is "tradition" and a fixed mindset of doing things. In this case, not considering all the risk factors caused executives to ignore the following effects:

1. The cost of transporting materials back and forth from Michigan to Mexico was allocated to overhead, not to the cost of operating the new facility.
2. The cost of the in-process transit inventory, which previously was a few days, was now measured in weeks, and that cost was allocated to overhead.
3. The total manufacturing lead time for the finished vehicle had significantly increased because of the transport time.

DOI: 10.4324/9781003224747-6

4. Occasional border delays also increased the lead time.
5. One of the brass gears in the transmission had to be cut precisely, and the machining in Mexico did not meet the required specs, causing a large amount of waste. The decision was made to have the gear produced in Japan and then transported to Mexico to be installed into the transmission. All of these additional costs were also allocated to overhead.
6. Overhead costs were allocated across all plants, not just to the Mexico plant.

The KPIs show that moving the plant was an intelligent move. Nevertheless, if all the overhead specific to the new location was added back to the Mexico plant, the cost of the new facility was higher than the cost of the old facility in Michigan. The message is simple, "Don't take the risk of trusting 'tradition' rather than looking at the big picture."

Financial service industries face risk challenges every day. There has been a strong focus on process risk controls in this industry, particularly considering the major external threats it faces. The usual reaction is to create risk committees to mitigate risks and further control processes and procedures. Instead of reducing the risk, this approach reduces the "thinking" of employees and managers, and as a result, they are no longer able to react to unplanned threats. Employees and managers are now more focused on the compliance with procedures and controls imposed by these risk committees thinking that this is the only way to avoid risk implications. However, breaches and problems continue to occur. It indicates that there must be another way to deal with risks. Risk should be controlled and managed in other ways driven by regulations and mindsets. Managers and leaders should now consider embedding risk behaviors within their organization's cultures in risky situations.

Background on Risk in Financial Service

Financial services are exposed to various landscapes on a global scale. These landscapes are one reason for the changing risks that financial services are exposed to. All industries are exposed to the same risks, but such dangers can affect the institution's financial services. Thus, financial industry leaders should think of tools to leverage the capability of organizations to control this risk. Nevertheless, they should consider the financial industry's common threats before managing the risk. Some of these risks are as follows.

Compliance Governing and Management

In attempting to control risks, financial services may impose some regulations and laws, which in turn act as a potential risk. In addition, most financial organizations are managed by state-related entities that set regulatory requirements for managing these organizations. The problem here lies in complying with these regulations, as this usually needs time, steps, and procedures. In some cases, failing to comply with these regulations may oblige the organization to pay penalties.

Cybersecurity

While technology has limited manual errors and human fraud, it introduced another threat: cybersecurity. Cybersecurity is a risk that threatens all industries working with technology. The financial sector, in particular, is a targeted entity for the benefits cyber attackers may get. A considerable investment has been made to confront this risk, but individual efforts will be useless if risk behavior is not entirely incorporated into the organizational culture.

Third Party

Most financial organizations work with third parties to continue to provide their services. These third parties may need confidential data from their customers, which adds to the ordinary risks of financial services. Providing data to third parties may expose this data to loss or disruption. The biggest problem for financial services is that they are usually held accountable for any data loss or steal. Therefore, managing the security of third parties and their access to data is one of the risk controls that financial services should consider.

Process Risk Controls

Organizations have developed several models and frameworks to control risks. They all have cultures and behaviors as the main elements of their risk management and control. One of the standard models used to embed an influential organizational risk culture is the A-B-C model. The ABC of risk culture approach by David explains that there is diverseness in organizational culture across companies and that attitudes shape behaviors that lead to an organization's culture when repeated. According to the model, culture will influence and shape attitudes and behaviors.

A-B-C Model

Many organizations adopt the A-B-C model to set in an organizational culture of desired behaviors and attitudes. It starts with attitudes, then behavior resulting in culture; these are the A-B-C. Adopting this model for creating a risk management culture is outlined as follows:

a. **Risk attitude:** This is the position individuals inside organizations take in response to their risks. The organizational culture toward risk usually influences this position.
b. **Risk behavior** is how employees and managers respond or react to a particular risk. Behaviors are also influenced and shaped by culture and attitude.
c. **Risk culture:** This is the organization's overall understanding and perception of risk. It consists of the values, beliefs, and behaviors in the organization.

According to this model, culture is formed by behaviors shaped by attitudes. Additionally, culture will influence attitudes and behaviors, so it becomes a loop that starts with culture. Creating a positive risk culture is crucial for risk management and control. Having a positive risk culture can help with higher compliance with regulations for financial services. Although compliance is one of the risks financial organizations face, having a risk-taking culture can convert this potential risk into improvements. When risk management policy aligns with positive risk culture, this contributes to further compliance. Risk culture influences the attitudes of leaders, who further influence employees. As a result, this culture shapes and affects the strategies and decisions related to risk taking.

Risk Behaviors

As mentioned above, attitudes and behaviors form culture. Having a set of risk behaviors promotes a positive risk culture. These behaviors are common in all organizations, and they include the following.

Ethical Role Modeling

When ethical issues emerge, managers are more concerned with the vast implications on their internal performance and external reputation. Risk increases when these ethical issues are customer-related, especially for financial industries. As most organizations care about their customers and their number one goal is to satisfy them, customer-related issues are a high-level risk. When the issue is of ethical consideration, it challenges the organization to solve the problem to satisfy the customer and not harm the reputation. An essential behavior here is leaders' role modeling of the ethical conduct of the organization. Even if the problem is not of a high-risk level, modeling such behavior will urge other employees to act similarly.

Challenge Management

Unlike the previous behavior, challenge management is a behavior that employees should exhibit. It is about considering diverse perspectives. Organizations that allow their employees to share their visions and suggestions can deploy a positive risk management culture. Instead of showing employees what they should do, employees are encouraged to show managers how they should act. Accordingly, this shows the difference between an organization with challenging management behavior and organizations with unidirectional management. Allowing different views to be expressed may yield alternative approaches managers do not consider.

Nonblame Behavior

Fostering a risk culture requires holding employees accountable for their decisions. However, such behavior may lead to a culture of blaming, where they are blamed for the negative consequences of their actions and, consequently, employees will not want to take risks so that they cannot be blamed for any failures. Adopting nonblame behavior can be challenging to managers. They should trust employees to make decisions. Simultaneously, blaming employees for mistakes should not lead to negative behavior that discourages openness and learning from mistakes. Adopting these behaviors and others will contribute to a risk mindset that is always accepted as a challenge, not something to prevent. How people think affects how they will act. Thus, a risk mindset is essential for a positive risk management and control culture.

Risk Mindset

People face risks in their everyday life. Risk levels vary but shared with all risk levels is the need for a quick response. More often, people facing threats do not think before they act. Their reaction is usually driven by their feelings and embedded behaviors in reacting to a similar situation. Expanding this to the organizational level, managers and employees respond to risk according to the culture's embedded behaviors. The goal thus is to reach a risk mindset that responds to those risks instead of reacting. Ideally, this mindset bases its decisions on thoughts and reasoning rather than feelings. People respond to a risk according to their perspective of risk. For example, if the risk is avoided, the organization will lose many opportunities.

On the other hand, if the risk is seen as a challenge, managers and employees may go to the extreme of taking every risk, which is also not the best response. Risk management needs a risk mindset to think appropriately about the potential threats and respond to each risky situation. Before thinking about fostering a risk mindset inside the organization, one should first understand the concept of risk. A better understanding of risk will lead to better management and control. When building a risk mindset, these values about risk should be embedded in the organizational culture:

a. **Risk is inevitable:** People should not always try to prevent risk. Risks are a natural occurrence that happens daily. The goal thus is not to avoid risks or prevent their occurrence but rather to deal with them appropriately.

b. **Risk is manageable:** At an organizational level, most risks are predicted, either by using data and insights or through reflecting on similar situations, maybe in other organizations. Thus, risk can be managed. In the worst cases, risk mindsets can deal with the effects and mitigate them when it occurs before it is predicted.

c. **Risk is sometimes an opportunity:** As mentioned before, it depends on the risk perspective. It may be seen as a threat or an opportunity. For example, a particular risk may cause delays in the business but results in reduced costs. Dealing with threats and opportunities and discovering the opening within the danger is the key to a positive risk mindset.

d. **Risk matters:** Avoiding risk does not mean never thinking about risk. If prevented or challenged, risk will affect the business processes in one way or another. Thus, risk should always be considered, and its impact on the business should be assessed.

e. **Risk is the responsibility of all people:** All employees face risk in their job unless they are not doing it correctly. A risk mindset knows that the employee is accountable for any risk that affects their performance in the organization.

Risk should be faced with proactivity: Risk is not managed by waiting for its impacts. There is a remarkable difference between reacting and responding to risk. Reacting is waiting for the implications to manifest and then taking action while responding initiates the action before it is all done.

How to Develop a Risk Mindset

First, organizations should make sure that the previous values are well embedded in the minds of all employees. There should be a clear, shared understanding of risk. The following steps may help in implementing a risk mindset within the organization:

1. **Start one by one:** If the organization does not have a risk mindset, it is impossible to shift the thinking of the whole organization. Leaders should start by implementing each value and related behavior one by one and work on them until they become a habit.
2. **Focus on minds:** Although a risk mindset appears as behavior, it starts with the mind. Leaders should focus on changing people's minds and thinking about risk instead of telling them how to behave.
3. **Seek help:** It is always good to seek help when you cannot do it independently. Organizations trying to transform their cultures can seek mentors and coaches to help set the general rules or guidelines for dealing with risk.

Risk Culture

Definition

Risk cultures are the traditions and norms of behaviors of people or groups of individuals in a company that determines their process of risk identification, comprehension, discussion, and action for risks taken or confronted by the organization.

Organizations have regulatory approaches and controls to minimize the risk in response to threats. These regulations do not necessarily prevent risk-taking behavior, but they may define the boundaries for acceptable risk taking. However, risk controls can also hinder the performance of the organization. In attempting to control risks, managers impose a high level of corporate governance. The governance varies. It may reside only in the top managerial positions where critical decisions are governed, or it may go down to employees' relations and individual behaviors. Governance frameworks imply an understanding of risk oversight as imposing more controls to prevent as much risk as possible. Compliance with such frameworks is then a voluntary action stemming from the fear of financial penalties rather than underlying conduct. Such cases cannot be regarded as organizations applying risk culture.

Managers and leaders must advocate compliance with risk controls instead of implementing a risk culture. Risk controls are derived from metrics that, in most cases, rely on factual data. The management will prevent risk, but avoiding the risk is not always the goal. Some risks are worth taking as they have business opportunities behind them. Thus, there is a need to have a risk culture. Developing an organizational culture that promotes positive risk behavior is inevitable for an organization's success in the challenging market companies are competing in today. Risk culture is how organizations manage risks influenced by their organizational culture. A positive risk culture determines how the organization will perform in different situations. Risk culture can have the following effects:

1. It influences the attitudes of all employees toward risk. According to their organizational culture, employees will be either willing to take risks or afraid or avoid them.
2. It affects the decision-making process. Managers responsible for critical decisions within the organization will either take risks or withdraw as their organizational culture informs.
3. Risk culture will improve risk behavior. When people of the organization are used to taking risks, they can determine when it is right to take a specific threat.
4. Risk culture promotes a mistakes-tolerable environment, though, at the same time, wrong behaviors are not condoned.

Developing a culture that encourages employees to act in risky situations and make decisions based on their risk perception is key to healthy risk oversight. Organizations have two approaches in developing a risk culture; both emphasize behaviors.

Top-to-Bottom Approach

In this approach, embedding a positive risk culture starts at the top. Managers and leaders will clearly state their definitions of risk and the desired behaviors they expect in response to risk. Leaders should, for instance, lay out their visions and regulations for managing risk. The behaviors should be communicated to all organization staff, and leaders should be at the forefront to role model these behaviors.

Bottom-to-Top Approach

This approach does not tell employees exactly what to do to manage risk. Instead, they are given the tools and necessary policy guidelines to manage risk and allow a positive culture to develop naturally. The advantage of this approach is that the intended behavior is put into practice, and employees are left to figure out risk management. When certain risk behaviors show positive results, employees are encouraged to continue with the same behavior, and thus, risk culture is created.

The two approaches have their advantages and disadvantages. In the first approach, desired behaviors are defined, and employees are told what they are expected to do. There is little scope for them to develop their perception and estimation of risk. This should not be removed with simple compliance to risk controls as in the second approach. The risk is avoided in the best possible ways. No risk is better than the risk with potential positive outcomes. However, in the top-to-bottom approach, employees are decision makers and take risks within a behavioral framework. In the second approach, behaviors are practiced rather than communicated. Employees will discover the intended behavior themselves when they see the results. It takes more time, and mistakes are more likely to occur in the second approach. However, it is sustainable for a longer time when behavior is practiced.

How to Develop a Risk Culture

To achieve a risk-mature organization, one should start with behaviors. Several indicators can predict whether an organization is cultivating risk behaviors or not. These indicators are called key risk indicators (KRIs). Similar to KPIs, which measure performance, KRIs measure risk behaviors.

Some KRIs are as follows:

■ Consistent risk-taking behaviors starting from the top managers down to all employees.
■ Ethical and legal considerations.
■ Deep understanding among all employees of the meaning of risk and the benefits of risk management to the organization.

■ Transparency regarding the outcomes of risk behaviors.
■ Wrong behavior condoning is not standard, and risk reporting is encouraged.
■ Desired risk behaviors are rewarded.
■ The status quo is challenged, and risk taking is prevalent.
■ The ongoing learning process of developing risk-management skills and previous incidents.

Organizations looking to implement a risk culture should use the above indicators to assess their risk behaviors. A situational analysis of the existing risk culture may also be required to determine the current situation and build upon it. The following steps may be undertaken:

Step 1: Where Are We Now?
In this step, organizations should define their risk behaviors and culture. The above KRIs can determine whether the organization already has part of the desired risk behaviors or starts from the beginning.

Step 2: Where Do We Want to Go?
Organizations should then define the desired position they want to be in. Using the same KRIs, organizations can determine the expected behaviors in response to risk and the overall intended culture.

Step 3: What Needs Changing?
Here, organizations can address the gap. After defining their current situation and the intended one, they know what is missing. The next step will work on the missing elements to reach the goals.

Step 4: How to Do It?
Now, it is time to implement a risk culture program or framework. One of the approaches mentioned above (top-to-bottom or bottom-to-top) could be executed. Organizations can also use both approaches and develop a very different strategy.

Step 5: Did It Succeed?
This step is a repetition of the first step. This time, the assessment is done after risk behaviors are promoted. Changes in the risk culture are assessed, and then the cycle is repeated all over again.

The Ideal Risk Behaviors

Ideal behaviors are different from one organization to another. So too are risk behaviors. Organizations should be able to identify perfect risk behaviors. One example of how behaviors should be determined is as follows: A manager wants employees and teams to continuously look at data on their actual performance and compare it to the targets. If there is a gap, they should identify it and identify whether it can be fixed. Closing this gap may require risky decisions, such as putting in more money and resources to get an immediate fix or using a structured risk assessment. Different decisions could be made, but, in all cases, the desired behavior here is as follows: The individual/team uses data to understand the gap between actual and targets and clearly define actions to close the gap permanently.

Leaders must clearly describe these behaviors as something that can be observed (seen and heard). By this, risk behaviors can be assessed, and KRIs can be used to measure a risk culture's success. Vague definitions of desired risk behaviors can leave each employee to their perceptions. On the other hand, strict but ideal risk-defining behaviors will not leave room for employees to think and react independently. If they are faced with situations other than the described ones, they probably will not respond in the desired way, as they did not develop the behaviors. They were told what to do, not taught how to react. Therefore, leaders can start by identifying and classifying the risks. Risks can be classified according to different criteria. One of the most used criteria of classification is the risk level. This classification offers a comprehensive model of dealing with risk according to how it might affect the organization. Different risk levels require alternative behaviors. Similarly, other managerial and employee levels should react differently according to their authority. However, the general behavioral framework can be similar for most managers and employees.

Therefore, the main steps for defining the ideal risk behaviors for any organization are as follows:

- Identifying and classifying the risks.
- Defining the behaviors that may lead to the best possible outcomes for each risk level.
- Creating a comprehensive framework for managerial and employee groups.
- Generalizing the framework to all the organization.
- Monitoring the adoption of those behaviors and the performance after implementing the behaviors.
- Using KRIs to measure the success of the behavioral framework.

For most organizations, a general corporate competencies framework categorized by the level of risk is as follows (Table 6.1).

Table 6.1 Risk Behavioral Framework

Decision Making/Judgment—Making Sound Decisions Based on Understanding Business, Analyzing Data, and Applying Common Sense.

	Team Member	Team Leader/ Manager	Executive Manager	General Manager	Executive General Manager	Group Executive/ CEO
Understands organisation group	Understands the organization's strategies and how own role, team, and department contribute.	Explains the business value and drivers for own team in relation to the organization's strategies.	Articulates the business value, drivers, and accountabilities of business units/divisions within the organization.	Understands own business operations and the organizational levers that drive profitable growth.	Understands own business operations and the organizational levers that drive profitable growth.	Articulates the shareholder value proposition of the organization to internal and external stakeholders.
	Understands the interrelationships of the organisation Group's functions/divisions.	Articulates and ensures the team understands the interrelationships of the organisation Group's functions/divisions on their responsibilities.	Articulates the organizations position, products, and services when compared with other organizations.	Articulates the shareholder value proposition of the business.	Articulates the shareholder value proposition of the business/division.	
		Understands the key business metrics that drive the organisation group's results.	Optimizes business results by actively managing operational levers.	Optimizes business results by actively managing operational levers.	Optimizes business/division results by actively managing operational levers.	

Table 6.1 (Continued) Risk Behavioral Framework

Decision Making/Judgment — Making Sound Decisions Based on Understanding Business, Analyzing Data, and Applying Common Sense.

	Team Member	Team Leader/ Manager	Executive Manager	General Manager	Executive General Manager	Group Executive/ CEO
Understands the industry	Understands how the organisation Group is differentiated from competitors.	Monitors industry trends and articulates the potential impact. Understands how the organisation Group is differentiated from competitors.	Monitors industry trends and articulates the potential impact Integrates understanding of the industry into decision-making.	Monitors and anticipates global trends that impact being a leading provider of financial services. Plans for impact of regulatory or commercial changes. Integrates understanding of the industry into decision-making.	Monitors and anticipates global trends. Manages financial impact of regulatory or commercial changes and proposes strategies to mitigate. Incorporates industry best practice into business/division plans.	Monitors and anticipates global trends that impact being a leading provider of financial services. Anticipates the impact of economic policy issues and/or industry regulations. Incorporates industry best practice and understanding of the external environment into organizational strategy.

(Continued)

Table 6.1 (Continued) Risk Behavioral Framework

	Team Leader/ Manager	Executive Manager	General Manager	Executive General Manager	Group Executive/ CEO
Decision Making/Judgment—*Making Sound Decisions Based on Understanding Business, Analyzing Data, and Applying Common Sense.*					
Team Member			Knowledgeable in current and possible future policies, practices, trends, technology, and information that impact the organization.	Knowledgeable in current and possible future policies, practices, trends, technology, and information that impact the organization.	Knowledgeable in current and possible future policies, practices, trends, technology, and information that impact the organization.

Table 6.1 (Continued)   Risk Behavioral Framework

	Team Member	Team Leader/ Manager	Executive Manager	General Manager	Executive General Manager	Group Executive/ CEO
Decision Making/Judgment—*Making Sound Decisions Based on Understanding Business, Analyzing Data, and Applying Common Sense.*						
Reaches measured decisions	Identifies important information and data relevant to role.	Identifies and analyzes important data relevant to the role and recommends actions.	Analyzes data to shape business decisions; separates the important from the unimportant.	Analyzes complex data and metrics to shape business decisions; gets to the heart of issues.	Analyzes complex data and metrics with rigor; is decisive in adjusting business/division strategies.	Demonstrates decisiveness and commitment in order to pursue organizational advantage.
	Considers broader implications of actions.	Considers broader implications of actions.	Considers broader implications and practicality of decisions.	Evaluates options considering depth and breadth of impact and consequences.	Evaluates options considering depth and breadth of impact and consequence.	Actively seeks to simplify complicated issues by isolating the most important elements and creates clarity when in ambiguous situations.
				Actively seeks to create clarity and simplicity in complex or ambiguous situations.	Actively seeks to create clarity and simplicity in complex or ambiguous situations.	

(Continued)

Table 6.1 (Continued)   Risk Behavioral Framework

	Team Member	Team Leader/ Manager	Executive Manager	General Manager	Executive General Manager	Group Executive/ CEO
Decision Making/Judgment — Making Sound Decisions Based on Understanding Business, Analyzing Data, and Applying Common Sense.						
Enhances brand and reputation	Understands organization brand proposition and the importance of reputation to the organization's success.	Understands organization brand proposition and the importance of reputation to the organization's success and encourages the team to do the same.	Actively supports the brand proposition and understands the importance of mitigating the risk of erosion.	Proactively sponsors the brand proposition and the importance of mitigating the risk of erosion.	Cascades the brand proposition and proactively sponsors the importance of mitigating the risk of erosion.	Ensures that the organization has a clear brand proposition that will deliver shareholder value.
	Considers organization's reputation and potential risks when taking action or making decisions.	Considers organization's reputation and potential risks when taking action or making decisions.	Manages reputational risk with internal and external stakeholders, escalating as required.	Proactively manages reputational risk with internal and external stakeholders, escalating as required.	Objectively manages reputation risk in consideration of business/division and organization brand.	Proactively manages reputational risks to the organization through expert judgment in critical decision-making.

Table 6.1 (Continued) Risk Behavioral Framework

	Team Member	Team Leader/ Manager	Executive Manager	General Manager	Executive General Manager	Group Executive/ CEO
Decision Making/Judgment – *Making Sound Decisions Based on Understanding Business, Analyzing Data, and Applying Common Sense.*						
Applies good judgment	Makes good decisions based on a mixture of analysis, wisdom, experience, and judgment.	Makes good decisions based on a mixture of analysis, wisdom, experience, and judgment.	Makes good decisions based on a mixture of analysis, wisdom, experience, and judgment.	Makes good decisions based on a mixture of analysis, wisdom, experience, and judgment.	Makes good decisions based on a mixture of analysis, wisdom, experience, and judgment.	Makes good decisions based on a mixture of analysis, wisdom, experience, and judgment.
		Aware of the importance of perception when making good decisions.	Understands that good decisions need to be perceived as in the best interest of customers, organisation, and employees.	Ensures good decisions are perceived as in the best interest of customers, organization, and employees.	Balances the conflicting interests of multiple stakeholders to an equitable outcome.	Balances the conflicting interests of multiple stakeholders to an equitable outcome.

Framework

This behavioral framework advocates for certain behaviors related to the decision-making process. Managers of the highest managerial levels have different roles from other employees. For example, managers are responsible for conveying the organization's ideal risk behaviors to the shareholders to imply transparency and deal with various situations.

Some of the ideal risk behaviors that the framework advocates are as follows:

a. **Understanding the organization**
   Understanding the organization involves understanding what works well for its approach to continuous improvement (CI) that it can build on. It also consists of understanding the areas of improvement to help the organization progress and measure its progress. Understanding the organization is the responsibility of all leaders and employees. Yet, leaders should initiate this behavior and promote the value of understanding throughout the organization. Each team member is then responsible for understanding their role and contribution to the organization. Thus, they will understand their role in risk situations.

b. **Understand the industry**
   This behavior helps leaders know the critical activities needed to take them to the next level. Leaders are advocates for the behavioral system and actively promote its value. They know that ideal behaviors will deliver outstanding results, so they will pull for the behaviors needed to be undertaken. It is related to understanding the industry, as understanding the competitive market means making better decisions and mitigating risks. Leaders continuously seek to refine the behavioral framework to drive the intended results.

c. **Reach measured decisions**
   Risk decisions are closely related to risk behaviors. Leaders continually strive to embed ideal risk behaviors to foster decision-making skills in all employees. Leaders respond positively to assessment findings and results of different behaviors to make better decisions. Consequently, they can proactively develop and implement action plans based on feedback.

d. **Enhance brand recognition**
   A well-defined behavioral framework provides opportunities for recognition. Employees proactively seek out and implement opportunities to improve throughout this behavioral framework. Leaders

and employees should know that there are constant recognition and reinforcement of ideal behaviors at every opportunity. Defining the ideal risk behaviors convey a good image for the organization and, thus, enhances brand recognition.

e. **Applies good judgment**

Good judgment means making decisions based on accurate analysis. Managers should make decisions based on their assessment of the customer's best interests. Managers should also consider employees when judging and making decisions.

Defining Ideal Risk Behaviors

The Shingo Institute model points to three insights when building a culture in any organization. These key insights are as follows:

a. **to deliver ideal results, you require ideal behaviors**

The results and outcomes of an organization are dependent on the culture and thus the way its people behave. Whether an employee makes a specific, risky decision will influence the overall results and outcomes, even for a small risk. To achieve the ideal results (risk mindset), ideal risk behaviors should be promoted within the organizational culture.

b. **Principles guide behaviors**

The more profound people understand an organization's principles and values, the better they adopt a behavior. In a risk culture, ethical and legal regulations are the principles to be considered. Organizations should design their risk culture to follow these regulations and other organizational values.

c. **System drive behaviors**

Systems are the frameworks or procedures designed to implement the behavior. These systems can drive a positive risk behavior if designed to do so. Organizations that foster a risk culture cannot develop systems where employees cannot make decisions regarding their day-to-day jobs.

Cultures that form accidentally or without attention can have significant and far-reaching adverse effects. A culture built around "firefighting" rewards and promotes the "firefighters" rather than identifying and fixing the problems that caused the emergencies. In a culture that supports the "power-hungry," people might withhold information except where it can benefit them personally. They keep the decision-making authority as close as possible rather than trusting others to make appropriate choices. This means the organization responds much more slowly to issues and is less likely to make the best decisions. Likewise, it is not difficult to imagine the behaviors that might arise in organizations that foster cultures of fear, survival, anger, power, and blaming.

Applying this to a risk behavior focus, cultures that mitigate each risk situation emerge without developing a risk mindset or a risk behavior framework to take advantage of available opportunities. In contrast, organizations that follow the operational excellence model and start with behaviors will foster positive risk culture. Such a culture promotes risk mindsets and allows employees to take accountability for their decisions.

Benefits of Risk-Defining Behavior

Organizations have the business goals of growing, sustaining this growth, and interacting with stakeholders. These goals may be interrelated or sequential, as one follows the other. In all cases, such plans require a kind of system or framework to define potential risks and the behaviors needed to deal with these risks. Consequently, organizations can adapt and grow within the current situation. Risk-defining behavior has several benefits, for example:

1. **Regulatory requirements**
   Risk-defining behaviors provide a set of regulations for dealing with different risks. These risks may be explicitly related to the business or the organization's community.
2. **Reduce uncertainty**
   Risk is associated with uncertainty. Situations defined as risky for organizations are usually those where the outcome is uncertain. This uncertainty leaves the decision-makers not knowing what to do or how to deal with such cases. Risk-defining behaviors guide employees to react and move forward when faced with one of these uncertain situations.
3. **Learning and improvement**
   Risk-defining behaviors are opportunities for learning and development. When employees face different risk situations and react to the defined behaviors, they can learn from the experience. This enables employees to develop skills to deal with future risk situations with different risk levels.

4. **Awareness**

   A set of behavioral frameworks for risk situations increases the awareness of managers and employees of potential risk situations. Knowing what the organization can go through is essential for plans and business decisions.

5. **Decision-making**

   Expanding on the previous point, defining risk behaviors help managers, leaders, and even employees to make the right decisions in their everyday work. When employees know the expected behavior in a particular situation, they can determine the anticipated decision or the best decision to drive the best possible outcomes.

6. **Proper projection of performance results**

   Awareness of potential risks followed by the right decisions will properly project the performance outcomes. This means that managers and employees can predict their performance when they have risk-defining behaviors and respond to threats according to these behaviors.

7. **Improved culture**

   Finally, risk-defining behaviors and the previously discussed benefits will improve organizational culture. Behaviors are one of the main elements of improving and sustaining corporate culture and risk behavior.

A Practical Case

A contact center employed a new manager to help them achieve organizational targets, reach optimal performance, and sustain these achievements. On his first day in the position, he decided to gain an insight into the corporate culture. He focused on understanding how the system flowed in the contact center, what the existing behaviors were, and what prevented the organization from achieving the optimal performance it was striving for. In doing so, the manager decided to look and listen to the employees and leaders. He wanted to get an idea of the whole thing from different points of view. He observed and spoke with colleagues, managers, and leaders. Several issues arose from these observations.

First, there were incidences of poor behavior and discipline within the call center. The leadership focused on the organization's monthly targets and the individual targets of the employees only. They did not care much about the behaviors of the employees and how these behaviors affected performance. A related problem was the recruitment process. It was heavily weighted toward technical ability, and there was no behavioral assessment. Therefore, much focus was given to the prerequisite skills to work in a contact center when recruiting team members. Still, they did not necessarily fit the organization's culture. Second, the high turnover resulted from, as the new manager assumed, uncertainty around reacting in different situations, holding one accountable for his actions. In addition, the lack of a predefined risk behavioral framework enhanced the problem. Such a framework will direct employees in most risk situations they face in their daily work. Instead, employees were left to act independently and then assessed on their actions. In high-risk situations, managers will give orders directly, and no employee is allowed to perform upon his perception or experience.

The organization had not defined a set of "expected behaviors" and, as the saying goes, "The behavior you walk past is the behavior you accept." It was a priority for the new manager to put together an agreed set of behaviors that the whole organization would live by. Thus, when any new member is recruited, or even with existing colleagues, they would clearly understand the organizational culture and how they operate. Before anything else, the manager decided to solve the above problems. He believed that organizational performance could be improved by adopting a behavioral framework that enhanced a CI culture. Further, the high turnover level could be reduced by having a risk behavioral framework to foster the employees' risk mindset to act independently in risk situations. Such acts should be coupled with a valuation from the managers of employees' actions and performance to foster their loyalty to the organization and reduce turnover.

Solving these two factors required a long-term strategy that involved senior leaders buying into the expected behaviors and reinforcing them through constant and consistent assessments. With the help of leaders and employees, the manager created a behavioral framework to help every individual in the organization make decisions and apply good judgment in different business situations. For the first problem, a behavioral framework was a perfect solution. Further, the manager decided to integrate an assessment of the desired behaviors into the recruitment process. This helped address the problem's first causation and ensured colleagues' alignment with what was required from both skills and cultural perspectives. To solve the second problem of the high turnover levels, the manager decided to have a risk behavioral framework and assess this risk using KRIs. The manager himself applied this competency risk behavioral framework on his first workday. He managed to comprehend the organizational culture and understand the industry he is working in. This understanding then helped him reach his decisions on incorporating risk behaviors in the organization. The adopted risk behavioral framework encouraged employees to refuse a compliance mindset to process orders and instead focus on understanding their roles in managing risk.

The next stage for the organization was to move toward Shingo. At this level of maturity, leader roles shift from workplace systems to systems of thinking and behaviors. A well-established and embedded maturity risk assessment was already implemented, but the manager wanted to extend this to embed ideal behaviors further. Therefore, he decided to make behaviors explicit in the overall evaluation. The general behavioral framework and the risk behavioral framework were promising. There was a dramatic improvement in the quality of recruits coming into the contact center, resulting in leaders' increased capacity. Leaders are now spending less time managing poor behaviors and more time on quality coaching and development conversations. Additionally, the KRIs used for assessing the risk behaviors helped the managers decide the ideal risk behaviors to promote. Employees were now more knowledgeable about the proper behaviors and ready to take accountability for their actions, even in the riskiest business decisions.

Risks Beyond Financial Services

The *Atlanta Journal-Constitution* published an article in July 2021 titled, "Supply chain troubles leave customers wanting." The article focused on the COVID virus and its effect on shutting borders. It discusses several examples of price jumps, including the price of lumber nearly tripling in the United States. It stressed that the more complex the supply chain, the higher risk of supply chain failure and disruption. The article concludes by saying, "The shorter and simpler the chain, the quicker it will adapt, said Sanchoy Das, a supply chain expert at the New Jersey Institute of Technology." Numerous studies have been performed that focus on risk management throughout the organization. Unfortunately, what happens is that these intensive studies are triggered by some catastrophic event, like a pandemic or a tsunami. Thorough investigations focus on what happened and how the event and disruptions should have been managed. Over time, these studies are often followed by ever-decreasing interest, as if the event never occurred and we will never have another catastrophic event in the future. In addition, when another severe event occurs, we are once again found unprepared.

The severe earthquake, followed by a devastating tsunami, which brought Japan to a standstill, triggered a study of this type. Supply chain channels were brought to a halt throughout Asia, devastatingly impacting worldwide. One of the authors participated in one of these studies, which he did in conjunction with APICS (name has now changed to Association for Supply Chain Management) focused on supply chain disruption and focuses on supply chain resilience. The full document can be found at (view-the-full-chronic-disruption-report.pdf [apics.org]). Enterprise resilience is foundational to the long-term sustainability of any organization. Resilience and preparedness are CI behavioral elements foundational in creating a bridge supporting long-term effective performance systems, as this chapter has thoroughly discussed.

Measuring Success

The traditional approach to measuring success is through the use of KPIs. To enhance the sustainability of embedding CI behaviors, there are also suggested key behavioral indicators (KBIs) to be used in conjunction with the KPIs.

Traditional KPIs for risk behavior are as follows:

a. Considerations of operational costs
b. Check the lead time as affected by different geographical locations
c. Assess the risks of exposing the financial services of the organization
d. Observe the efficiency of the models and frameworks being used to control risks in organizations

Suggested KBIs for risk behavior are as follows:

a. Avoid acting based on the tradition that "it has always been done like that."
b. Assess the attitude-behavior and culture exhibited due to risk.
c. Ability to operate ethically when dealing with risk.
d. Ability to build resilience

Banking Royal Commission

The government conducted the Banking Royal Commission, or the Royal Commission into Misconduct in the Banking, Superannuation, and Financial

Services Industry, to report on misconduct in financial services. The Royal Commission was created after the media made allegations of agreed culture within Australian financial institutions. Consequently, the Commission discovered that several of these institutions were involved in money laundering, illegal money exchange trading, and other misconduct. Before the Commission was established, there were several attempts to prevent misconduct in financial institutions, especially the banking sector. One attempt was Steve Sedgwick's (a former senior Australian public servant) initiative to end the employees' bonus system. In his view, this system was the most significant incentive for misconduct, as employees and leaders were solely focused on achieving targets. Such focus blinds the eyes from the employees' illegal actions and misconduct as their only purpose is reaching the target.

The Commission was created to investigate this alleged misconduct and discover its reasons. The government wanted to protect consumer interests and build trust between the financial service givers and clients. It also strived to increase transparency and accountability within economic organizations. After public hearings with consumers, managers, SMEs, and other stakeholders, the Royal Commission presented its report. The report addressed two main points: why the misconduct occurred and how to solve mischief in the future. The first point of why it happened suggested that misconduct results from behaviors. Most financial institutions' culture is focused on "the pursuit of short-term profit at the expense of basic standards of honesty." Employees and managers were assessed on their performance, which was translated into how much profit they had achieved. No behavioral assessment was ever conducted. Further, when misconduct was discovered, it was usually neglected if targets were met.

Answering the second question—how to solve the problem—the Royal Commission did not promote adding more laws. The Commission believed that a new law is just "an extra layer of legal complexity to an already complex regulatory regime." Employees, staff, and managers should comply with regulations from an intrinsic belief that this is the best way. Their organizations should embed a culture of acting in consumers' interests instead of achieving profits. In brief, the Royal Commission found that using KPIs only drove undesired behaviors. These behaviors were focused only on outcomes and did not care about building a sustainable culture.

On the other hand, using KPIs, KBIs, and key activity indicators (KAIs) can yield more positive results. Using these tools, people are assessed on their performance and behaviors. Applying this to risk situations, employees will already have the guidelines of expected behaviors, and they will react accordingly.

Summary

Risk behavior might be what an organization needs for success. Still, it is crucial to appreciate that the risks in an organization can result in devastating financial and managerial implications. Thus, it should not be based on a particular tradition that would make organization leaders think the results would be the same. As a result, organizations need to adopt a constant background check on the risk to financial services, which is essential in minimizing risks. This chapter reveals the various risks that influence the financial industry as compliance governing and management, cybersecurity, and third party, detailing their consequences on its performance. Multiple organizations have established different models and frameworks that can be used to control risks in organizations based on culture, behavior, and attitude. The chapter explores the A-B-C risk control model that many organizations adopt to develop an organizational culture of desired behaviors and attitudes. The model starts with attitudes and then behavior that results in an organization's culture, enabling the employees to understand the organization's risks and cultivate a positive perception of risk control in their place of work.

Risk is a common part of organizational processes. Having a set of risk behaviors promotes a positive risk culture in an organization. Ethical role modeling, challenge management, and nonblame behaviors are the expected behaviors encountered in all organizations. As a result, both the employees and managers need to embrace a risk mindset to tackle it strategically. By doing this, they would be developing a risk culture that promotes positive behavior at the time of risk. Further, it would lead to ideal risk behaviors that would strengthen the current risk culture. Organizations need to define their ideal risk behaviors to build a culture that will enable them to deliver results, guide them on how to handle the risks, and act as a driver of positive risk behaviors for organizations' financial operations.

The benefits of risk-defining behavior enable organizations to develop the business goals of growing, sustaining this growth, and interacting with stakeholders. The goals are interrelated or sequential, as one follows the other. Such purposes require a system or framework to define potential risks and the behaviors needed to deal with these risks in an organization. As a result, organizations may adapt and grow within the current risk situations. Organizations need to: understand the organization to enable it to measure the progress and understand the industry in which they operate to move to the next levels.

In addition, they need to reach measured decisions by focusing on all employees' engagement and involving their feedback on decision-making. They also need to enhance brand recognition since a well-defined behavioral framework provides opportunities in an organization for recognition. Leaders and employees should know that there are constant recognition and reinforcement of ideal behaviors at every opportunity. Defining the ideal risk behaviors convey a good image for the organization and, thus, enhances brand recognition. All needed in an organization is the combinative utilization of KPIs, KBIs, and KAIs to achieve the desired outcome of financial risk management and control.

Measuring Success

The traditional approach to measuring success is through the use of KPIs. To enhance the sustainability of embedding CI behaviors, there are also suggested KBIs to be used in conjunction with the KPIs

Traditional KPIs for risk behaviors are as follows:

a. Number of risk controls triggered
b. Time taken to mitigate risk triggering
c. Triggers activated prior to receipt at customer
d. Number of level 4(X) risk controls triggered this month

Suggested KBIs for risk behavior are as follows:

a. Number of leading risk controls activated before a customer lagging risk control is activated
b. Opportunities/learnings generated from a risk control being activated
c. Teams actively looking for opportunities to improve before risk control activated
d. Percent Team meeting where risk controls are discussed

Suggested KAIs for risk behaviors are as follows:

a. How many actions have been generated to reduce risk this week/month?
b. How many risk observations have been completed this week/month?

Chapter 7

Customer Experience

An example of shifting cultures and shifting behaviors as they relate to the customer's experience was found in a hospital project that one of the authors was involved with. In this case, the hospital president and his senior staff were directed by their board to come up with a strategic plan. The board was frustrated by the long wait times and high costs of hospital's operation, and they wanted to get it under control. Potential patients preferred to go to nearby hospitals that were more responsive to patient's needs. The hospital leadership was directed to put a focus on improving customer quality, which included responsiveness, and cost reduction.

The author led the strategy workshops, which were a series of half-day workshops each week over a month. A preferred off-site 2-day option was deemed unacceptable by hospital administration. However, the space between the sessions was used to the advantage of the author in that; it allowed intermediate time for data collection. In the end, the weekly meetings continued well beyond the initial 2 months.

The hospital leadership was convinced that what they needed to do was focus on cost and run some statistics on the inventory stockrooms, and that this would identify where cost waste was occurring. The author did not agree. He challenged them to focus first on customer satisfaction and identifying where customer failures were occurring, and that costs would be reduced by first focusing on the hospital's culture and their attitude toward customer satisfaction. Hospital administration was slightly offended at the idea that maybe they were not as responsive to their patient's needs as they should have been. The author stressed that their looking at cost as a higher

DOI: 10.4324/9781003224747-7

priority than customer satisfaction exemplified that the culture was pointed in the wrong direction.

The author challenged the leadership to start by focusing on customer satisfaction, starting by looking first at their highest priced real estate within the hospital. This, of course, was the OR (operating room). They were currently using a scheduling methodology for OR where doctors blocked off a segment of time, and that time was locked up for that doctor, no matter how little of that time he or she actually utilized. In conjunction with the leadership of the hospital, a new scheduling system was designed that would allow smaller time segments whose length was specific to the procedure that would be performed. Using a Gemba approach of "Go and Observe" they also realized that a lot of what was done in the OR (preparation and equipment cleanup work) could be done outside of the OR either before or after the procedure. By making these basic changes, and after about 3 months of using the new scheduling methodology, the hospital was able to triple the amount of procedures that were being run through the OR, significantly reducing the cost of each procedure, and enormously increasing utilization and capacity. Of course, customer satisfaction was improved when patients no longer needed to wait months for the care they needed. There was a chain-reaction ripple effect of shifting workloads throughout the hospital as a result of this scheduling change, and numerous departments were affected, but in the end, customer satisfaction was significantly increased.

Then, the strategy team moved on to the next most expensive real estate in the hospital, which was the ER (emergency room). Similar Gemba observations of the ER quickly identified that the delays in the ER were caused primarily due to a lack of responsiveness of the labs and a lack of efficiency in scheduling beds in the main hospital. Patients would be on hold in the ER for hours waiting for lab work or waiting for a bed. This made turnaround in the ER extremely slow. The Gemba, Go and Observe, shifted to a focus on studying the lab systems and the bed scheduling systems. In the end, the poor performance of both of these systems turned out to be the result of the labs and bed schedulers not knowing the impact that they were having on ER. They had not been able to see the big picture. No one was watching the performance of the overall ER flow and the systems connected with that flow. The labs changed several of their procedures focusing on improving their responsiveness to ER, and bed scheduling also changed procedures which allowed the ER improved information on bed availability. Once again, now that the big system perspective had been identified and appropriate changes were made to the various subsystems, performance was dramatically affected. Wait time in the ER waiting room was reduced from, in the worst case, several hours, down to minutes. The ER soon prided itself on trying to keep wait times down to single-digit minutes.

The big change that occurred was in the behaviors and the culture. Hospital leadership no longer focused on cost reduction, previously thinking of themselves as a factory. They realized that customer satisfaction needed to be the focus. Along with this, the cultural transformation of the leadership trickled down to management and the associates. Each felt more pride in their work when their customers were satisfied by the reduced response times and the improved results.

The other big change was the system perspective where the hospital saw itself as a large patient (customer) response system with numerous interconnecting subsystems, each of which affected the overall performance of the larger system. This new, system perspective changed the way hospital leadership thought of their specific roles. The hospital was no longer focused on keeping doctors happy. Administration and the doctors all shifted their focus to keeping the patients happy, and that turned out to be a major critical behavioral cultural shift.

The author stepped out of this project at this point, which was about 6 months into the transformation effort, but the leadership continued having their weekly strategy meetings and made that a permanent part of their new culture. They continued working and reworking the different systems within the hospital with an eye on customer satisfaction.

Which Flavor Is Your Customer Experience (CX)?

Customer experience (CX) thinking and practice should not be confused with CX research. In this domain of research, companies using various methods from analyzing the market and understanding customer satisfaction "Rooted in advertising and marketing ... expanded to almost every sector by the 1970s."[1]

CXs have, in fact, always existed, from the bartering exchanges of cavemen to modern-day digital transactions. It has only become a significant business discipline since the late 1990s when companies such as Apple perceived CX as a substantial differentiator in their market. As such, CXs field and development have emerged in the last two decades as an alternative to traditional ways of improving organizational performance. It is almost as if some people have discovered CX is a new thing. "They will say things like, "we need to start doing customer experience!" Every company that has ever existed and every company that will ever exist has done and will 'do customer experience'; it is not a choice that you can make. The only choice you have is to take notice or not, and just because you have not taken notice of it before doesn't mean that it hasn't existed." Foundations for Customer Centricity (Page 23), James Dodkins (2014).

These days CX management is at the heart of the world's most successful companies in terms of shareholder value, customer satisfaction, business performance, and employee empowerment.

CX—A Sea Change in How Work Gets Done

In 1997 and at the annual Apple World Developers conference (May 1997), Steve Jobs returned to Apple and explained his perspective regarding customers. He challenged organizations to rethink how they approach business change by contrasting the traditional approaches with a new view. Instead of starting with the technology and product, you should start with the customer and their associated experiences.[2] This idea underpinned Apple's rapid transformation and growth; it is worth considering that CX impact as a stock investment of USD $1 in May 1997 was worth $880 in December 2020.[3]

In a similar vein, Jeff Bezos coined the phrase "working backward" to describe the same approach. He extolled organizations to become "customer obsessed" and overcome many traditional business challenges caused by legacy industrial age practices.[4] That strategic and operational shift to emphasize the creation and management of CXs is discussed extensively in the book "Working Backwards (2021)" written by two former Amazon executives.[5]

Despite the success of companies such as Amazon, Apple, Zara, Emirates, and BMW, "Customer Experience" is still however, perceived by many as being "soft and fluffy." The contrast of the top-performing companies, who approach CX objectively and scientifically, is stark. The formula is simple: happy customers come back for more,[6] reduce customer churn, and do that constantly. This is often because the poor performers define CX in very narrow terms from their perspective—and not the customers.

Not just in private industry but across public sectors, the same is often true due to misunderstanding real CX. Let's review some of the typical shortfalls.

Challenges with CX

1. **They are conflating CX research with the discipline and science of CX.**
   There is no doubt that CX should be data driven; however, historically, marketing is the people doing this work and can mistakenly view CX as just another part of their discipline. This misalignment is fostered by research firms who derive their income from "Marketing" departments where selective backward-looking perceptual data gets mixed in with genuine insights. The result? When business performance fails to improve, the top team naturally loses faith and will relate, "oh yes, we tried that CX thing, and it didn't work for us."

2. **Approaching CX as if it is nice to have**, rather than a critical ingredient for organization success. Put that in contrast with Jeff Bezos's letter to shareholders in 2010 "We have an unshakeable belief that the long-term interests of shareholders are perfectly aligned with the interests of customers."[7]

3. **Perceiving CX as another functional silo**, as opposed to something everyone contributes to. CX is a new paradigm, it isn't another department or swim lane to be approached with an industrial-age mindset. It requires a complete rethink along the lines of Steve Jobs "start with the customer experience and work backward toward the technology."[8] Recent academic research (2020) does nothing to dispel this myth of seeing CX as a marketing initiative.[9]

4. **Establishing CX as a report to executives** who do not have the remit and influence to change the way an organization works, the alternative may seem paradoxical. To get the top team's ears, you need to play the politics and ensure CX delivers on its promise objectively at speed.

5. **Justifying CX as a means to improve customer satisfaction** and linking that to bonuses/reward systems. You will really be encouraging poor behaviors and potentially terrible CXs.[10]

6. **Evangelizing CX as the new religion.**
   The examples of CX initiatives integrate the best from the old with the good from the new and are inclusive of everyone. Having a clearly defined set of goals and outcomes. "The basics are that the organization

of companies has to follow the processes (and experiences), which follow the priorities, which follow the goals (outcomes), which follow the vision and mission of the company." Alexander Breskvar, Corporate VP of Quality, Siemens Gamesa Renewable Energy.[11]

7. **Becoming distracted by CX digitization** to the cost of improving processes and experiences before automation. It is less about the technology and more about moving "Outside-In"; it is a way to deliver rapid and sustainable success (Examples, Pharma pandemic).

8. **Overlaying the CX approaches onto existing organization structures.**
   Traditional top-down structures with functional specializations were developed to improve throughput, efficiency, and effectiveness and boost unit productivity. Lean out waste and removing variation from processes clashes directly with the third decade of 21c to personalize, differentiate, and excel with successful customer outcomes, without exception.

9. **Hiring consultants to have CX "done for you."**
   You can't have CX done for you. Embracing CX is about empowering people to make decisions at touch points. It is about collaboration and cocreation.

10. **Understanding that customer interactions are critical to an organization's success.**
    Why do so many companies put their most precious resource (the customer) with the most inexperienced lowest-paid people? If you are working in the customer contact center and perform well, what happens? Yes, you are promoted away from the customer! And the better your performance, the less contact you have with customers. Imagine if a soccer team did that. We would immediately pull the best striker off the pitch and promote them to become a Director. We would score fewer goals, and our fans would become dissatisfied very quickly.

The Justification and Benefits for Evolving to a Customer-Centric View

In almost every regard, the customer has become "enlightened" and insists on a different treatment, whether in the private or public sectors, healthcare, defense, or countless other industries.

We discuss the "enlightened customer" at length in "Outside-In The Secret of the 21st century leading companies,"[12] but here is a brief synopsis. Customers demand choice; they are persistent in exercising that choice, become rebellious if they can't get what they want, have high expectations, wish to operate across many channels simultaneously, and in fact have become prosumers (professional consumers).

Ignore this at your peril. It just isn't good enough to overlay our functional specialist pyramids with these additional capabilities. The past industrial age approaches were never designed to cope with the current times' speed and complexity.

In auditing customer-obsessed organizations, the litmus test of success is the ability to win the Triple Crown—simultaneously reducing costs, growing revenues, and enhancing service. If you are not doing that, whatever you are doing is not Outside-In (Figure 7.1).

Business Transformation via CX Thinking and Practice

As a process transformation leader, you need to craft a plan detailing why, how, and what to transform in your company, alongside with when the transformation will start showing results. A pragmatic CX approach builds a

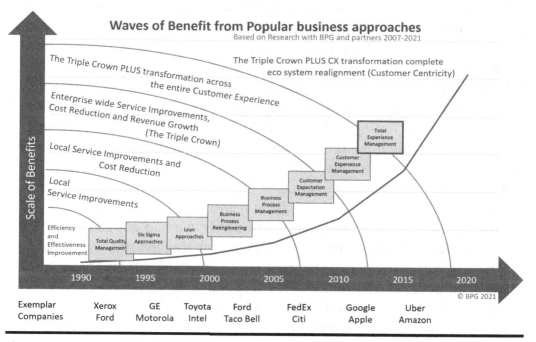

Figure 7.1   The evolution of total experience model (TEM) approaches.

program that guides you through the challenges and steps to help to chart a successful course toward change.

Critical to success is ensuring that your company, stakeholders, and employees understand and can practically articulate the why, what, and how of transforming the process to become a customer-centric company.

A Strategy for CX Success

- Step 1: CX leadership: Developing a laser-like focus on successful business and customer outcomes
- Step 2: A total experience framework: Introduce a process and CX competency framework
- Step 3: Migrating the company to True North Alignment.

Step 1: CX Leadership—Organizing for Success

"We trained hard—but it seemed that every time we were beginning to form up into teams, we were reorganized. I was to learn later in life that we tend to meet any new situation by reorganizing, and what a wonderful method it can be for creating the illusion of progress while actually producing confusion, inefficiency, and demoralization." Petronius, AD43

Critical to success is going beyond the industrial age idea that we continually improve what we are doing already.

Organizing for success requires a robust challenge of looking at what we do through the Outside-In lens. Implicit is the idea that we may need to be doing things in a radically different way from the past. Just improving efficiencies and effectiveness is no longer good enough.

There are many examples of companies outperforming their previous best but then wholly missing the point that customer needs had shifted, causing those companies to struggle. On the surface, the metrics were looking good, so what was the issue?

One senior automotive leader (having helped successfully with an enterprise-wide transformation) said, "Effectively, we had got good at doing the wrong things. People were saying to us, 'you are fantastic at making cars no one wants anymore!' You must make sure the tools and techniques, coupled with outcome-based metrics guide you at every turn."

Additionally, it isn't about just process improvements and tweaks to the reward systems and organization structure. Often it requires a complete rewiring of the total ecosystem.

Recent research (2021) published by Gartner identifies the need to embrace four elements in this ecosystem:

"By 2024, organizations providing a total experience will outperform competitors by 25% in satisfaction metrics for both customer and employee experience."[13]

Step 2: A Total Experience Management Framework

An all-too-often take on CX is that it is the new marketing.[14] That is, about as far from the truth as you can get; so much so that organizations who follow this mistaken credo quickly fail in their quest to harness the real power of CX thinking and practice.

Those failed companies will say CX doesn't work and then move on to try the latest guru-inspired snake oil. They see CX as another silo that is destined for failure. So how do those that consistently deliver outstanding business and customer results achieve this alchemy?

Practical CX thinking requires a connection of the dots between everyone and everything. At a basic level, this involves drawing the lines between the customer and the employee through the channels, into the systems, and across the metrics. It isn't just the customer journey—it touches everything the organisation does.

Additionally, a pragmatic approach to implementing this framework revolves around the customer lifecycle for products and services coupled with the actual delivery of outcomes via the employee experience.

The BP Group Total Experience Model

The BP Group has programs[15] that explore this territory in detail; however, for our purposes, the connecting of everything with everyone can be seen in Figure 7.2 "Total Experience Management."

Step 3: Migrating the Organization to True North Alignment

What is North Star Alignment about? Well, the North Star idea comes about from ancient mariners in the Northern Seas, who used to navigate with the North Star as a means to calibrate where they were and how much further they had to go. The North Star, also called Polaris, is the star that sits directly above the Earth's North Pole. In the night sky, the star doesn't appear to move, while all the other stars appear to circulate it. It looks like they're all circling the North Star. It's the only one that has a fixed position.

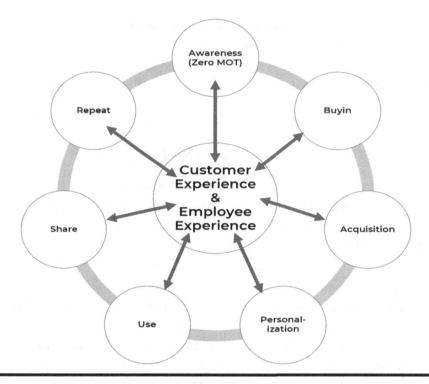

Figure 7.2 Triple Crown = simultaneously reducing costs, growing revenues, and enhancing service.

However, let's examine this simplified version that individuals, teams, or the entire organization can use. There are also emerging examples of people using the North Star Alignment template (NSAT) for the whole supply/value chain. So, what this is about is two dimensions. There's the organizational. As you can see, ABC and then over on the right the individual team, a larger part of the organization (or whatever) from D to I.

Let's get practical about it and move to the NSAT. This thinking forms the guiding principles behind several leading "Outside-In" companies such as Amazon. Naturally, you can add/exchange certain information more pertinent to your company, such as progress assessment, other metrics, and organization trends (Figure 7.3).

Have you got the North Star metric? It is a fundamental part of any organization seeking to grow and improve its efficiency, effectiveness, and CX delivery. If you haven't already identified one, you should seriously consider taking the time to figure it out.

The North Star metric is the critical measure that consistently delivers successful business and customer outcomes that drive performance and sustainable growth when you focus on above all else.

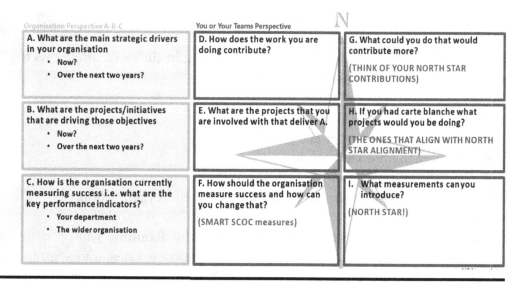

Organisation Perspective A-B-C	You or Your Teams Perspective	
A. What are the main strategic drivers in your organisation • Now? • Over the next two years?	**D. How does the work you are doing contribute?**	**G. What could you do that would contribute more?** (THINK OF YOUR NORTH STAR CONTRIBUTIONS)
B. What are the projects/initiatives that are driving those objectives • Now? • Over the next two years?	**E. What are the projects that you are involved with that deliver A.**	**H. If you had carte blanche what projects would you be doing?** (THE ONES THAT ALIGN WITH NORTH STAR ALIGNMENT)
C. How is the organisation currently measuring success i.e. what are the key performance indicators? • Your department • The wider organisation	**F. How should the organisation measure success and how can you change that?** (SMART SCOC measures)	**I. What measurements can you introduce?** (NORTH STAR!)

Figure 7.3   North Star Alignment template.

Facebook is daily active users, Airbnb is nights booked, and **ours is monthly organization upskilling.**

Why is having one important?

It is because delivering successful outcomes and consistently improving performance is heavy lifting for most, and it's easy to waste your resources on things that don't move the needle. Plus, it's easy to get distracted with the latest and shiniest new ideas. So having a fantastic metric keeps everyone in your company focused on the most critical metric for your company's success, connecting the dots from the frontline to the top team.

So What Is the Process to Define Your North Star Metric Effectively?

Identifying the North Star metric can significantly impact all stakeholders, including immediate customers, employees, and partners. In fact, on how your company operates overall.

The North Star metric is unique to each organization, as is how it's rolled out and communicated.

Anyone involved in delivering successful customer outcomes and driving growth for your company, from the marketing people, across the sales teams, and all of your partners, should have a clear line of sight of your North Star metric and how they can contribute to moving it forward.

This alignment is a significant part of the strategic and operational effort of leading CX organizations. Not having a North Star metric increases complexity and uncertainty, with people pulling in different directions to pursue their "local" measures.

- Set up a time with key stakeholders,
- identify your customer categories,
- agree on the SMART needs,
- choose the most important one, and then
- brainstorm what it should be across the entire organization.

Identify who are your best customers and why. Examine vital organizational metrics, focus on the critical to success ones, and seek to identify the one metric that rules them all. It is the metric that has the most significant impact on your business performance.

It needs to be a rigorous process of sorting and sifting to ensure the metrics that count are the ones that matter (Tables 7.1 and 7.2).

Summary

Customer satisfaction is a fundamental aspect of determining the success of an organization. Various companies experience challenges meeting the needs of their customers in time while operating at a cost-efficient scale. In the contemporary times, customers have become quite enlightened, which necessitates the need to create a customer-centered approach that would see the satisfaction levels that clients need are achieved. This implies that as organizations aim to create a culture and behavior that would increase performance, some part of the strategies involved should have the interest of customers at heart.

This chapter reveals that transforming the business entity with a focus on CX and practice can help to guide the organization through the challenges, thereby creating a successful course toward achieving change. To do this, many strategies are involved. However, it is essential for the ambassadors of change to ensure that everyone in the company understands the practical articulation of the why, what, and how of the transformation process from a customer-centered perspective. The next chapter reviews some of the techniques used to improve the efficiency of an organization particularly agile management and its use in improving organizational culture.

Table 7.1   Customer Focus Behavior Framework

		Customer Experience— Delivering Value Across the Total Customer Experience from the Customer Need Arising through to the Need Being Satisfied.					
	Lifecycle Stage	*Team Member*	*Team Lead/ Supervisor*	*Manager*	*General Manager*	*Executive General Manager*	*Group Executive/CEO*
Customer lifecycle	**Awareness**	Generates and reinforces customers understanding.	Identifies CX improvements.	Negotiates improvement priorities across teams and stakeholders.	Coordinates and collaborates with peers and the C suite to connect the dots between the strategy and execution.		
	Buy-in	Encourages information access and provides supporting advice.	Negotiates with stakeholders' improvement implementation.	Provides guidance and support by connecting the dots and drawing the lines across the organization and its operations.	Provides directional support to ensure priorities are understood and acted upon.	Links everything and everybody to understanding customer obsession.	

(Continued)

Table 7.1 (Continued) Customer Focus Behavior Framework

		Customer Experience— Delivering Value Across the Total Customer Experience from the Customer Need Arising through to the Need Being Satisfied.					
Lifecycle Stage	*Team Member*	*Team Lead/ Supervisor*	*Manager*	*General Manager*	*Executive General Manager*	*Group Executive/CEO*
Acquisition	Provides the means to purchase/ access the product or service.	Supports implementation of improvements.	Oversees and reports on multiple experiences to ensure alignment to the North Star.	Manages the politics of change throughout the organization and its stakeholders.	Supports and assists CX discussions at the top table.	Provides internal and external leadership to establish North Star principles and alignment.
Customization	Understands the customer need(s) to align the product or service.	Tracks and reports CX performance.	Determines how to implement the strategy and enable operations to deliver on those strategic objectives.	Develops initiatives and gains support for maturing customer experiences.	Identifies and gains support for business-wide CX improvements across people, processes, and technology.	Leads from the front with the customer-obsessed mantra.

Table 7.1 (Continued)   Customer Focus Behavior Framework

Customer Experience—Delivering Value Across the Total Customer Experience from the Customer Need Arising through to the Need Being Satisfied.

Lifecycle Stage	Team Member	Team Lead/ Supervisor	Manager	General Manager	Executive General Manager	Group Executive/CEO
Use	Ensures the customer understands and uses the product/service efficiently and effectively.	Collaborates with stakeholders to mature the experience(s).	Facilitates internal and external discussions to continually improve process, systems, and experience.	Presents strategic and operational options to enhance organization effectiveness.	Provides infrastructure support to ensure the appropriate attitudes, behaviors, and culture.	Liaises with industry and partners to ensure ongoing improvements/ innovations of strategy and operations.
Share	Creates the means to socialize the experience.	Communicates across teams and the organization the evolution of their experience(s).	Maintains the CX real-time dashboards.		Agrees on resource allocations and effective utilization of those resources.	
Repeat	Reinforces the customer relationship to ensure greater product/service penetration.	Identifies "in the moment" risks and ensures necessary actions to mitigate failure.	Creates visibility of dashboards across all stakeholders.			

(Continued)

Table 7.1 (Continued)   Customer Focus Behavior Framework

Customer Experience—Delivering Value Across the Total Customer Experience from the Customer Need Arising through to the Need Being Satisfied.

Lifecycle Stage	Team Member	Team Lead/ Supervisor	Manager	General Manager	Executive General Manager	Group Executive/CEO
Creates value	Ensures every customer interaction delivers Triple Crown Plus benefits.	Breaks value of Triple Crown Plus into team metrics.	Identifies Triple Crown Plus dependencies.	Focuses attention on the Triple Crown Plus to guide all behaviors.	Determines the strategic and operational focus to delivering congruently Triple Crown Plus benefits and North Star Alignment.	Faces off to external stakeholders by sharing, explaining, and clarifying the organization CX strategy as embodied in North Star Alignment.
	Reports and Acts upon misalignment against Triple Crown Plus objectives.	Tracks and reports on value past/ present and future.	Implements action in the moment capability across the value streams.	Coordinates and collaborates with peers and the C suite to connect the dots across Triple Crown Plus objectives.	Reinforces the creation of shareholder value is determined by consistently delivering Triple Crown Plus benefits.	

Table 7.1 (Continued)   Customer Focus Behavior Framework

Customer Experience— Delivering Value Across the Total Customer Experience from the Customer Need Arising through to the Need Being Satisfied.

Lifecycle Stage	Team Member	Team Lead/ Supervisor	Manager	General Manager	Executive General Manager	Group Executive/CEO
Identifies opportunities	Participates in Innovation thinking and actions to implement opportunities to improve the CX.	Coordinates and provides guidance to team members through the chosen innovation approach.	Utilizes "Innovation approaches" to identify and prioritize potential improvements.	Connects the strategic objectives with execution actions to ensure opportunities are identified and realized.	Balances across stakeholder groups the prioritization of opportunities.	Establishes the culture to ensure opportunities are identified and acted upon "from the board room to the lunch room."
Resolves issues	Collaborates with colleagues to understand and share issues.	Highlights and prioritizes challenges.	Provides a forum for negotiating and managing challenges.	Liaises with other GMs to ensure a coordinated-approach to overcoming issues.	Maintains a long-sighted view of Issue resolution to balance immediate challenges with long-term goals and objective.	Demonstrates that the learning organization embraces challenges as opportunities to make things progressively better
	Practices "Action In the Moment" to overcome immediate Issues.	Agrees resolution actions and enables "Action in the Moment" capability.				

(Continued)

Table 7.1 (Continued)   Customer Focus Behavior Framework

***Customer Experience**—Delivering Value Across the Total Customer Experience from the Customer Need Arising through to the Customer Need Being Satisfied.*

Lifecycle Stage	Team Member	Team Lead/ Supervisor	Manager	General Manager	Executive General Manager	Group Executive/CEO
Customer obsession	Ensures every interaction is informed by customer-obsessed goals and outcomes.	Guides team members in the day-to-day management of customer-obsessive goals and outcomes.	Provides a customer obsession framework to link the principles, measures, and mechanisms across teams and individuals.	Coordinates and collaborates with peers and the C suite to connect the dots with customer obsession objectives.	Develops the measures and mechanisms to make customer obsession actionable.	Articulates the principles associated with customer obsession.
						Lives, eats, and breathes customer obsession across all internal and external relationships.

Table 7.2 Customer Experience Behavior Framework

		Corporate Transformation/CI Competencies				
		Customer Focus— Creating Value in Each Customer Interaction and Focusing on the Total Customer Experience.				
	Team Member	*Team Leader/ Supervisor*	*Executive Manager*	*General Manager*	*Executive General Manager*	*Group Executive/CEO*
Understands the customer	Actively listens to customers and other stakeholders.	Leverages the voice of customers and other stakeholders in understanding customer information to anticipate their needs.	Leverages the voice of customers and other stakeholders understanding customer information to anticipate their needs and future priorities.	Maintains an understanding and current knowledge of customer's needs and potential issues.	Maintains an understanding and current knowledge of customer's needs and potential issues.	Analyzes domestic and global data to anticipate changing customer expectations.
	Proactively asking questions to understand their needs.	Stays abreast of customer service best practices.	Understands the key end-to-end processes that create value for the customer.	Evaluates internal and external data to anticipate changing customer expectations.	Analyzes domestic and global data to anticipate changing customer expectations.	Gathers and responds to stakeholder feedback on expectations of organization.
			Stays abreast of customer service best practices.	Articulates the key end-to-end processes that create value for the customer.	Articulates the key end-to-end processes that create value for the customer.	Articulates the organization's customer value proposition.

(Continued)

Table 7.2 (Continued)   Customer Experience Behavior Framework

	Team Member	Team Leader/Supervisor	Executive Manager	General Manager	Executive General Manager	Group Executive/CEO
Corporate Transformation/CI Competencies						
Customer Focus—Creating Value in Each Customer Interaction and Focusing on the Total Customer Experience.						
Creates value	Demonstrates a positive attitude, builds rapport, and treats customers with care and courtesy.	Establishes and grows strong, value add relationships with customers and stakeholders.	Develops a partnering relationship with customers and stakeholders and adopts a long-term perspective.	Develops a partnering relationship with customers and stakeholders and adopts a long-term perspective.	Structures the business to best serve customer needs and build sustainable relationships.	Structures the organization to best serve customer needs and build sustainable relationships.
	Provides solutions that meet the customers' needs.	Creates win/win solutions with customers and other stakeholders.	Creates win/win solutions with customers and other stakeholders.	Uses an understanding of customer needs and supporting data to institute products, processes, and services that will ensure customer satisfaction.	Ensures products, processes, and services will assure customer satisfaction.	Ensures products, processes, and services will assure customer satisfaction.
		Encourages team to consider the impact on customers when making decisions.	Monitors customer satisfaction to ensure high levels are being achieved.	Champions a customer-first approach to business decisions.	Champions a customer-first approach to business decisions.	Champions a customer-first approach to business decisions.
			Encourages team to consider the impact on customers when making decisions.			

Table 7.2 (Continued)   Customer Experience Behavior Framework

	Team Member	Team Leader/ Supervisor	Executive Manager	General Manager	Executive General Manager	Group Executive/CEO
Corporate Transformation/CI Competencies						
***Customer Focus**—Creating Value in Each Customer Interaction and Focusing on the Total Customer Experience.*						
Resolves issues	Empathizes and takes personal responsibility for resolving issues.	Recognizes potential service issues and takes corrective action.	Recognizes potential service issues and takes corrective action.	Resolves complex customer issues that have been escalated.	Resolves complex customer issues where reputational damage is at risk.	Resolves escalated complex customer issues where reputational damage is at risk.
	Escalates customer concerns when required.	Identifies and removes root causes of locally generated issues.	Identifies systemic issues to remove root causes.	Identifies systemic issues to remove root causes.		
		Resolves customer issues escalated by the team in a timely manner.	Resolves customer issues escalated by the team in a timely manner.			
Lives sales and service	Consistently demonstrates group sales and service principles.	Demonstrates the sales and service principles and ensures the team applies them effectively.	Embeds sales and service principles in their business.	Champions sales and service principles within the business.	Champions sales and service principles across the business/ division.	Champions sales and service principles across the organization.

(Continued)

Table 7.2 (Continued)   Customer Experience Behavior Framework

Corporate Transformation/CI Competencies

Customer Focus— Creating Value in Each Customer Interaction and Focusing on the Total Customer Experience.

	Team Member	Team Leader/ Manager	Executive Manager	General Manager	Executive General Manager	Group Executive/CEO
Understands the customer	Actively listens to customers and other stakeholders.	Leverages the voice of customers and other stakeholders in understanding customer information to anticipate their needs.	Leverages the voice of customers and other stakeholders understanding customer information to anticipate their needs and future priorities.	Maintains an understanding and current knowledge of customer's needs and potential issues.	Maintains an understanding and current knowledge of customer's needs and potential issues.	Analyzes domestic and global data to anticipate changing customer expectations.
	Proactively asking questions to understand their needs.	Stays abreast of customer service best practices.	Understands the key end-to-end processes that create value for the customer.	Evaluates internal and external data to anticipate changing customer expectations.	Analyzes domestic and global data to anticipate changing customer expectations.	Gathers and responds to stakeholder feedback on expectations of organisation.
			Stays abreast of customer service best practices.	Articulates the key end-to-end processes that create value for the customer.	Articulates the key end-to-end processes that create value for the customer.	Articulates the organization's customer value proposition.

Table 7.2 (Continued) Customer Experience Behavior Framework

Corporate Transformation/CI Competencies					
Customer Focus—Creating Value in Each Customer Interaction and Focusing on the Total Customer Experience.					
Team Member	*Team Leader/ Manager*	*Executive Manager*	*General Manager*	*Executive General Manager*	*Group Executive/CEO*
Demonstrates a positive attitude, builds rapport, and treats customers with care and courtesy.	Establishes and grows strong, value add relationships with customers and stakeholders.	Develops a partnering relationship with customers and stakeholders and adopts a long-term perspective.	Develops a partnering relationship with customers and stakeholders and adopts a long-term perspective.	Structures the business to best serve customer needs and build sustainable relationships.	Structures the organization to best serve customer needs and build sustainable relationships.
Provides solutions that meet the customers' needs.	Creates win/win solutions with customers and other stakeholders.	Creates win/win solutions with customers and other stakeholders.	Uses an understanding of customer needs and supporting data to institute products, processes, and services that will ensure customer satisfaction.	Ensures products, processes, and services will assure customer satisfaction.	Ensures products, processes, and services will assure customer satisfaction.
	Encourages team to consider the impact on customers when making decisions.	Monitors customer satisfaction to ensure high levels are being achieved.	Champions a customer-first approach to business decisions.	Champions a customer-first approach to business decisions.	Champions a customer-first approach to business decisions.
		Encourages team to consider the impact on customers when making decisions.			

Creates value

(Continued)

Table 7.2 (Continued) Customer Experience Behavior Framework

Corporate Transformation/CI Competencies

Customer Focus—Creating Value in Each Customer Interaction and Focusing on the Total Customer Experience.

	Team Member	Team Leader/ Manager	Executive Manager	General Manager	Executive General Manager	Group Executive/CEO
Resolves issues	Empathizes and takes personal responsibility for resolving issues.	Recognizes potential service issues and takes corrective action.	Recognizes potential service issues and takes corrective action.	Resolves complex customer issues that have been escalated.	Resolves complex customer issues where reputational damage is at risk.	Resolves escalated complex customer issues where reputational damage is at risk.
	Escalates customer concerns when required.	Identifies and removes root causes of locally generated issues.	Identifies systemic issues to remove root causes.	Identifies systemic issues to remove root causes.		
		Resolves customer issues escalated by the team in a timely manner.	Resolves customer issues escalated by the team in a timely manner.			
Lives sales and service	Consistently demonstrates group sales and service principles.	Demonstrates the sales and service principles and ensures the team applies them effectively.	Embeds sales and service principles in their business.	Champions sales and service principles within the business.	Champions sales and service principles across the business/division.	Champions sales and service principles across the organization.

Measuring Success

Traditional key performance indicators (KPIs) for CX initiative or programs are as follows:

a. Net promoter score
b. Ability of the leadership to promote CX
c. Successful alignment of CX strategies with those of the organization
d. An efficient framework revolving around employees, customers, and the management at large.

Suggested key behavioral indicators (KBIs) for CX initiatives or programs are as follows:

a. The behavior exhibited by employees when dealing with customers
b. Putting the interest of the customer first
c. Ability to resolve issues empathically
d. Analyze employee experience in delivering outcomes from a perspective of CX.

Suggested key activity indicators (KAIs) for CX initiatives or programs are as follows:

a. Number of net promoter surveys conducted
b. Number of customer surveys at the end of each interaction
c. The number of returning customers
d. The average $ amount per order of returning customers

Notes

1. https://customerthink.com/a-brief-history-of-customer-experience/
2. https://youtu.be/EMdzBm3QUtI
3. https://www.macrotrends.net/stocks/charts/AAPL/apple/stock-price-history
4. https://youtu.be/Yr_vQgzAgDM
5. https://www.amazon.co.uk/dp/1529033829?tag=amz-mkt-chr-uk-21&ascsubtag=1ba00-01000-org00-win10-other-smile-uk000-pcomp-feature-scomp-wm-5&ref=aa_scomp&pldnSite=1
6. https://www.forbes.com/sites/forrester/2020/11/20/how-banks-and-insurers-can-connect-cx-with-business-impact/?sh=19c2d4e67972

7. https://www.sec.gov/Archives/edgar/data/1018724/000119312511110797/dex991.htm
8. https://youtu.be/EMdzBm3QUtI
9. https://link.springer.com/article/10.1007/s11747-019-00718-x
10. https://twitter.com/JDODKINS/status/1182209113696165888
11. "Dare! Behind the Scenes of the Best Business Transformation Project in the World" Amazon Best seller 2020: https://www.amazon.com/DARE-Behind-Business-Transformation-Project/dp/1916312004
12. https://www.stevetowers.com/outsidein.html
13. Gartner Strategic Planning Assumption—from the webinar "The Top Strategic Technology Trends for 2021"
14. Becker and Jaakkola "Customer experience: fundamental premises and implications for research"
    https://link.springer.com/article/10.1007/s11747-019-00718-x
    https://link.springer.com/article/10.1007/s11747-019-00718-x
15. BP Groups Certified Process Professional and Accredited Customer Experience programs: https://www.bpgroup.org

Chapter 8

Safety

We have talked about the importance of changing behaviors while creating and designing a culture that supports sustainable results. Changing behaviors is one of the most important things that leaders do in businesses, yet too often we see that this change in behavior is only temporary, for example, each new year we make resolutions, but in a few months' time, they are all but forgotten. At the time we make the resolution to change our behavior, we have high confidence that we are going to be successful; this year is the year! In business, we follow the same pattern and have a great plan going into the year, but we quickly lose focus because of all the other issues that arise, and, in many cases, we accomplish very little. No better example of this exists than in creating a safety culture.

When most people think about safety they think about physical safety, and most companies do a great job with safety awareness. In an operational excellence culture, you will not only see an enhanced version of this physical safety focus but also an emphasis on psychological safety, or in other words, it is ok to make mistakes because we learn from them and get better. Without this psychological safety net, it's very hard to change the culture and be successful with an operational excellence transformation. In this chapter, we will explore these two aspects of safety in depth.

One of the most famous representations of this is Maslow's Hierarchy of needs (Figure 8.1). There are Basic needs, Psychological needs, and Self-fulfillment needs in that order. As in the Shingo model, if you don't create the culture without addressing the Basic needs (Cultural

DOI: 10.4324/9781003224747-8

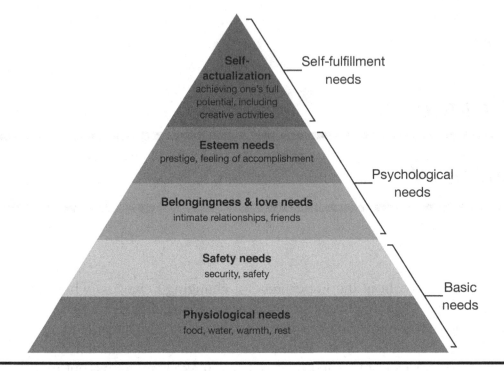

Figure 8.1 Maslow's hierarchy of needs.

Enablers), it's difficult, if not impossible to implement the rest of the dimensions.

- The Basic needs are made up of Physiological and Safety needs. Physiological needs are food, water, warmth, and rest. The Safety needs are security and safety. Again, if the Basic needs are not met, it is almost impossible to address the other needs.
- The Psychological needs are comprised of Belongingness and love needs and esteem needs. The Belongingness and love needs comprise intimate relationships and friends, while the Esteem needs are prestige and a feeling of accomplishment. In the Shingo model, we would talk about respect for the individual.
- Self-fulfillment needs—in this dimension, we realize self-actualization which is reaching one's full potential and including creative activities, again very parallel with the Shingo model and Lean Thinking.

Physical Safety

Safety in most companies is tool based—we put up signs, have all-hands meetings where we review the safety program, and have a safety manager to manage the safety program. It was always interesting to watch as the safety manager or anyone from the leadership team walk around the floor; all of a sudden, everyone is doing everything the safe way, which quickly went back to a focus of getting the work out once the leader passed by! In my own experience with this approach, I would always wonder: Are we truly being safe or are we just lucky! Usually, it was a little of both, but at times it felt that we had very little control and we were just waiting for the next accident to happen. I always thought there had to be a better way.

In the Shingo model, we talk about how everything is based on principles, and the first principle is **Respect for the Individual**. This is a foundational principle, and if you do not get this one right, it is very hard to implement and sustain a continuous improvement culture. An example of this is Toyota, where safety is based on this principle, and they never design a system or create a situation where someone could get hurt, that is, true respect for the Individual and drives the right behaviors. In many businesses, we talk about safety, but then in the next breath, we talk about whether we are meeting shipments, cost, and other issues that inevitably come up. This sends a mixed message to teams and creates bad behaviors all in the name of "getting the job done" or "making the numbers."

In my experience of running operations, we always had what we thought were great safety programs, with daily huddles, safety moments, and visual safety reminders throughout the facility. However, every time we had a safety incident, and I investigated, inevitably, I would hear the same thing, "Oh, they do that all the time but today they got hurt!" How could this happen? The reason it could happen is that we had a strong safety program but not a strong safety culture or safety behaviors. People would take shortcuts to get the "job done" because there were conflicting perceptions about what was important and the team, in many cases, they wouldn't bring unsafe behaviors to the attention of the person doing it because "that isn't my job" or "We have always done it that way!" In addition, we would use lagging indicators such as Lost Time Incident Rate, OSHA recordables, instead of leading indicators such as Safety Observations. This formed the behavior of not reacting to safety incidents until after they happened, and one of the foundational elements of operational excellence is reacting to deviations from the expected as soon as possible.

So, what does this safety culture look like based on the Shingo model? In a safety culture that is based on Respect for the Individual, safety becomes so ingrained in the daily work that people are not even consciously thinking about safety. There are no safety moments because every moment is a safety moment. One of the ways this culture forms is through changing

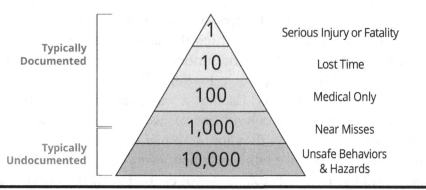

Figure 8.2 Safety injury dimension.

the perception of what safety is in a business, and this is where the Shingo principles of "Respect Every Individual" and "Lead with Humility" become vitally important.

Behavior-Based Safety

Many of you are aware of the safety pyramid illustrated in Figure 8.2, which looks at unsafe behaviors as the foundation of the pyramid and escalates up to serious injury or fatality at the top. The thinking is that if we can capture these unsafe behaviors and hazards as they are happening, coach the team as they are happening or remove the hazard right away, and then we reduce the chance of a serious injury or fatality.

At many companies, they use Behavior safety as the foundation for safety, where we ask the team to capture other team members doing safe and unsafe behaviors, and if they are unsafe, we fix them immediately. This starts to form a safety culture where, instead of having one safety manager, everyone is a safety manager and looking out for each other. It also recognizes people doing the RIGHT thing instead of always focusing on the wrong thing.

We also incentivize this by donating to a local charity of their choosing for each card they hand in.

I also use Quality and 5S/6S metrics as leading indicators of potential safety issues occurring. If our 5S/6S and Quality metrics are dropping, it is a leading indicator that we are not focused on the right things and creating the wrong behaviors such as rushing in our work and that is causing us to have poor housekeeping and organization; we are not focused on quality. All of this is a leading indicator that we are not focused on the right things and are taking shortcuts or workarounds when it comes to safety (Figure 8.3).

Behavior Based Safety
Awareness Based Safety Observation

Area			Date/Time	
Observer			# of People	
Shift			Task	

Action	Safe	Concern	Notes
Observe			
Correct Ergonomics/ Lifting			
Safe Position			
Grip			
Hand Safety			
Tools & Equipment Usage			

Please make a 51 Donation to (circle one):
Utah Food Bank , St. Jude's Children's Hospital or Huntsman Cancer Institute

Figure 8.3   Safety observation card.

A Real-Life Example

Recently, our 16-year-old daughter started to drive, and we gave her the proper tools: a safe car with antilock brakes, air bags, and driving lessons; in other words, what most parents do, but we took it a step further and used operational excellence and Shingo principles to create leading indicators of poor behaviors, the goal or results that we wanted are that every time she drives she is safe.

So in this example, if we just used lagging indicators, we would see speeding tickets or accidents, which could possibly lead to catastrophic consequences for our family, not the results we want! If we followed a traditional approach and waited until she received a speeding ticket or was in an accident, we would then take "corrective actions," like most businesses, and put things in place—usually more tools or systems to counteract it from happening again. The effectiveness of these actions is unknown, and we would never really address the behavior that caused the problem in the first place. So how did we apply the Shingo principles to make sure that she was safe.

Our Goal

Every time she drives, she is safe and comes home every time. Everything my wife and I do is aligned with this goal and we speak with the same voice, which means we are always giving the same message.

Set Expectations and Observe

- You must wear your seatbelt and everyone in the car with you must wear his or her seatbelt.
  - Key behavioral indicator (KBI): **Observation/Leading indicator**: Is she wearing her seatbelt? Is everyone in the car wearing their seatbelts?
- When you back out of the garage, you need to make sure that there is no one behind you and use your backup camera.
  - KBI: **Observation/Leading indicator**: Is she watching as she backs out of the garage?
- Is she distracted?
- You can only have one friend in the car at a time.
  - KBI: **Observation/Leading indicator:** Does she have multiple friends in the car when she is driving. Talk to her friends and ask if there were other people in the car
- You cannot talk on the phone or text while you are driving.
  - KBI: **Observation/Leading indicator**: Is she talking or texting as she drives?

Use Technology

We have also installed a monitor in her car that lets us know if she is driving too fast, braking too hard, and so on. (I will discuss how technology is playing a much bigger role in CI in Chapter 10.) All of these are leading indicators of unsafe behaviors that could lead to accidents and have serious consequences. By setting clear expectations and observing, we are designing and laying the foundation of a safe driving system.

Coaching

If we do notice that she is performing an unsafe behavior, we take immediate action by coaching her. We point out how her behavior did not meet the expectations we had set and the possible consequences of continuing to do this behavior.

Leadership

As parents, we must also set the example for her with our behaviors, and as leaders, we must set the example for our teams by modeling the right behaviors. If she is driving with us and we are talking on the phone or texting, then we are not modeling the right behaviors or "walking the walk" and she could very easily say, "I know you told me not to do this behavior, but you do it all the time." It is the same with our teams; if we are not modeling the right behaviors, then our teams will not either. They will say things such as, "I know you said that safety is the most important thing we do, but every time I talk to you all you talk about is if we made our numbers, so I really don't feel like safety is the most important thing at our company."

If your team sees you modeling the right behaviors and hear you talking about safety and see you doing observations and coaching, then they will believe that safety is the most important thing at your company. I observed this at a company I used to work for where I could talk to the teams at different plants around the world and, without telling me what division the plant was in, I could tell you who the Vice President was of that division just by the behaviors of the teams. That is how strong an influence a leader has on culture.

The most interesting thing in the example I just gave is that my wife and I were not even consciously thinking about what I described. We did it automatically because it is so ingrained in our daily actions that we are always looking for the things I described and are looking for anything else that may come up that we did not plan for. In Utah, it snows in the winter, and the first time it did, my wife talked through driving in snow with our daughter. Then, we observed her driving, and if we saw anything that we were concerned about, we coached her right away: Respect for the Individual.

Keys to Success

A clearly aligned safety focus—organizations will at times reinforce safety thru visual displays, safety huddles, audits, etc., but then counteract all this work with a focus on another metric. Observe the behaviors of leadership as they talk to the teams, are they starting with a safety message, or are they asking about production numbers or some other related metric. As the saying goes people will respond to how they are measured. Again, in my experiences, if our 5S scores were dropping or we were having quality issues, I knew a safety issue wasn't far behind because all systems are interconnected. It meant that we were focusing on the wrong things and sending the wrong message; in other words, we weren't "Walking the Walk!"

Psychological Safety

I know of one company that decided to introduce OKRs (objectives and key results) as a new initiative because one of the leaders had read about

Table 8.1   Safety Behavioral Framework

Safety (*Management*)—*Creating a Physically and Psychologically Safe Environment for All Employees to Reduce the Risk to a Level that Is as Low as Is Reasonably Practicable to Prevent Harm to People or the Environment*

	Team Member	Team Leader/ Manager	Executive Manager	General Manager	Executive General Manager	Group Executive/CEO
Fosters a culture of safety	Explores new ways of doing things. Works hard to implement the safety measures in place by being observant of any loopholes. In other words, he/she sets expectations and observes them.	Challenges the status quo among the team members by encouraging them to try out the new safety measures. The team leader supports the strategic initiatives and recognizes the efforts of his/her team members.	Oversees the implementation of safety measures. They are responsible for ensuring that all the measures put in place are followed adequately in his department.	Drafts the strategies that would be used to foster a safety culture in the organization. Manages the staff to ensure that they conform to the standards of safety guidelines developed.	Collaborate with the CEO and the board to create policies for a safer work environment. Works closely with other managers to foster a new safety culture.	Provides strategic and operational leadership that would help to create a safer environment for work. He sets goals and ensures that they are executed separately using other managers down the hierarchy.

Table 8.1 (Continued)   Safety Behavioral Framework

Safety (Management)—*Creating a Physically and Psychologically Safe Environment for All Employees to Reduce the Risk to a Level that Is as Low as Is Reasonably Practicable to Prevent Harm to People or the Environment*

	Team Member	Team Leader/Manager	Executive Manager	General Manager	Executive General Manager	Group Executive/CEO
Develops & implements solutions	Identifies safety opportunities to eliminate workplace injuries. Improves and simplifies the process of adopting safety measures by being positive about the change.	Translates the safety policies from the upstream managers to actions that would be adopted downstream. Ensures safety improvement among the team members while aiming for a solution and considering the impact that would be experienced both upstream and downstream.	Oversees the implementation of safety policies and guides the downstream members on other simpler ways of achieving success using the new strategies. Ensures that the new strategies will deliver optimum outcomes and solve the safety issues facing the organization.	Oversees the implementation of safety policies and guides the downstream members on other simpler ways of achieving success using the new strategies. Decides on which improvement initiatives to resource.	Measures the results and modifies the solution to ensure that the change is within the parameters of sustainability and capable of leading to positive outcomes. Monitors the progress of policy implementation to ensure it is within the niche of sustainability and positivity.	Measures the results from the reports received and modifies the solution to ensure that the change is within the parameters of sustainability and capable of leading to positive outcomes.

(Continued)

Table 8.1 (Continued)   Safety Behavioral Framework

Safety (Management) — *Creating a Physically and Psychologically Safe Environment for All Employees to Reduce the Risk to a Level that Is as Low as Is Reasonably Practicable to Prevent Harm to People or the Environment*

	Team Member	Team Leader/ Manager	Executive Manager	General Manager	Executive General Manager	Group Executive/CEO
Leads safety	Shows readiness in adopting safety measures by acknowledging that it is the only way to grow.	Accepts the changes brought about by safety policies by participating actively in the process while showing respect to his team members.	Actively monitors performance and output across the leaders downstream and reduces the variability that would lead to undesired outcomes.	Actively monitors performance and output across the leaders downstream and reduces the variability that would lead to undesired outcomes.	Understands the values of the group and applies them frequently when developing policies and making decisions. Continuously looks for ways of making the organization more functional and productive.	Understands the values of the group and applies them frequently when developing policies and making decisions. Continuously looks for ways of making the organization more functional and productive.

Table 8.1 (*Continued*) Safety Behavioral Framework

	Team Member	Team Leader/ Manager	Executive Manager	General Manager	Executive General Manager	Group Executive/CEO
Safety (Management)—*Creating a Physically and Psychologically Safe Environment for All Employees to Reduce the Risk to a Level that Is as Low as Is Reasonably Practicable to Prevent Harm to People or the Environment*						
Lives safety	Understands the values of the group and applies them frequently.	Understands the values of the group and applies them quite often.	Understands the values of the group and regularly applies them. Monitors the performance of the employees actively in terms of output as related to safety output measures. Continuously looks for other ways of being productive.	Understands the values of safety policies and finds a way of ensuring they are implemented efficiently.	Understands the values of the new policies and continuously looks for ways of enhancing the organizational functionality to make it more productive.	Understands the values of the new policies and continuously looks for ways of enhancing the organizational functionality to make it more productive.

it in a book by John Doerr and believed it would change the culture at the company. The idea of OKRs started with Andy Grove at Intel and the idea was to set short-term objectives that focused on the most important things facing the company at the moment, with the idea that this would lead to breakthrough performance. Andy Grove demanded high performance, but he also knew that there would be failure, and as long as Intel learned from the failure, the company would move forward. The interesting thing is at this company that decided to implement OKRs, people believed that failure was not an option, you didn't miss your numbers, and if you did, there was a price to pay. This is what people believed and implementing a program like OKRs, which depended on trust and psychological safety, would be an uphill battle to say the least. Unfortunately, companies do this all the time.

In the Shingo model, we talk about Respect for the Individual and one of the beliefs is that people are going to fail and that's ok if we learn from the failure. When I worked for OC Tanner, one of the beliefs that were instilled in us by Obert Tanner was to seek perfection, we may never reach it, but we will get better each day just from the mere act of trying to reach perfection each day. We all knew that it was a psychologically safe environment to work in, so we constantly pushed ourselves to get better.

In companies that aren't based on the Shingo model's principles this can be a very hard concept to follow and they might not even know they are creating this culture. In one situation, a site believed that the cause of their quality issues was people not following the process steps; in reality, the processes weren't capable but that's for another chapter! In an effort to solve the issue, they granted a 2-week "clemency" period to anyone who came forward and admitted that they hadn't or couldn't follow a process step, and after that, if anyone didn't follow a process step, they would be terminated. Of course, no one came forward because in addition to an "offer they couldn't refuse," a few weeks prior, they had terminated someone for....not following a process step! There was no trust in leadership that if they did bring a process problem to leadership's attention that bad things wouldn't happen to them, there was no Respect for the Individual.

This is why the first dimension of the Shingo model is so critical for a successful outcome; without Respect for the Individual and Humility, it's very hard, if not impossible to move on to the next dimensions, but in many cases, companies skip this first dimension and move on to the second or tool dimension and end up with poor results. Hopefully, you are starting to see the importance of "Psychological Safety" in a culture where people can come forward and openly and honestly discuss the issues that are affecting them in the workplace. In high-level Shingo Prize-winning companies, this sometimes extends to outside the workplace, and such a strong cultural safety net has been established that people will confide personal problems they are facing with the knowledge that they are in a safe environment.

As examiners, we often say that as soon as you walk in the door you can "feel the positive Culture," people are excited to talk to you and share their accomplishments; I have heard it referred to as bright and shiny faces. Unfortunately, this is also true for poor cultures, and you can feel it as soon as you walk in the door, people won't look at you or share with you anything about their work because they fear that they will get in trouble. As Taiichi Ohno famously said, "The work area is a reflection of Leadership."

Traditionally, we categorize safety either "being safe" or "not safe" and assign colors of GREEN to safe environments and behaviors and RED to unsafe environments and behaviors. If we consider safety on a continuum and make a point on there, that is our minimum standard and anything above this line is colored green and unsafe to be red. There is a region that has not caused injury or danger but could potentially. Figure 8.4 illustrates

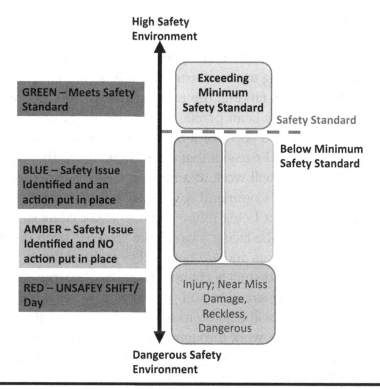

Figure 8.4   Color coding of the safety spectrum.

this continuum and what we want is to encourage people to talk about unsafe things colored BLUE and AMBER.

- GREEN is behaviors and environment that is at or above the minimum standard defined and communicated to employees.
- RED to unsafe environments and behaviors that cause harm, damage to equipment or the environment.
- AMBER to unsafe environments and behaviors that have been identified and not actually caused harm or damages. NO action has been implemented to address the hazard or behaviors from causing harm or damage.
- BLUE to unsafe environments and behaviors that have been identified and have not actually caused harm or damages. However, action(s) have been implemented to address the hazard or behaviors before causing harm or damage.

What we want to do is create a safe environment for people to feel psychologically safe to speak up about AMBER categories so that we can put some actions in place to turn them initially BLUE and then ideally GREEN.

Psychological Safety and the Lean Practitioner

As Lean practitioners, we have to take special care to ensure physiological safety when we are working to transform sites. It is all too easy to go in and start change without understanding the existing culture and the impact you may have on the people. As Lean practitioners, we have all studied the theory and, in some cases, have led successful transformations at a site and may have even won the Shingo Prize but that doesn't guarantee that the same process and methodology will work at a new site. This is especially true if the previous culture has been "Command & Control" based and people are not used to making decisions or being empowered to make changes.

In many cases, you may be facing a workforce who has been doing the same processes for many years and are not used to change, and as we are transforming a site, there is definitely change! They may be worried about how they will fit in with the new structure and process flow or what if they can't adapt to the changes, what will happen to me! Building trust with the team (Psychological Safety) as you work through this transition is essential and can mean the difference between a successful transition and one that falters. I always see people doing benchmarking site visits at high-level lean companies and making a list of all the things they are going to take back and implement at their sites, not realizing that in most cases what they are seeing took many years of

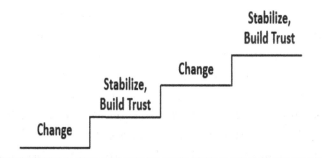

Figure 8.5   Safety stabilization ladder.

building the culture and trust for it to work the way it is today; in other words, they don't see all the pain and failures it took to get there. A life lesson from all of this is take time to understand the culture at your site, build trust, and allow changes to stabilize before you move on to the next change (Figure 8.5).

This will create a safe psychological environment for change and also start empowering the teams to make changes. They will start thinking "Hey!, we made this change and it wasn't so bad and it actually made things better, I can get more done with less work!" If you can get this chain started, at some point, it will take on a critical mass and it's amazing to watch what happens. As a leader, you will see the team running the business; they will understand the expectations, know the processes, and focus on the customer. There have been many times where I thought "this is crazy, it's not going to work," and then, all of a sudden you see this change and things are just flowing. As a leader, this should be your goal because if you can transform your business to this point, you are truly a leader and have created physiological safety in your culture.

Summary

Physical as well as physiological safety are critical to the successful transformation of a site. In Maslow's hierarchy of needs, these are the Basic needs, and it's very hard to move on to anything else without satisfying these needs. The same is true of the Shingo model and Cultural Enablers, if you don't address this first dimension by showing Respect for Every Individual and Humility, it's very hard to progress and you won't be able to sustain any change.

- Respect for Every Individual and Humility are fundamental for creating a strong safety culture in an organization.
- Use the Behavioral triangle to identify hazards that have the potential to cause serious or fatal injuries and identify the leadership metrics or expectations that may be driving this and change them.

■ Celebrate and reward good safety behavior, both physical and physiological, to create a strong safety culture where everyone feels empowered to identify potential risks as well as recognizing good things people are doing. The objective is that instead of having a safety manager, everyone is a safety manager, and you have the eyes of the entire workforce looking at safety, not just one person. Remember, recognizing the right behaviors reinforces the desired behaviors.

■ Productivity and safety are two sides of the same corn and are not mutually exclusive. In the same token, Quality and 5S can be a leading indicator of potential Safety issues and are indicators of metrics that may be driving the wrong behaviors.

Psychological safety is the confidence for teams to step into a work environment and ask questions and/or challenge. The next chapter reviews personality and behaviors in regard to specific traits that would fit certain organizational culture and how they would impose organizational change.

Measuring Success

Traditional key performance indicators (KPIs) for safety initiatives or programs are as follows:

a. Incident rate
b. Lost time rate
c. Severity rate
d. Near misses

Suggested KBIs for safety initiatives or programs are as follows:

a. Leaders directly coaching in safety
b. Identification of desired safety patterns
c. Modeled value-based behavior
d. Correcting near misses

Suggested key activity indicators (KAIs) for safety initiatives or programs are as follows:

a. Number of safety coaching sessions
b. Number incident investigations complete
c. Number behavioral-based observation checklists

Chapter 9

Personality Types and Behaviors

One of the authors was working with Toyota academics and executives on a new book, and in the evening, he would often discuss various topics. One discussion centered around change management, behaviors, and personalities. The discussion in Japan focused on cultural shift and what you needed in order to get people on board. The executives asked the question, "Where are the largest pockets of resistance to change? Who is the strongest in their resistance to a cultural shift?"

The academics, who had the most experience in teaching Toyota Principles, were quick to respond, There are three groups who give us the most trouble. They do not want to change. They like the status quo and want everything to stay just the way it is. They feel change is good for everyone else, but not for them. They become argumentative and try to find reasons why the changes they are being asked to make should not be made. They arrogantly seem to feel that they are smarter than their customers and that the customers should be happy with their product, just the way it's handed to them. Ironically, they are also the same individuals that are always pushing for everyone and everything else to change.

The author asked, "What are those three groups?"

The academics explained, "Doctors, Lawyers (which for them includes Politicians), and Academics."

What makes this conversation interesting is that these are indeed the groups that are always pushing for everyone else to make changes and improvements. Yet, they are found to have the most resistive cultures.

DOI: 10.4324/9781003224747-9

In a similar conversation, a group of change managers was asked, "Where do you received the most resistance to change within an organization?"

The answer was quick and unanimous, "Middle Management."

The next question was, "Why do you think that's the case?"

The answer was also quick, "Because in many cases they are the ones that own the processes that are being used. They are often the individuals that created these systems and so they have pride and ownership in them. They don't see the need for change or improvement to what they created. They are the personalities who were successful at firefighting and that's what got them promoted. They like the way everything is running."

Impact of Personalities on Behavioral Change

From the information presented in the previous chapters, it is clear that cultures are influenced by behaviors and behaviors influence culture. In this chapter, the underlying personality traits behind particular behaviors will be discussed, as well as the effect that these personalities have on organizational culture.

Organizational Culture

Organizational culture can be divided into three levels in terms of depth and manifestation to others, whether inside or outside an organization. These levels as described by Schein (2010) are the following.

Artifacts

Artifacts are the first level of organizational culture. These are the manifestations of the culture that appear to any observer from outside an organization. Examples of these artifacts are the language people speak, the way they dress, the mission and vision statements, and the physical environment. Although these things can give an idea about the organization, it is a very basic idea that cannot explain the underlying behaviors.

Beliefs and Values

Organization's values are sometimes announced and made clear to employees, as with its vision and goals. In most cases, they are understood over time. However, some organizations don't have a set of values but rather have unspoken rules. Values are the reflection of beliefs (Giffen, 2015). When an organization is established on a certain belief, this usually appears in the values that later define the culture.

Underlying Assumptions

The expectations of business/corporate, the values, beliefs, and culture of the organizations are what urge employees to react or behave in a certain way. For example, new employees may join a business with a set of values that differ from that organization's current values. After spending some time in the new organization, they will assume the organization will react differently in certain situations. They tailor their values and behavior to suit the new organizational culture.

It is imperative to address these three levels when changing the culture of any organization. While the first level is easy to change, the second and third levels are harder as they require a change in beliefs and values. To change these fundamentals, the different personality traits of people should be considered. A personality trait is a pattern of feelings, thoughts, and behaviors (Soto, 2018). A commonly known model to study different personality traits is the Big Five Personality Traits model.

Big Five Personality Traits

The model was developed back in the 1980s. It consists of five bipolar broad traits, and each person should fall somewhere between the two extremes of each trait. This model was adopted by different researchers, especially in psychology. Later, it was adopted by organizations when studying employees and change. The five personality traits as described by Mallinger (2001) are the following.

Extraversion vs. Introversion

Extraversion means the ability of individuals to perform several activities with others at ease. Extroverts are open to new relationships and usually engage and interact with other people. The opposite of extraversion is introversion. Those are people who prefer not to appear in social settings. Further, they are less engaged in teamwork and other activities that require different types versus people to do them. Extraversion versus introversion has associated characteristics as follows:

Friendliness: This is related to how extroverts or introverts deal with people. Extroverts can form relationships quicker than introverts (Mallinger, 2001).

Gregariousness: This is also related to dealing with people but in a group context. Extroverts are comfortable to be in a group, whereas introverts prefer to be alone or at least be in a group with familiar people.

Activity level: Extroverts have higher activity levels and enjoy a fast-paced life (Mallinger, 2001). On the other hand, introverts don't engage in many social activities.

Agreeableness vs. Disagreeableness

Agreeableness is also related to how individuals deal with others. Agreeable people tend to trust others and be trusted. They can compromise their interests for the sake of the group. On the other hand, disagreeable people are more suspicious and are sometimes perceived as untrustworthy. Three characteristics are used to describe agreeable and disagreeable people. These are as follows:

Trust: The extent to which an individual trusts others and is perceived as trustworthy by others. Agreeable people both trust others and convey a sense of trustworthiness.

Altruism: The willingness to help others and perhaps prefer others to oneself. This is related to trust. Because agreeable people are willing to help others, they are in turn more trusted than disagreeable people.

Cooperation: Cooperation involves practically helping others. The difference between cooperation and altruism is that while cooperation involves the deed of helping others, altruism requires only a willingness to help. Agreeable people cooperate more than disagreeable people.

Conscientiousness vs. Unconscientiousness

Conscientiousness is a focus on achievements. Having high conscientiousness levels means being organized, planned, and paying attention to details. Low conscientiousness levels mean spontaneity and sometimes more flexibility. The characteristics related to conscientiousness are as follows:

Self-efficacy: Showing self-discipline and being confident in achieving the intended goals.

Achievement striving: This is related to the value of social recognition. Conscientiousness means the need to be recognized as an achieving person. On the other side, unconscientiousness is related to satisfaction with one's person with no need to be socially recognized.

Cautiousness: People with high conscientiousness levels always think before they say or do something. They are more cautious about their behaviors, unlike low conscientiousness level people who react without much thinking.

High Neuroticism vs. Low Neuroticism

Neuroticism is related to negative emotions. People with high neuroticism levels tend to get angry and irritated easier. Small things can frustrate them, and they may experience a sense of emotional instability. The related characteristic is as follows:

Self-consciousness: The extent to which a person is affected by others' judgment of them. High neuroticism levels mean more sensitivity to criticism.

Openness vs. Closeness to Experience

This is about curiosity and willingness to try new things. People who are open to experience will appreciate art more than closed people. Also, they usually have unconventional beliefs and are more likely to challenge the status quo. The two related characteristics are as follows:

Adventurousness: This relates to the extent that people are willing to undertake new experiences. Open people dislike routine and always look for change, whereas closed people feel uncomfortable with change, especially those that are sudden or unpredicted.

Liberalism: This is also related to challenging the status quo, but it is more related to challenging authority. Open people don't mind going against norms and traditions. On the other hand, closed people strive for stability.

Predictions for Work Outcomes

Each of the above traits can predict certain occupational outcomes. For example, extroverts perform better in social jobs and can be better community leaders (Soto, 2018). They are more optimistic than introverts and can adapt better to changes (Aidla, 2003). Likewise, people with high agreeableness scores are better social leaders and are more liked by others (Soto, 2018). Usually, extraversion and agreeableness are directly proportional (Aidla, 2003). Conscientiousness is related to achievement; therefore, people with high scores in this trait can hold more demanding jobs. On the contrary, highly neurotic people are more subject to stress and dissatisfaction. So, they are not good at critical jobs. It is better to place highly neurotic people in less stressful jobs (Aidla, 2003). Finally, people who exhibit an openness to experience are best at creative and artistic tasks (Soto, 2018).

Agreeable people are uncomfortable with conflict. Consequently, less agreeableness is a prediction of an ability to better fit in market cultures where conflict and competitiveness are predominant (Gardner et al., 2012). Further, extroverts and disagreeable people prefer to work in outcome-oriented organizations where results are valued more than anything else (Gardner et al., 2012). Organizations that are open to innovation, such as start-ups, are certainly more preferred by open people who like to try new things (Gardner et al., 2012).

Peeters et al. (2006) found that similarity to other team members is also a predictor of performance, that is, the degree to which an individual has similar traits to his team members affects the overall performance of the team. Conscientiousness is more task-related, whereas agreeableness and extraversion are team related (Mohammed, Mathieu, and Bartlett, 2002). The distinction between both affects performance. Peeters et al. (2006) found that team-related traits directly affect the satisfaction with the team. The degree of similarity between team members for task-related traits affects the team. For example, more similar conscientiousness predicts more satisfaction with the team.

Just as personality traits can predict certain work outcomes, they can also predict the overall organizational culture. In a study conducted at various organizations, researchers found that organizational culture is affected by the CEO's personality type. Moreover, certain personality types are more effective than others, and the effect can be seen in the overall performance (Palmquist, 2015).

For example, CEOs with high levels of conscientiousness foster a culture of attention to detail and hard work to achieve results. Likewise, more agreeable CEOs mean a more flexible culture. Organizations with those types of CEOs are more adaptable to changes, and they have a general culture of risk taking and innovation (Palmquist, 2015).

In general, the combination of agreeableness and conscientiousness always leads to more positive outcomes. These two traits, in particular, work very well when present in a person holding a managerial position, as they foster taking opportunities and implementing changes (Palmquist, 2015).

The Eight Personalities

The combination of different personality traits forms a personality type. There are different classifications to define personalities and differentiate between them. For this book, two classifications will be addressed. The first is adopted from Wyles (2013). In this classification, eight personalities are defined. For a change management program to occur, these different personalities should be considered.

Champion

Champions are advocates of the organizations or certain projects implemented by the organizations. They are people who believe in the goals of a project and will work hard not only to achieve these goals but also to bring other people around the same goals. For any transformational project, organizations need champions in frontlines. Those will help a lot in convincing others about the project and ease the roles of the managers. Sometimes, champions are more useful than managers in these particular roles.

One of the important characteristics of champions is the ability to communicate persuasively with others. They tend to show great flexibility in different situations, and they can resolve conflicts. Further, they have high conscientiousness scores and openness to experience and low neuroticism scores. So, they are self-motivated and more willing to challenge the current situation.

Ambassador

Ambassadors are like champions to a certain point, which is accepting the change and willingness to change. However, ambassadors are different in that they don't promote the change like champions. Thus, champions are more useful when attempting to do any transformations in an organization.

To better benefit from ambassadors, they need to work with champions in the same team. Putting them in senior management roles with champions in their teams where they are required to work more proactively.

Challenger

Challengers, as the name suggests, challenge anything, including change. They have high personal satisfaction but lower belief in change. They will question the change and ask about the reasons behind this change. This may be perceived by the organization and its managers as being unsupportive and resistant to change. However, challengers just need sufficient reasons for the change.

Since they are personally satisfied, they need to have a personal reason for changing their behaviors and performance. Providing them with more details is a way to bring them along with the change. They also need to connect the organizational change with their personal change. In other words, they need to see a positive future outcome for themselves, along with positive outcomes for the organization to be willing to adopt the change.

Skeptic

Skeptics are similar to challengers; in that, they always question the need for any change. The difference between them is in the personal satisfaction level. Skeptics have high neuroticism levels, low agreeableness, and low openness to experience. Consequently, they are less satisfied with themselves than challengers and are not willing to undergo any change. Further, they have difficulty trusting others and, by extension, trusting changes proposed by others.

However, questioning changes can be seen as positive behavior, which may draw the change advocates to certain details questioned by skeptics. Organizations will need to provide sufficient details to challengers but more details and evidence for skeptics. It may be hard to work with skeptics, but they will perform the best in positions such as quality control if the organization can align them with the change.

Saboteur

Saboteurs are negatively proactive people. They have similar characteristics as skeptics, but they are more effective as they react to their thoughts.

Saboteurs will resist the change and work to prevent it from happening. They are neither satisfied with themselves nor with the organization. Working with saboteurs in a way that conveys that a change will happen even without their consent is not a wise thing to do. This is because they will exploit any chance to prove that the change was not good. In this way, they will work against the organization, not with it.

The best way to deal with saboteurs is to change them to skeptics and then to challengers. This can be done in the early stages of the change by spending enough time with them explaining the change and the positive outcomes it will bring to them first and then to the organization.

Thief

Unfortunately, thieves cannot be part of any organizational change. The reason is that thieves already have negative intentions for the change, and they are not willing to even communicate with their managers. If they unwillingly take part in any communication, they will be passive listeners. They are dissatisfied with the whole organization and believe it is not doing them any good and so they won't be willing to do anything for the organization in return.

If the organization already has thieves, the best way to deal with them is to disengage them from the change. Those personalities may benefit from special help (e.g., HR, counselling) that cannot be addressed with the usual communication and meetings with other leaders. The reason behind being a thief should be determined first, separate from the change. It might be a low salary or a bad working environment. Then, working on this reason will gradually change the thief to one of the other personalities.

Prisoner

Prisoners have very high conscientiousness levels and can become trapped in organizing and planning for their job roles. They have the potential of being high performers, but they are limited by the boundary they draw around themselves. They can also have a degree of high neuroticism, as they are not always satisfied with themselves.

To get the best from prisoners, they need to release their potential. Working closely with an ambassador or a champion is a good way to do so. Providing them with the social recognition they need is a valuable way to get them out of the prison they have put themselves in.

Passenger

Passengers are people who are working for a certain reason, and they will move once this reason is no longer available. They are highly unsatisfied with the job and the organization. They don't care about the change, even if they believe it is positive. They usually have a high openness-to-experience score, but this means that they are not loyal to a certain place.

To deal with passengers, it is advisable to discover their motivation and always challenge them. Passengers become dissatisfied quickly, so organizations should always give them a new challenge or role they can engage in.

Myers & Briggs 16 Personalities

A second and more detailed understanding of personalities is the Myers & Briggs 16 personalities. While there is no one personality type better than the other, understanding types is important to best position people in specific job roles. Different personalities can support different job functions, such as managing others, advocating for change, leadership, and other roles.

The personality types are divided across four categories, and each one has two alternatives. These four categories, according to Myers-Briggs (2021a), are the following.

Extraversion (E)—Introversion (I)

Similar to the Big Five Personality Traits model, extraversion and introversion determine the way people interact with others. However, in this classification, they also determine the effect of outer and inner worlds on people. Also, they assess how people reenergize.

Extroverts are action oriented. They love to socially interact with others and feel their best times are spent within a group. The outer world has more effect on them than their inner world. They feel they are energized by being in a socially active contest. On the other hand, introverts are thought-oriented, and their inner world has more effect on them. Deep inner thoughts and alone time are what energize them more.

Sensing (S)—Intuition (N)

This is related to gathering information from the outside world. It is worth noting that people may be sensing in some situations and intuitive in others.

However, most people tend to do one more than the other. This category explains the difference between people who are more attentive to physical evidence and those who depend on their intuition.

Sensing people are those who prefer realities. They need to see, hear, or feel evidence using one of the five senses. That's why they are better in practical jobs and studies that offer hands-on experience. These people usually start with details and then develop the bigger picture. Alternatively, intuitive people pay more attention to impressions and things they can draw on using their minds. They think about different options and possibilities and then form patterns. They always think about the future more than about the realities between their hands.

Thinking (T)—Feeling (F)

In this category, people are divided across the thinking and feeling scale. It is related to how people make their decisions based on the facts and information they gathered using one of the previous ways (sensing and intuition).

Thinking means using facts and logic. Thinkers build their decisions on the objective use of data. They tend to be impersonal and depend more on objectiveness when making a decision. Feelers use their emotions. Their decisions or conclusions consider people and their circumstances.

Judging (J)—Perceiving (P)

Finally, there is a structure that people use to deal with the outside world. People fall somewhere between judging and perceiving in terms of how they structure their life. This scale is also related to the other three scales. However, it is not about their level of organization, as both judgers and perceivers can be organized in their way.

Judgers prefer to get things decided, and they dislike the many options in life. They are less flexible and want everything to be done as they have decided. Perceivers are adaptable and open to options. They love to have different choices and always want to keep the door open.

The 16 Personalities

While each person should have one trait from each of the four divisions, all alternatives make up the 16 personalities. These 16 personalities are described by Myers-Briggs, 2021b) as below. Note that the first letter of each trait forms up the acronym of the personality.

ISTJ (Logistician)

Logisticians are practical people who rely on facts and objectivity when making decisions. They are very logical and prefer to have everything in their life organized. They are loyal people and can devote a great part of their life to things they appreciate. They also value other loyal persons. Logisticians are people whom managers can rely on and be assured that they will get tasks done. Even with difficult tasks, logisticians can work steadily and isolate themselves from distractions. They can work independently as well.

ISFJ (Defender)

Similar to logisticians, defenders are also committed people and can noticeably achieve results. They are responsible and loyal to whatever they are working on. They also show a great deal of conscientiousness. Yet, they are different from the ISTJ personality in that they care about people. They always consider how other people feel, and they are concerned with making everyone feel at ease. Perhaps their most notable feature is that they can defend others' ideas and behaviors as long as they love them. Those people would be good champions of new projects in an organization if it succeeded in gaining their loyalty.

INFJ (Advocate)

Advocates are inspiring people. They can inspire others with their idealistic values and behaviors. They are also committed to their organizations especially if the organizations have clear values. Advocates are good at connecting ideas and developing visions to serve their organization and also relate this vision to the common good. Further, they are organized in their way of implementing their visions. They also prefer firm decisions and hate the gray zone.

INTJ (Architect)

These are people who think before they act. They are strategic thinkers and can perform well in jobs that require planning. Architects can see patterns very well. They are able to imagine and prepare for the future using their minds. In a working environment, architects are skeptical and question things, but they will try to get answers independently. They hold high standards on job performance and commit themselves to reach these standards. They also hold high standards for others, so if they are in a managerial position, they will expect more from each team member.

ISTP (Virtuoso)

They are highly skilled people in different tools. They are flexible and can learn from the situations they face. They are tolerant and don't react unless there is a problem. They are not proactive as they prefer to observe and analyze the situation before reacting. Virtuosos are good at solving long-term problems, as they take their time to analyze the cause-and-effect relationship, develop patterns, and then develop a solution. Yet, they are not procrastinators; they can work quickly once they realize there is a problem that needs a solution.

ISFP (Adventurer)

They are flexible and willing to try different things. Adventurers prefer to work alone within their defined work and time frame. They know their abilities, and they take only tasks that they know they can perform. Once they have a task, they are committed to it and will find the best way to do it. Adventurers also value differences and respect other people's opinions and attitudes. They do not like conflict and will distance themselves from conflict in a working environment.

INFP (Mediator)

Like advocates, mediators are also idealistic people. They love to hold themselves accountable for a good cause. They also care about values and love to work in a place where values are defined. They prefer to have different choices, and they seek to choose the best option that is aligned with their values. They also care about people, and they are eager to help others achieve their goals. They can be flexible and adapt to different conditions so long as their values are not challenged.

INTP (Logician)

Logicians are different from logisticians in many things. Logicians are like logisticians in that they both base their decisions on logic. However, logicians are more analytical and seek to understand what is behind an idea. They depend on their interpretations more than realities. They are also innovative and can come up with new ideas, especially in areas of their interest. Logicians are more flexible and adaptable than logisticians, and they can assess the different options they have.

ESTP (Entrepreneur)

Entrepreneurs are energetic people who want to see quick results. Entrepreneurs prefer to have hands-on experience with whatever they are interested in rather than listen to theories and concepts. When faced with a problem, they will try to solve it using their experience and the facts they gathered from dealing directly with the problem. Entrepreneurs are spontaneous and deal with the present more than the future. They want to enjoy whatever they are doing in the best way and prefer to enjoy themselves with others.

ESFP (Entertainer)

These are friendly people who make the environment around them more lovely and inviting. Those people have a special charm that attracts others to them. They enjoy working with others and people also enjoy working with them. They perform the best in roles that require dealing with people. Entertainers are also spontaneous, flexible, and open to different options. They are open to new experiences and learn better if they can do everything on their own. Entertainers are optimistic and can be good advocates of a certain cause or project.

ENFP (Campaigner)

Campaigners are enthusiastic people who see different possibilities and options in everything. They are imaginative and can come up with ideas that no one else thinks of. However, they need social recognition and want assurance from others. In return, they offer support and appreciate others' work. Campaigners are also smart and can quickly use connections to draw conclusions. They can rely on their imagination to predict what is coming and act accordingly.

ENTP (Debater)

They are intellectually triggered people. To get the best out of the debaters, one should challenge their minds. Debaters will find themselves curious and speaking about their thoughts in every social context allowing for this. They are good at generating possibilities and critically analyzing those possibilities using their interpretations. They are also good at understanding people and are intuitive. Debaters will look for new challenges or at least new ways to do things.

ESTJ (Executive)

Executives are very decisive people, who qualify them to be good managers or administrators. They rely on facts when judging things and they like to see results. Their top-most goal is to achieve results and get others to achieve results as well. They are also logical and prefer to have a system to follow in their day-to-day work. They don't mind routine as long as it helps in achieving the results they want. They will do whatever it takes to implement the plan they believe will yield the best outcomes.

ESFJ (Consul)

These people are extraordinarily cooperative and caring people who value helping others more than anything else. These people are the best coaches and other jobs that require teaching people. They will do their best to help others, and they prefer working in teams where they have the leading role in ensuring the tasks are completed perfectly and on time. Yet, they won't take all the credit themselves. Consuls are also loyal to organizations and people. When they feel appreciated for who they are, they can give more than what is expected from them.

ENFJ (Protagonist)

As advocates, protagonists are inspiring people. They can help others to find their motivation and potential. They are also responsive and caring people who consider others' feelings and emotions. The difference between them and advocates is that protagonists work better in groups. They can be change leaders and motivate others to change and grow. Further, protagonists see the good in everything and they are open to criticism.

ENTJ (Commander)

Commanders are leaders who are bold, decisive, and can always find a way. They can quickly spot problems and inconsistencies within systems and then find a way to solve these problems. They are good at planning and creating strategic goals for their organizations. They are also good at presenting their ideas and convincing others to believe in their ideas. Commanders usually tend to read, learn, and know more about everything so they have an argument ready when trying to promote a particular vision.

Different Personalities and Imposing Change

There is no one personality that is better than another. Every combination from the 16 personalities has its own merits and can perform better in certain job roles. Consequently, when implementing an organizational change, it is important that every employee should be assessed to know how they might be thinking or feeling about the change. In this way, different approaches can be applied to change different people.

Organizational culture is a determinant of how an individual fits into an organization. This term is referred to as "person-organization fit" in research (Giffen, 2015). The term is about the values a person holds before entering the organization. When these values are aligned with the organizational values, the employee will feel satisfied and will accept the change more willingly than those whose values do not align with the organizational values (Giffen, 2015).

Influential organizations with strong values will affect employees who have different values. If an employee's personality is adaptable and open to change, the strong organizational influence will change their values to align with the organization's. On the other hand, if employees are not open to change, they are more likely to refuse to adopt the organizational culture change and choose to leave (Giffen, 2015).

Before attempting to impose any change, organizations should consider three elements related to the people of the organization (Mallinger, 2001). The change and the approach that will be taken to implement the change should enable different team members to:

■ Work comfortably in the organization and have a good working environment.
■ Have their motivations triggered and always get motivated to do more.
■ Work in an environment that helps them to deliver the intended results.

Here, we will discuss some tips for working with the abovementioned 16 personalities.

ISTJ—They prefer organization (Son, 2016) and will need to have a plan for the upcoming change ahead of time.

ISFJ—They are attentive to detail and can be very loyal. They are better placed in moderating roles (Son, 2016) or quality assurance.

INFJ—They work better behind the scenes (Thompson-Atlassian, 2020). Placing them in the center of the action is not a good idea. They will advocate for the new change once they believe in it.

INTJ—They don't need the effort to be convinced with change. They are already innovators and love to explore new things. Yet, they can tend to rush things out of their eagerness to try new experiences. It is better to place them in teams with other personalities.

ISTP—They are good at problem-solving and analyzing complex problems. They will perform better if placed in auditing positions and can be responsible for identifying mistakes and areas for further improvement in the new change program.

ISFP—They work at their own pace (Son, 2016). To implement a change, they need time to get acquainted with this change. Thus, they need direction from a supervisor.

INFP—They greatly appreciate values. If the proposed change can be related to their values, they will be more willing to implement the change.

INTP—They are quick to notice problems, and they care about ideas (Son, 2016). When imposing a change, they need to be listened to and have their ideas considered.

ESTP—They are fast-paced people who can be influential as well. They need a set of short-term goals results or milestones throughout the change process to be convinced of the benefit of the change and to help work toward achieving them.

ESFP—They prefer to be recognized. To bring them along with the change, they will need to be spoken to about their role in the change before moving on to the overall picture.

ENFP—They are more motivated by social outcomes than financial results (Thompson-Atlassian, 2020). Focus more on these outcomes when proposing change and offer them ways, they can help others as they love to see their positive effect on others.

ENTP—They are rational and will appreciate the change that is based on realities and facts. Provide them with details and they will even convince others of the change.

ESTJ—Although they are organized and want everything around to be so, this can be perceived as being bossy (Thompson-Atlassian, 2020). Those people are good at being leaders, and it is always better to place them in managerial roles.

ESFJ—They are the best caregivers within the team. They are also good leaders; therefore, putting them at the head of a team of juniors to teach them about the change is the best way to benefit from their abilities.

ENFJ—They are also good leaders who care about others. To convince them of a change, ask them to speak about it with others.

ENTJ—They want to see clear goals and long-term results. Introduce the big picture to them, and if the proposed change is efficient, they will surely support it.

Influences on Behavior

According to a report issued by the UK cabinet, nine elements influence behavior (Dolan et al., 2009). These elements are summarized in the acronym MINDSPACE. When attempting to change behavior, one should pay attention to these elements and how they differ according to each person's personality. These nine elements are the following.

Messenger

People are greatly influenced by the person delivering the communication. For example, when the message is delivered by a higher-level authority, they are more likely to accept the message than when it is delivered by the same or lower-level authority. Likewise, the degree to which people accept the messenger or can relate to them also affects their acceptance of the message. Another determinant of a message being accepted is the cognitive process that people undergo when receiving a message. People tend to respond to those whom they believe that the behavior of the person delivering the message is consistent with the and are more reliable than others.

Consequently, communication between organizational members and interpersonal relationships are both affected by the perception that each person has of the messenger, among other things (Giffen, 2015). Just as personalities are different, perspectives will be different as well. Some people will be greatly influenced by others' messages, while others will use more rational means to process the messages first. In other cases, people will get influenced by the majority acceptance of a certain message, that is, they will tend to believe or accept something if it is widely accepted by other people.

To convey a message, leaders and managers should consider different personality traits and, accordingly, use different methods to convey their messages.

Incentives

Incentives are the rewards that people get in return for performing certain actions. According to McGee and McGee (2020), people are either incentivized or nonincentivized according to the extent of their motivation for reward. At the two extremes, people are either highly motivated by incentives, to the point where they won't do a job unless they receive some kind of reward, or they won't be motivated by incentives at all. Most people usually lie between these two extremes.

However, there are general rules that control incentives. One of these rules is that people dislike losses more than they like gains of the same value. Therefore, a reward should be offered in a way that conveys that someone has avoided losing something rather than that they have gained something else. Yet, there might be exceptions to this rule. Another rule is that most people would prefer to get an immediate though smaller reward rather than a delayed but bigger reward (Dolan et al., 2009), so it would seem that it is usually more productive to have monthly targets or quarterly bonuses instead of yearly ones.

The impact of incentives varies to when an incentive is offered, the type of incentive being offered, and its compatibility with the particular personality it is being offered to. For example, some people are greatly influenced by intrinsic incentives, such as getting more recognition or having a better status among others. On the other hand, other people are influenced by extrinsic incentives, such as bonuses, financial rewards, and promotions.

Norms

Norms and behaviors affect each other. Norms are obtained from the observed behaviors of other people, whereas behaviors are the results of the commonly known norms of the group. Social norms are very powerful in promoting desired behaviors, as many people won't behave in a way that is perceived as being different from the larger group.

When aiming to change the behaviors of people, their norms should be considered. Although norms are a social acceptance of something, people behave differently in response to norms. For some people, being socially accepted and receiving social benefits is a matter of security and having a feeling of belonging. On the other hand, compliance with norms can occur out of a fear of incurring social penalties.

Although both types of people will accept norms and act upon them, they have different reasons for doing so. These reasons are related to each person's personality. Knowing how each person perceives norms is important to determine how managers or leaders are supposed to promote norms within their organization.

Defaults

Defaults are the options that are preselected or would be selected if no other decision is made. For the defaults to occur, there must be a set of choices or alternatives where people choose the most likely option to occur.

According to much research, defaults are the choices most made by people albeit for different reasons (Dinner et al., 2011). First, it is the most effortless option among other available options. Second, it is sometimes perceived as an already selected option and therefore the person has no other choice. Third, it is usually perceived as the reference point from which people should start acting.

Defaults are closely related to social norms. Managers and leaders should establish the defaults as well as the norms they want to foster in their organizations. Although norms are different from one personality to another, defaults are the same. Being able to determine the defaults is important to further change the behaviors.

Salience

Salience means prominence. This is the degree to which something is significant to someone. Behaviors are then affected by what people are attentive to. When there is nothing salient or different in a certain thing, people will look for anchors. These are reference points upon which they base decisions.

For example, if a manager is comparing several products to launch where they do not know much about the functionality differences, they will search for an anchor point, which may be the cost versus profit, to base their decision.

The information and knowledge someone has on a certain topic determines the degree of salience they will have for anything related to this topic. Similarly, different people have different experiences in their life, and these contribute to forming their personalities. Peak experiences are always more salient, and they will act as references that determine people's behavior in the future.

Priming

Priming is the effect of subconscious cues that influence the decision-making process. Primes can be as simple as certain words that direct the individual to a certain behavior. Alternatively, they can be unspoken cues, such as placing motivational pictures in the organization to prime a successful environment.

Priming can affect the personality perceptions of everyone (Nordlund, 2009). For example, a person working in an achieving organization that promotes the use of words like success and achievement and other acts of positive reinforcement will perceive themselves as an achiever. The achievement might be the result of other people's work, but as they are subjected to the same primes, they will be similarly affected.

By extension, priming will also affect behaviors (Nordlund, 2009). When people have different perceptions of their personality traits, they will behave according to their perceptions. Moreover, studies have shown that priming can affect, along with the specific personality traits of each person, their problem-solving skills (Yeh, Li, and Lin, 2020). Therefore, for organizations to change behaviors and consequently culture, they should pay attention to what primes they promote inside the organization.

Affect

Affect is linked to provoked emotions. This is the degree to which people emotionally respond to a certain trigger and how they show these emotions. Personality traits influence the impact, and reactivity to, emotions (Komulainen et al., 2014). This influence will consequently affect the decision-making process.

Thus, when studying emotions and their effect on behaviors, managers should pay attention to the specific personality traits of each team member. For example, the agreeableness personality trait is associated with more positive evaluations of incidents, whereas openness is associated with more reactivity to daily stress (Komulainen et al., 2014).

Mood can also affect behaviors. A person in a good mood will behave differently than if presented with the same situation while in a negative mood. Although emotions are not stable (i.e., emotions of the same person may change by changing the given situation), they are powerful in influencing the behavior.

Commitment

Commitment is a desirable behavior among all organizations. Yet, commitment here is how people oblige themselves to commit to do a particular thing. Studies have found that one of the ways to foster commitment is to make the commitment public (Dolan et al., 2009). This is related to the previously stated fact that people hate losses more than they love gains. Failing to achieve a public commitment means they will lose their reputation. Thus, public commitment always yields more positive results.

Commitment is also related to reciprocity. Employees work in return for money. They will commit to the organization in return for an added value or an advantage that they won't find in another organization. This is similar to the idea of incentives, where people do more in return for something.

Yet, not all personalities behave in the same way in relation to commitment (Ziapour et al., 2017). People with conscientiousness are more committed to their organization than others. Agreeableness is also related to commitment (Ziapour et al., 2017). Consequently, managers should consider such traits when hiring staff for sensitive positions that need the highest levels of commitment.

Ego

The last behavioral determinant is ego. Ego is how someone sees themselves. Generally, people will act in a way that presents them in a better way. Achievements are always favorable as they enhance the ego, whereas mistakes are always attributed to someone else or the conditions and circumstances.

According to Sigmund Freud, the ego is what balances the primal needs of a person, their morals, and the social reality they are living in (Cherry, 2020). People usually want to present a positive self-image. However, morals and social reality affect how a person behaves to achieve this positive self-image.

The ego itself is sometimes regarded as a personal trait as it is found on different levels for different people. The extent to which a team member has a positive or negative self-image will determine the most appropriate way of influencing their behavior. For example, people with low egos will always compare themselves with others. Thus, they need more reassurance and encouragement than others with high egos.

How to Persuade People

Changing the culture is important for any organizational change, but, for long-term change, one needs to understand that habits create behaviors that later form a culture. Organizations can face different barriers when attempting to change habits. They should start with changing those habits that will lead to the desired change. According to the personality type and traits discussed above, each individual may have one of the following barriers to change at different levels. These barriers, as mentioned by Grant (2021), are in the following.

Arrogance

Many people believe they know a lot, and whenever they are faced with a situation, they don't know more about they tend to resist. When implementing a change, it is better not to directly address the ignorance of people about what you are up to. Instead, help them to recognize the gaps in their knowledge so that they can fill them in.

Stubbornness

Some people mistake consistency with stubbornness. Trying to be consistent with their values and behaviors may change to stubbornness. These people will be defensive and resistant to any change. To solve this problem, ask the questions that will result in the desired answers. Do not directly tell people what they have to do. Instead, give them clues and ask the questions that will drive the intended answers.

Narcissism

Narcissist people are those who believe that they are always right. If a change conflicts with what they are doing, they are likely to resist. A proposed solution by Grant (2021) to deal with this barrier is to praise the person in relation to one side of his personality before trying to change another. When people are praised and believe that they are perfect in some areas, they are more open to improving deficiencies in others.

Integrated Cultural Framework

The Integrated Cultural Framework (ICF), developed by Mallinger and Rossy Mallinger (Mallinger, 2001), offers a way of measuring organizational culture so that organizations can align their change efforts with different personalities. This framework is divided into six dimensions, which are the following.

Ability to Influence

This describes the ability of organizational members to influence the organization itself. This includes the new ideas, suggestions, and input proposed by different team members and the willingness of the organizations to accept these propositions. Organizational cultures with a high ability to influence are more inviting for personalities who prefer leading and change. Those personalities will find themselves in such organizations as they can see their impact on the outcomes.

Comfort with Ambiguity

It is about the degree of comfort of organizational members in risk taking and challenging the status quo. Similarly, more agreeable personalities prefer working in cultures that promote comfort with ambiguity as they always want to try new things.

Achievement Orientation

It refers to how organizations see achievements. Cultures with high achievement orientation encourage every individual to achieve goals and perform better. Cultures with low achievement orientation don't care about high achievements and focus only on short-term financial results. High levels of conscientiousness are better performers in high achievement orientation cultures as both encourage reaching goals.

Individualism vs. Collectivism

Individualism means focusing on personal gain, while collectivism means focusing on group interests. Personalities that value cooperation and helping others are more into collectivism. Personalities that prefer working at their own pace and interest will prefer organizations with an individualism culture.

Time Orientation

It means whether organizations focus more on the present, past, or future. Organizations can have different time orientations at the same time. Imaginative personalities will prefer organizations with a more future time orientation, whereas organized personalities will prefer a present/future time orientation.

Space Orientation

It refers to how organizations physically exist. Do they have public access or private one or a mix of both? Different extraversion personalities prefer public orientation, while introverts prefer the opposite.

Summary

Culture can be influenced by behavior and the opposite is true. Similarly, the personality dictates the behavior of a person. In this chapter, the Big Five Personality Traits have been reviewed in terms of employees and change particularly in predicting occupational outcomes. These personality traits end up forming a certain personality type, which are majorly eight in total. However, there are certain kinds of personality specific to change management in an organization. Finally, the chapter reviews Myers & Briggs 16 personalities, where it is deduced that the different kinds of these personalities can support various work roles such as being a manager, advocating for change, leadership, etc.

However, in the context of an organization, there is no personality that can be proven to be better than the other. They all seem to influence behavior in what is termed as MINDSPACE. As a result, leaders who are trying to transform the organization should pay attention to these aspects of personality and the influence they pose on behavior. While doing this, it would be essential to discuss the aspect of technology that drives change in the contemporary society as seen in the next chapter.

Measuring Success

Traditional key performance indicators (KPIs) for personality and behavior are as follows:

a. Cultural framework based on different personalities
b. Assessing personality in relation to change
c. Leadership
d. Environment and ability to deliver expected results

Suggested key behavior indicators (KBIs) for personality and behavior are as follows:

a. The type of a person's personality in relation to job outcomes
b. The level of persuasiveness
c. Behavior exhibited by each person's personality
d. Work toward expectations

Chapter 10

Fourth Stage of the Industrial Revolution: Industry 4.0, Internet of Things (IoT), and Artificial Intelligence (AI)

I remember watching the first Marvel Ironman movie where Tony Starks's house is controlled by a "virtual assistant" who does everything like making reservations, sending out the dry cleaning, and giving weather updates among many, many tasks that traditionally humans did and remember thinking this is incredible! I remember seeing Tony Starks in his "hobby" shop using the same virtual assistant to design incredible machines by just waving his hands and manipulating drawings and thinking that it's so fantastic, "someday" my kids will probably have all of this; it seemed so far away!

Recently, I watched the movie again and realized that we have come a long way in just a little 12 years to achieve this realization. In our homes, we are using Amazon's Alexa to make our lives easier and find information instantly, as well as entertain ourselves with music and podcasts, self-driving cars, virtual assistants, and 3D printers; the list is endless and yet so subtle that we have easily adopted it into our lives. Gurmeet Mangat of DDB Inc,

> We can literally find anything on the web or buy anything with three clicks in our personal lives, in our business lives the change has also been very rapid also, but in many cases, we still find ourselves doing things the way we have always done them,

searching for information, losing information, being constrained by certain types of thinking, in essence a traditional "lean" problem can be extremely frustrating.

The formal terms for all of this are Industry 4.0, IoT (The Internet of Things) or IIoT (Industrial Internet of Things) and AI or artificial intelligence, or more simply the fourth stage of the Industrial Revolution simplified it as the concept of using technology to achieve the point where man and machine become more connected. That can be a scary thought and the stuff of science fiction movies, but it is already happening and has been happening for quite some time and will have a significant impact on the lean practitioner and the way we work (Figure 10.1).

As lean practitioners the question becomes how do we use this technology to implement lean so that we can move faster? It's a tough question, one which many people are thinking about, and it's a very important one for our success down the road.

So here is an example of how businesses are using it in real life, in this case managing wind farms.

Traditional Approach

In this case, the wind turbine went down at 7 pm and the technician was not able to get to the site to diagnose the problem until 7:00 am the next morning, it then took until 5:00 pm to get the wind turbine back up, which equals 22 hours of downtime. Also, looking at this from the case of the technician where was

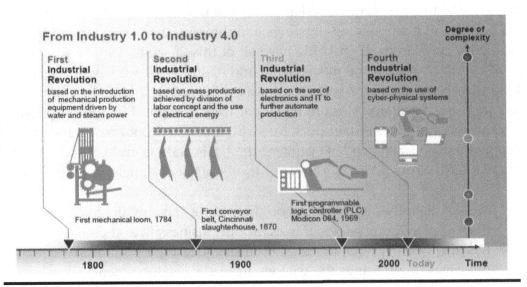

Figure 10.1 Industry evolution roadmap.

Wind Turbine Example

Turbine down at 7pm - 7am site drive and determine which asset is down - Visit turbine and log in to local terminal - diagnose fault - climb turbine - seized motor - climb down - drive to shop and collect parts - return to turbine and repair the asset. End time 5pm.

Figure 10.2   Traditional industry example roadmap.

Source: Courtesy of DDB Consulting.

the value-added time? Most of the time was spent in one of the eight wastes and not adding value to the customer to get the wind turbine back up and running. Now, let's apply Industry 4.0 and the IoT to this same process (Figure 10.2).

In this case, technology is diagnosing the problem and making changes to keep the unit up and running rather than going down. The technician is dispatched at 7:00 am with the right parts and its back up at full production by 9:00, or in only 2 hours. The technician's time is made better use of, and he has the remainder of his shift to do improvement activities or work on other issues.

Now let's look at a "Real life" example of how this technology will affect us moving forward; we start off with the traditional IT solution approach and then transition into an Industry 4.0 approach (Figure 10.3).

Wind Turbine Example

Turbine down at 7pm - technician notified via text msg - remote login to attempt fault reset - determines bearing temp is high and reduces output to lower the temperature - 7am huddle with team viewing centralized dashboard - parts collected and dispatched - turbine repaired by 9am.

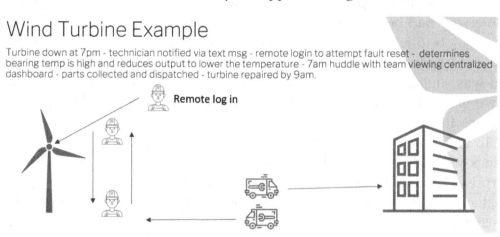

Remote log in

Figure 10.3   New thinking industry example roadmap.

Source: Courtesy of DDB Consulting.

Figure 10.4   Work being batched – no flow!

Real-life example – In 2019, we wanted to create a "Real-time" dashboard that would let the teams know if they were winning or losing against customer demand (Figure 10.4). To give the readers some background, orders would be processed throughout the day and piled up at the end of a table; people would look at the pile and decide that we had enough in the pile to meet the orders for the day; I'm totally serious!

There was no flow, everything was being batched, and this made perfect sense to the people doing the work and unfortunately created some very bad behaviors such as no cross-training, the attitude of "it's not my job to learn new skills or help others out" and on and on with the result being no focus on the customer! One of the first things we did was suggest that we try shipping orders as we go so, we could see if we were "winning or losing," they looked at me like I had two heads (Figure 10.5)!

To their credit, they tried it and the interesting thing is that it worked, things started flowing that day and it was much easier and better, not a surprise. The next step was to improve our dashboard that hung in shipping so that everyone could see if we were winning or losing very quickly, within 3 seconds.

Figure 10.5 Two heads.

This dashboard is a simple concept that is principle-based and really covers all of the ten Shingo principles:

- **Respect for the Individual** – By getting the team involved and owning the process.
- **Humility** – Management realizing that they can't control every second but allowing the team to adjust as needed.
- **Flow and Pull Value** – Change the behavior from a PUSH system to a pull/flow system.
- **Assure Quality at the Source** – Since we were batching, we would lose orders, labels would come off, packages would get damaged, and batching leads to a whole host of potential problems.
- **Focus on the Process** – We didn't have a stable, predictable process, so as a result, there was no way we could improve it because it changed daily.
- **Embrace Scientific Thinking** – Again, an unstable process caused unscientific fixes to be put in place randomly with no connection as to whether they improved the process.
- **Seek Perfection** – The idea of getting better each day was not in the mindset or behaviors; in many ways, people treated it as just a job with no connection to the customer.
- **Constancy of Purpose** – The organization was very siloed with the focus on each person's job, not on the customer and how things were flowing to the customer.

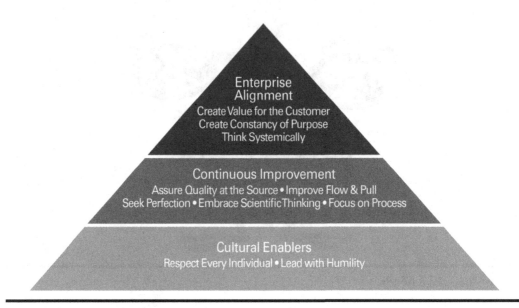

Figure 10.6   Shingo Institute Model 10 principles.

- **Think Systemically** – All the systems were linked, but we didn't treat them that way.
- **Create Value for the Customer** – This was one of the major pieces that were missing; no one was aligned on creating value (Figure 10.6).

So, as you can see, there were a lot of very good reasons to create a dashboard that would drive the right behaviors! The first step was talking to IT to see how to create and implement a dashboard. Over the course of my career, as I have approached any IT or information problem, there seems to be a few standard responses:

- We didn't buy that module of the software.
- We don't have the resources because we are working on this "big" project, and it will be years, months before we can even look at it.
- Put it on the list, and we put it on the schedule.

In this case, we had our own in-house developers, so the project was put on the list and scheduled, which was a few weeks out. We had a basic idea of what we wanted from an operational standpoint, but translating this vision proved challenging. The first drafts were much more complicated than we needed, and as often happens, we wanted a lot of information that wasn't value added and presented challenges to the developers. The problem was that it took a few weeks of development time to get to this realization

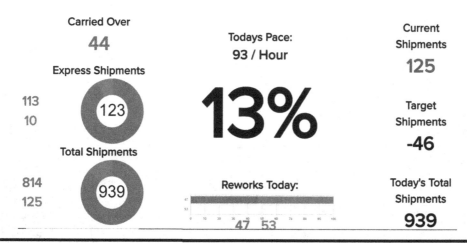

Figure 10.7   Production dashboard.

and resulted in many missteps; it was ok to fail; we just need to fail faster, learn, and move on. After a few weeks, the first version of the dashboard was ready; it was close, but again, once we saw it and as we started using it, we identified gaps (Figure 10.7).

The first problem we ran into was verifying information; we knew there were errors, but we didn't know where the information was being pulled from, so we couldn't identify what or where the errors were coming from, which became very frustrating. The second is that we immediately saw that there were improvements needed, but the only way to get the improvements implemented was to get back into the development cycle, which was an another weeks long process. This pattern went on for quite a few months, and eventually we had a working dashboard. A few highlights is as follows:

Today's Total Shipments – This is the total customer shipments for the day, and before the dashboard, there was no awareness as to what this number was. As I mentioned, there was a pile of work, and the focus was on reducing that pile, nothing else.

Today's Pace – This is TAKT time; we are working a 10-hour shipping shift, so in this example, we have to ship 93 per hour to meet customer demand. It is also a leading indicator that tells us information very quickly, such as in the morning if we are staffed correctly and also prompts other actions if the number is above capabilities or turns RED.

Target Shipments – This number is a calculation based on the Pace times the number of hours worked, so if the Pace is 93 and we have worked 2 hours, the target shipments would be showing 186.

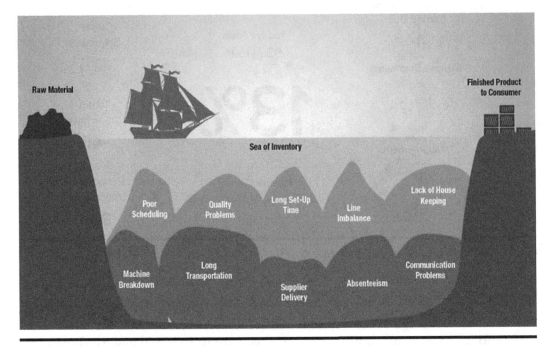

Figure 10.8   Sea of inventory hides problems.

Current Shipments (Displayed in Red/Green) – This is based on how many orders have shipped and then compared to the Target Shipments. If the Current Shipments are ahead of the Target Shipments, the number is Green; if it is behind, the number changes to Red.

Express Shipments – Shipments that need to be shipped for next-day delivery; the number is included in the overall Total Shipment number.

We placed the dashboard on the production floor; the behaviors did start to change with the team now focused on the dashboard, and we started to make our shipments much more easily and earlier in the day. One of the chief complaints and pain points for the team was having to work late to get everything out, and now, every 15 minutes, we knew exactly where we were. This also exposed the "rocks" of the process, as things started to flow thru more quickly; it was easier to see where the problems were and address them faster, essentially in "Real Time" (Figure 10.8).

As you can see from this illustration, if there is no flow, then there are a lot of hidden problems (The Hidden Factory) that don't get addressed.

As you start flowing, these problems become "exposed" and you are forced to address them, that's what happened when we instituted the dashboard and changed the behaviors; we started to have to address these problems (Figure 10.9).

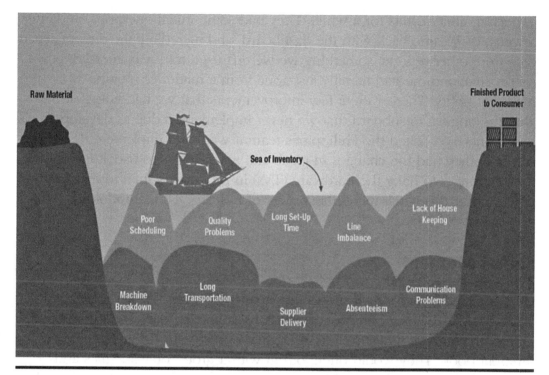

Figure 10.9   Flow exposes the problems.

Over the next year, we worked out the bugs in the dashboard; it was a cumbersome process working with the Development group and getting onto the list of priorities. Also, during this time, we started to investigate other methods for reporting based on Industry 4.0 methodology. The thought process was could we have a place where we gather the data (a data warehouse) and then use a reporting software, run from our desktops, to compile the dashboard the way we wanted to. It would be faster and allow us to try things very quickly and see what works and what doesn't. The initial trials were very promising with some successes and the ability to "prototype" what we wanted to rapidly see if the concept was even feasible. This saved countless hours of developer time, and ideas were vetted much more quickly and found to be viable or not. Toward the end of this time, the company was sold, and we became part of a much larger organization; this became a blessing in disguise.

The new organization had resources in the Philippines for writing these reports and a data repository similar to the one we had thought about. This was a great opportunity to try our theory and see if this was possible to create reports from a desktop software using a data warehouse without having to go through the IT/Developer process. I contacted the group and explained to them what I wanted, at this point, I was hopeful but not expecting great results for a while. They had some initial questions, and after a week, they came back with the dashboard, and incredibly the data matched data from other reports, something we weren't used to! I was amazed; our report creation time had literally just gone from a matter of months to a matter of hours. There were a few improvements that we had talked about with the original dashboard that we never implemented due to developer constraints, so I asked the Philippines team if we could implement them. The next day they had the changes in place and ready for us to use; it literally took us longer to hang the hardware (TVs) in production than to make the new reports; this is the incredible power of Industry 4.0 methodology.

Sensei Moment

Here is a small story which shows the Japanese perspective on creating value by adjusting our behaviors and not by collecting data and information. One of the authors was traveling in Japan working with his coauthor on a different book. They would often join in with a group of academics and Toyota executives to discuss Toyota Production System principles. One night, during one of these discussions, the conversation turned to the United States. One executive stated, "Do you want to know what's wrong with the United States?" Unfortunately, this is a conversation that occurs far too often during international travels. Everyone seems to know what is wrong with the United States, and they are eager to share their insights into how to fix it.

The author was tempted to answer by saying, "Nothing! We are perfect. But I can tell you what's wrong with Japan." However, instead, he did the courteous thing, trying to stay on their good side, and answered, "Tell me what you think is wrong with the US."

The executive came back with a very lean answer. He suggested, "You're creating far too much non-value-added content."

The author responded with, "What does that mean."

The executive drew a diagram on a piece of paper (see the chart below) as he said, "Look at the students that you are graduating from your universities. You are graduating an ever-increasing number of non-value-added students and an ever-decreasing number of value-added students. The non-value-added students are using up resources, or at best just moving them around. But the overall value of the nation is not increasing in proportion to the size of the population. The United States is not producing enough resources to sustain its current standard of living in the long run.

The value-added content is decreasing and so is the standard of living as a whole throughout the United States."

All the author could say was, "That's a very interesting perspective."

The executive ended with the comment, "You need to shift the culture in the United States to be more focused on creating value. You need to change the way people think so that your students will want to enter into professions that grow the country, rather than just burn up its value-added content."

The author responded by smiling and saying, "I'll hurry back and tell our president what he needs to do to fix America."

"Excellent," was the executive's response. I think he seriously expected me to do exactly that.

The purpose of this story is to make you the reader think. Are we creating value as a nation? As a government (federal, state, local)? As a company or agency? What do you, the reader, think? What about our culture? Is it based on principles? Is there a set of principles, like the Shingo Principles, that should be considered as a basis of principles for the nation as a whole? What behaviors need to shift in order for this goal to be accomplished?

Chapter Summary

In this chapter, we illustrated how you can change behaviors and add value by using the Shingo Model principles to create systems that transform behaviors. In this case, we created an information system that let team members know if they were winning or losing and tied them to creating value for the customer. We did this by showing an example of using the methodologies of Industry 4.0 to show the power of these technologies and how they will impact lean implementation and fundamentally change the way we get and use data in the future. In the next chapter, we will look at the aspect of leadership that is necessary for bringing about organizational change and behavior.

Measuring Success

Traditional key performance indicators (KPIs) for the fourth stage of the industrial revolution are as follows:

a. Alignment of enterprise to technology
b. Continuous improvement

    c. Cultural enablers

    d. Technology

Traditional key behavior indicators (KBIs) for the fourth stage of the industrial revolution are as follows:

    a. Are we running to our Dashboard/TAKT time?

    b. Is it taking more than three clicks to find information?

    c. Are we collecting information for the sake of collecting information?

    d. How many improvement ideas are getting turned in and implemented??

Suggested key activity indicators (KAIs) for the fourth stage of the industrial revolution are as follows:

    a. Mapping technology gaps

    b. Team dashboards with live information

    c. Number of improvement suggestions submitted via QR codes

Chapter 11

Leadership Responsibility

In a recent August 2021 *USA Today* article titled, "Can I get fired for not fitting in with a company's culture," the author, John C, Taylor Jr., stated, "Several work factors fall under the umbrella of culture including, but not limited to, work performance, personality, work style, work ethic or ability to work as a team." Later in the article, he says, "Over time, I have come to view culture as the fundamental defining element of the workplace. If the work is what an organization does, workplace culture is how an organization does it." His conclusion basically questions why you would want to work for an organization wherein you have a cultural clash. He says, "I challenge you to seek an organizational culture that aligns with your persona." Employees and leadership need to be culturally and behaviorally aligned in order for workplace harmony to exist.

The United States space program and NASA have shifted their focus, and there is a lot of confusion within the aerospace industry attempting to determine what they should work on next. The United States is using foreign rockets to launch satellites, and private companies are fighting their way toward becoming the first commercial provider of space transportation including tourism.

Being tangled up in these struggles finds American aerospace companies in a quandary attempting to redefine themselves. Companies that were once the primary industry in a community are now only supporting a small portion of the population.

One of the authors of this book was brought into a company of this type and was asked to help them redefine themselves. Unfortunately, the company was extremely siloed. The manufacturing silo was in direct conflict with the engineering silo. Engineering felt that the only way to save the

DOI: 10.4324/9781003224747-11

company was by coming up with creative technologies, like lift mechanisms into space that did not require rockets or hypersonic speed engines. Manufacturing was looking for ways to make cheaper rockets and was not interested in wasting time producing engineering's fantasies.

The author was involved in organizing an off-site strategy workshop where the leadership and senior management were brought together in the hope that a unified plan could be created. It was a disaster because it turned into a power struggle between the various factions of the organization. In the end, they came up with a vision and strategy that cemented rather than resolved the conflict between the divisions. The company's leadership was not forceful enough in their commitment to create a vision that the entire company could stand behind. They let the engineering and manufacturing organizations run over them. After this strategy workshop, the editor refused to work with them any longer. Since then, the company has seen major declines in its revenues, and it is on the verge of bankruptcy. A strong commitment to enterprise excellence success starts with leadership, and without it, there is no moving forward.

Leadership: In Chapter 8, we talked about the key role that leadership has in forming the safety culture of an organization. What is important to a leader, how they act, and their attitude will all be reflected in their teams. As Taiichi Ohno once said, "The Shop Floor is a reflection of Management (Leadership)." If you walked around your business right now, what would you see? Would you be proud of what you saw?

The Shingo Model discusses ten principles and three dimensions that form the Shingo Model. The foundation of the Shingo Model is the dimension Cultural Enables, made up of the principles of:

- **Respect for the Individual**
- **Lead with Humility**

For leaders, this is the most important dimension and the most important principles. In previous chapters, we discussed these principles but let us look at how they are applied in "Real-Life" scenarios.

Respect for the Individual

One time I was teaching a Shingo workshop on Cultural Enablers, and we were discussing Respect for the Individual, and one person in the class said, "That's just means you have to be nice to people!" and that is probably the thought that most people have when they hear this principle. The truth is to have true respect for a person means that you need to be honest and open with them about their abilities, where they need to improve and at times have some difficult conversations. When leadership has respect for the individual, they are coaching the team on a frequent basis so that there is alignment, everyone clearly knows what is expected, and the leader is supporting the team members to help them achieve their personal goals and the business's goals. The business goals are also clearly defined, and the team has a clear understanding of how their work matters and is aligned to achieving those goals. This empowers and engages the team because they are truly part of the business.

Lead with Humility

As Ritsuio Shingo says, when Leaders do Go & Observe walks they should have "Big Eyes, Big Ears, Small Mouth," unfortunately all too often leaders don't abide by this advice and revert to how they think leaders should act; they give all the answers! This is a huge disservice to the team and is not an example of Leading with Humility. I find out more about what is really happening by going and talking to people and listening to what their problems and frustrations are, rather than just looking at a spreadsheet. In almost every case, the problems are different from what leadership believes. As Taiichi Ohno said, "Leaders need to admit that they are wrong, even the weatherman is wrong half the time!"

As leaders adopt the Shingo model and remarkable things start to happen, they have time to do the work that leaders should be doing, such as coaching, working on strategy, root cause analysis, and the long-term direction of the business, rather than firefighting and doing workarounds. Processes start running the way they were designed to, with everyone doing them the same way (standard work) and you get the results you expected!

The main role and some would say the only important role of a leader is to create this culture. The leader that is able to not only follow but model/ emulate these principles in his behavior and get his leadership team aligned with following the same behaviors and principles will have a much easier time transforming the culture of the company. Once again, a leader who cannot model/emulate these principles and behaviors or has a team that is not aligned with principles and behaviors will likely fail or get results that are neither sustainable nor what they expect. This is really the secret between companies that have sustainable results and those that achieve good short-term results. Here are a few "Keys to Success" for helping leaders emulate these principles:

- **Set clear expectations of what is winning and what is losing and allow the team to know if they are winning or losing as soon as possible:** In most businesses, if you ask the teams if they are winning or losing or even what are the expectations for today, the team will not be able to answer. In most cases, they believe that their job is to come in and put parts in a machine or process paperwork, etc., not create value for the customer. This is not Respect for the Individual, and you are violating the eighth waste by not using their minds and creativity to get them involved in the process. Here is an example of a dashboard that is visible to everyone in the plant, and within 3 seconds, anyone can know if they are winning or losing.
- **Real-life example:** My epiphany on this thought process was when I visited the Toyota San Antonio truck plant, and they were running to a 60 second TAKT time. They explained that as long as they made their 60-second TAKT time, they knew that their safety, quality, delivery, and cost were good and didn't need a lot of more intricate measurements. Customer focus and winning or losing and knowing if you have a problem every 60 seconds!
- **Hold people accountable to the expectations:** In every organization, you have a bell curve of performance (Figure 11.1).

If a leader does not set performance expectations, which every company usually has, such as coming in on time, taking the right

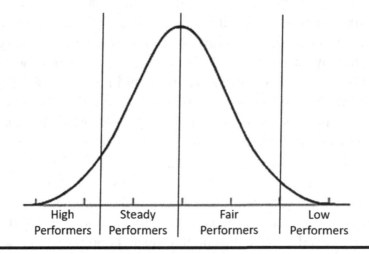

| High Performers | Steady Performers | Fair Performers | Low Performers |

Figure 11.1   Performance distribution bell curve.

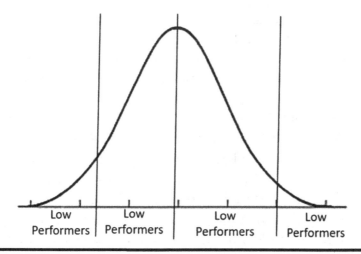

Figure 11.2   Basic performance distribution.

amount of time for breaks, cross-training, etc., then you will have chaos because no one knows what the rules are, and generally, people want to have rules or standards and have everyone held accountable to them. If the leader does not hold everyone accountable to these rules, then the leader will spend the majority of their time handling people issues within the team rather than focusing on improvement. Performance will also degrade to the lowest level of performance and your bell curve will look like this (Figure 11.2).

How can we prevent this? It is critical to coach low performers and hold them accountable, and really giving them the opportunities and support they need to be successful. It is also critical to show the rest of the team that performance problems are addressed.

Real-life example: We recently had one of the team members starting to miss time and come in late. It wasn't being effectively addressed, and after a short period of time, the rest of the team was coming to the manager and reminding him that they expected to be held to the same standards. This was a huge distraction and made it very hard to make improvements or even do the daily work as this was the main focus of conversation throughout the day. Again, if these situations are not addressed, it is disrespectful to the rest of the team, and the rest of the team will expect to be held to the same standards, so overall your performance starts to decrease because now there is no "standard" of when people will be at work, etc.

Lean champions/influencers: It is critical to find team members who support the transformation and have a passion for change and improvement. If these team members are also influencers, well respected, and trusted among their peers, then you have a much higher chance of success.

> **Real-life example:** I was working at an oil and gas plant in Texas building equipment for the fracking industry. We received a new piece of equipment to build and the first one took us 3 months; the demand was 15 per month! We started doing weekly Kaizen events and the same pattern started to repeat itself; Kaizen improvements during the week but then back to the "real job" the following Monday of getting orders out the door; nothing was changing. I approached the lead in the shop, Juan Serrato, who was well respected for his knowledge as well as his compassion, people would come to him with work problems as well as personal problems, and he would help them out. I explained to him how we were trying to "flow" this piece of equipment down a line and could he help us; his reply was very simple, "Of Course, no one has ever asked me to help before!" The change was astonishing, he would direct his team on what to do each day, and the next day, when I came in, there would be another piece in place. In a matter of only a few weeks, we were flowing the new piece of equipment down the line and completing one in a little over a day. A huge accomplishment in a very short period of time, and all it took was getting the right lean champion in place to form the right culture.

Tools to do the job/listen to the people: As lean practitioners, most of us have a standard process we follow when we go into a site or try to improve our own site; we usually start with 5S, standard work, vision/mission statement, huddle boards, etc. In other words, we focus on the tools and not always on making things easier for the team. It's important to remember that you may have seen the benefits of these tools in other places, but to the average person, they aren't sure what it's all about yet and they are trying to figure out whether to trust you or not.

> **Real-life example:** I am guilty as anyone of doing this, when you have been doing this for a while it's easy to walk into a site and "see" what needs to change but not take the time to listen to the people to see what their pain points are. I see this all the time when I'm teaching Shingo workshops at Shingo award-winning

sites; many of the participants will see things in place at the host site and want to take the ideas back as "best practices" and "copy" them at their site. What they don't realize is that it has taken many years, many steps along the way, and many failures for that site to develop their culture to get to that point where that "best practice" works for them. If you bring back one of these "Best Practices" and the teams are struggling with not having the right tools to do their jobs, bad material, or a host of other frustrating issues, and if you don't address this or implement a tool that doesn't address it, you will start to lose credibility. Address the pain points of the team first and get them what they need to do their jobs!

Make it flow/create value streams: Early in my career, I worked with a Japanese Sensei, Mr. Shimbo, and the first thing he always wanted us to do is to make the process/value stream flow. The reason is that when you start flowing you start to see all the problems that are occurring, and they aren't hidden any longer. This is called the "Hidden Factory" and "Fire Fighting" and "work arounds" are the norms.

Once you start flowing, these hidden problems become visible and force you to address them. The fear is that this change will disrupt shipments, the way we do things, etc., but the question is "are you really in control" with the current system?

Alignment of leadership team: In many businesses, if you asked the leadership team what the deliverables are to the customer you would get different answers depending on their job functions. This misalignment is like rowers in the same boat but everyone rowing in a different direction, everyone is working extremely hard but little progress is being made in the direction they want or need to go. There is also blaming for lack of progress or not hitting goals and very little teamwork occurring because everyone is pushing their own agenda (Figure 11.3).

In Shingo prize-winning organizations, you don't see this, there is a clear direction, and everyone can articulate that direction, from the top-level leadership team to the team in the production or office area. In addition, any improvement activity is tied into this direction or the "why" we exist as a company and improvements or changes are only made if it is aligned with this direction. This provides an easy framework for decision-making; the teams ask if this improvement is in line with our purpose (deliverables to the customer), and if not, the improvement is not done. This also helps prevent localized improvements that don't tie in with the overall purpose of the organization or the value stream.

Figure 11.3   Alignment or misalignment of leadership teams.

Servant leadership: An important concept for leaders is servant leadership. Simply it is the leader adopting the attitude that the leader works for the team and not the other way around. In this relationship, the leader is focused on getting the team what they need to do their jobs and be successful, asking the team what they think, and valuing their opinion on improving the processes. It is also providing clear expectations to the team and making it clear to the team if they are winning or losing.

Multigenerational workforce: We wanted to touch briefly on a challenge for leaders in today's world, a multigenerational workforce. There are currently five different generations in the workforce, which there have ever been before. This multigenerational workforce presents new challenges for leaders because each generation has different wants, needs, and reasons for why they work. The challenge for the leader is to address these concerns so that each person feels understood and their needs are met. In today's world, the Shingo Cultural Enabler principles have never been more relevant or hold truer as to their true meaning. As a leader, if you follow the Respect for the Individual principle, you would be doing, among other things, performance coaching, career planning, and setting clear expectations that all transcend generations.

- Traditionalists: born 1925–1945
- Baby boomers: born 1946–1964
- Generation X: born 1965–1980
- Millennials: born 1981–2000
- Generation Z: born 2001–2020

Decision-Making Framework

Table 11.1 Leadership Decision-Making Behavior Framework

	Team Member	Team Leader/ Manager	Executive Manager	General Manager	Executive General Manager	Group Executive/ CEO
Corporate Transformation/CI Competencies						
Drive Results—Initiating Action and Committing to Achieving Business Outcomes by Taking Accountability for Goals						
Sets goals and drives accountability	Understands personal accountabilities and expected results.	Understands personal and team accountabilities and expected results.	Understands personal and team accountabilities and expected results.	Understands personal and business accountabilities and expected results.	Sets the strategies and goals for the business, translating them into short- and long-term goals.	Sets the organizational vision and strategic priorities that will result in sustainable growth.
	Accepts responsibility for outcomes.	Cascades goals and sets expectations.	Translates the department's goals and expected results.	Communicates organization goals and translates them for their business.	Articulates expected business/ division results and challenges the team to take accountability.	Articulates expected results and challenges the team to take accountability.
		Aligns resources and communicates accountabilities.	Aligns resources and holds others accountable.	Aligns resources and holds others accountable.		

(Continued)

Table 11.1 (Continued) Leadership Decision-Making Behavior Framework

	Team Member	Team Leader/ Manager	Executive Manager	General Manager	Executive General Manager	Group Executive/ CEO
	Corporate Transformation/CI Competencies					
	Drive Results—Initiating Action and Committing to Achieving Business Outcomes by Taking Accountability for Goals					
Stays focused to execute	Plans work and prioritizes tasks.	Plans and prioritizes work, leveraging resources to complete work on time, to agreed quality and within budget.	Prioritizes work, leveraging resources, and adjusting as circumstances change.	Prioritizes goals and leverages resources across the business to deliver results.	Prioritizes goals and leverages resources across the business/ division to deliver results.	Leverages resources across the organization to remove systemic obstacles to delivering results.
	Overcomes obstacles, finds solutions, and persists to completion.	Anticipates and removes obstacles.	Proactively removes obstacles.	Works relentlessly to overcome obstacles.		
			Measures and tracks progress and outcomes, taking corrective action when required.	Measures and tracks progress and outcomes, taking corrective action when required.	Measures and tracks performance and takes corrective action.	Measures and tracks organizational performance and takes corrective action.

Table 11.1 (*Continued*) Leadership Decision-Making Behavior Framework

	Team Member	Team Leader/ Manager	Executive Manager	General Manager	Executive General Manager	Group Executive/ CEO
Corporate Transformation/CI Competencies						
Drive Results — Initiating Action and Committing to Achieving Business Outcomes by Taking Accountability for Goals						
Manages risks prudently	Identifies and manages risk when appropriate; escalates where required.	Identifies, manages, and mitigates risk; escalates where required.	Identifies, manages, and mitigates risk; escalates where required.	Practices and actively promotes culture of risk awareness and risk management.	Practices and actively promotes culture of risk awareness and risk management.	Practices and actively promotes culture of risk awareness and risk management.
		Makes decisions in consideration of organisation risk practices.	Makes decisions in consideration of organisation risk practices.	Makes decisions in consideration of the organisation Group risk appetite.	Makes decisions in consideration of the organisation Group risk appetite.	Determines the organization's risk appetite.
		Observes the business and ensures products, processes, and services are within the risk appetite of the business.	Observes the business and ensures products, processes, and services are within the risk appetite of the business.	Observes the business and ensures products, processes, and services are within the risk appetite of the business.	Observes the business and ensures products, processes, and services are within the risk appetite of the business.	

(*Continued*)

Table 11.1 (*Continued*) Leadership Decision-Making Behavior Framework

		Team Member	Team Leader/ Manager	Executive Manager	General Manager	Executive General Manager	Group Executive/ CEO
Corporate Transformation/CI Competencies							
Customer Focus—Creating Value in Each Customer Interaction and Focusing on the Total Customer Experience							
Understands the customer		Actively listens to customers and other stakeholders.	Leverages the voice of customers and other stakeholders in understanding customer information to anticipate their needs.	Leverages the voice of customers and other stakeholders understanding customer information to anticipate their needs and future priorities.	Maintains an understanding and current knowledge of customer's needs and potential issues.	Maintains an understanding and current knowledge of customer's needs and potential issues.	Analyzes domestic and global data to anticipate changing customer expectations.
		Proactively asking questions to understand their needs.	Stays abreast of customer service best practices.	Understands the key end-to-end processes that create value for the customer.	Evaluates internal and external data to anticipate changing customer expectations.	Analyzes domestic and global data to anticipate changing customer expectations.	Gathers and responds to stakeholder feedback on expectations of organisation.
				Stays abreast of customer service best practices.	Articulates the key end-to-end processes that create value for the customer.	Articulates the key end-to-end processes that create value for the customer.	Articulates the organization's customer value proposition.

Table 11.1 (*Continued*) Leadership Decision-Making Behavior Framework

			Team Leader/ Manager	Executive Manager	General Manager	Executive General Manager	Group Executive/ CEO
Corporate Transformation/CI Competencies							
Customer Focus—Creating Value in Each Customer Interaction and Focusing on the Total Customer Experience							
		Team Member					
Creates value		Demonstrates a positive attitude, builds rapport, and treats customers with care and courtesy.	Establishes and grows strong, value add relationships with customers and stakeholders.	Develops a partnering relationship with customers and stakeholders and adopts a long-term perspective.	Develops a partnering relationship with customers and stakeholders and adopts a long-term perspective.	Structures the business to best serve customer needs and build sustainable relationships.	Structures the organization to best serve customer needs and build sustainable relationships.
		Provides solutions that meet the customers' needs.	Creates win/win solutions with customers and other stakeholders.	Creates win/win solutions with customers and other stakeholders.	Uses the understanding of customer needs and supporting data to institute products, processes, and services that will ensure customer satisfaction.	Ensures products, processes, and services will assure customer satisfaction.	Ensures products, processes, and services will assure customer satisfaction.
			Encourages team to consider the impact on customers when making decisions.	Monitors customer satisfaction to ensure high levels are being achieved.	Champions a customer-first approach to business decisions.	Champions a customer-first approach to business decisions.	Champions a customer-first approach to business decisions.

(Continued)

Table 11.1 (Continued) Leadership Decision-Making Behavior Framework

| | Corporate Transformation/CI Competencies | | | | | |
| | Customer Focus—Creating Value in Each Customer Interaction and Focusing on the Total Customer Experience | | | | | |
	Team Member	Team Leader/Manager	Executive Manager	General Manager	Executive General Manager	Group Executive/CEO
Resolves issues			Encourages team to consider the impact on customers when making decisions.			
	Empathizes and takes personal responsibility for resolving issues.	Recognizes potential service issues and takes corrective action.	Recognizes potential service issues and takes corrective action.	Resolves complex customer issues that have been escalated.	Resolves complex customer issues where reputational damage is at risk.	Resolves escalated complex customer issues where reputational damage is at risk.
	Escalates customer concerns when required.	Identifies and removes root causes of locally generated issues.	Identifies systemic issues to remove root causes.	Identifies systemic issues to remove root causes.		
		Resolves customer issues escalated by the team in a timely manner.	Resolves customer issues escalated by the team in a timely manner.			
Lives sales and service	Consistently demonstrates Group Sales and Service principles.	Demonstrates the Sales and Service principles and ensures the team applies them effectively.	Embeds Sales and Service principles in their business.	Champions Sales and Service principles within the business.	Champions Sales and Service principles across the business/division.	Champions Sales and Service principles across the organization.

Summary

Businesses will form a culture either by accident or design; the purpose of the Shingo model is to help you design this culture so that you get the results you want and expect and sustain this culture. The most important role of leadership is creating this company culture, and those leaders who don't will find most of their time spent on firefighting, work arounds, and not getting the results they expect, rather than improving the processes and getting the results they expect. The Shingo model cultural enablers are based on two principles:

- **Respect for the Individual**
- **Lead with Humility**

It is difficult for leaders to really live these principles and develop them in their teams. A few ways for leaders to live and develop these principles are as follows:

- Set clear expectations of what is winning and what is losing and allow the team to know if they are winning or losing as soon as possible.
- Hold people accountable to those expectations.
- Find the lean champions/influencers in your organization.
- Give people the tools they need to do the work and really listen to what their problems are.
- Make sure the leadership team is aligned.
- Make it flow.
- Servant leadership.
- Multigenerational workforce and Respect for the Individual.

With all the dimensions of change in place, it would be significant to now look at the roadmap for implementation in the next chapter.

Measuring Success

Traditional key performance indicators (KPIs) for leadership responsibility are as follows:

a. Leadership that fosters humility and respect
b. Teamwork

c. Accountability
d. Leadership style

Suggested key behavior indicators (KBIs) for leadership responsibility are as follows:

a. Are leaders modeling the behaviors they expect the team to emulate? Are leaders listening during Go & Observes or are they giving all the answers?
b. Are leaders paying attention during the Go & Observes or are they distracted, looking at their phones?
c. Is decision-making being pushed down to the front-line workers?

Chapter 12

Roadmap for Implementation

NUMMI was a joint venture between General Motors in the United States and Toyota in Japan. There were a lot of struggles in blending the two management styles, and there have been a lot of books published about the United States' perspective on this merger. In the Discover Excellence workshop, the first in the Shingo series of workshops, we have a case study on the NUMMI implementation.

One interesting story that came out of this implementation occurred when a Japanese executive came to visit the NUMMI plant in the San Francisco Bay Area. He was walking on a plant tour with an American executive, and he asked him, "What problems are you having in the plant?"

The GM executive's response was, "We're not having any problems. Things have been running very smoothly."

The Toyota executive turned to the American, shook his finger at him, and said, "No Problem is Problem!"

The job of the leader is to search for opportunities for improvement. It is the leader's job to focus continuously on making things better. His job is to search for systems and behavior shortcomings. If the leader/executive is not working on a problem, then he or she is simply not doing their job. Hence, "No Problem is Problem."

If you want to read a detailed account of the NUMMI implementation from the Japanese/Toyota perspective, rather than the dozens of books written from a western perspective (which aren't very useful because, looking at GM, they didn't work), take a look at the book ***Toyota's Global Marketing Strategy: Innovation through Breakthrough Thinking and Kaizen,*** Taylor and Francis Group, CRC Press, 2017 and authored by Kouichiro Noguchi, a former

DOI: 10.4324/9781003224747-12

director of Toyota, Shozo Hibino the author of the "Breakthrough Thinking" series, and Gerhard Plenert an author of this current book. The primary messages are that we should make your organization one that continuously struggles to become better. It talks about culture and behavioral shifts. And it talks about continuously looking for ways to make things better.

One of the tools that is stressed in the Toyota book is the need for something they call a Purpose Expansion. A Purpose Expansion is where, before we make any change, we first ask, "What is the purpose of making that change?" Then, if that purpose does not point directly toward the goals of the company like customer satisfaction or improved product quality, then you ask the question, "What is the purpose of that purpose." It's a second layered step, much like the Five Whys except that it drills upward rather than downward. Then, if after answering this second question, we are still not pointed toward the goals of the company, then we simply do not do the change process. There is no gain in it.

Making Behavioral Change Real

In this last chapter, we will discuss how to pull together all the previous chapters together and then develop a way forward to plan to bring this to life in your organization.

In most transformations, the lean transformation leader will go in with a set of tools that they have used before, or they may have come from a highly functional lean transformation where the culture has been embedded and try to start at this point at this new company. The chances of succeeding are very low, it's not unusual to see as we teach Shingo workshops at Shingo Prize winning organizations to hear people say they want to take this "piece" back to their own company and not really understanding how many years it took for the host company to get there or how all the systems are interdependent to support this "piece." They usually will take it back to their site, and it will fail because culturally their site isn't ready for it. Here are some guidelines to help you plan this transformation and not only change behaviors but sustain the change. The Shingo Prize is set up with three dimensions, and you should start at the base dimension and work your way up, but also remember that results are part of each dimension.

Dimension 1:

1. **Respect for the Individual/Humility** – Leadership at any organization needs to embrace and live these principles. What does this mean and how does it look? The first changes you want to begin seeing are that leaders

are going to the "Gemba" and see the work taking place and asking questions about why systems are not working the way they were intended or designed; in most cases, they weren't properly designed or came about by accident, aren't interdependent on each other, so it is critical to start understanding this. In my experiences, as I walk around the "Gemba" I'm looking at the systems and the results we are getting and am asking myself, "Why is that system driving that behavior that's giving us a bad result?"

The second change that you want to start seeing is leadership stop blaming all problems on people. It's important for leaders to truly believe that as Dr. Demming famously said "People come to work wanting to do a good job, but the system won't let them." This is a critical change and without it the transformation process will not work well because this mindset starts to make leaders question their systems and how they can be improved.

One of the common questions that you will hear from leadership and managers is how am I going to do lean along with all of the other things I am already do, I won't have time! The entire structure of the Shingo model is to create a culture where this "Fire-Fighting" and "work arounds" go away and leaders and managers are making sure the systems are working the way they were designed rather than constantly trying to "patch" poorly designed systems that aren't focused on delivering to the customer (Figure 12.1).

Guiding Principles **Dimensions**

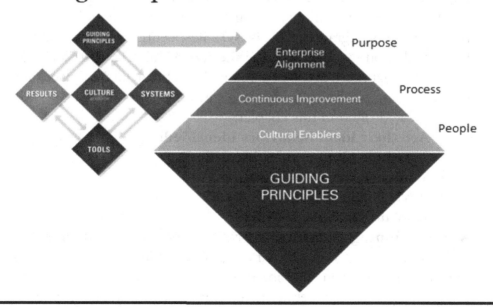

Figure 12.1   Shingo model.

Another critical step at this point is to address poor behaviors in the team. It is critical that you have the right team in place that want to change, it will make implementing the tools so much easier. **Respect for the Individual** means having these tough conversations with members of the team who aren't performing to expectations; interestingly enough in many, many cases you will find that there are no expectations in place. So, the first step is to set expectations and then hold people to them. If you have poor performers who aren't meeting expectations, what you will find is that the entire team sinks to these low expectations, even your high performers! An example that I experienced is people coming in late; managers will tell you that they talked to the person, but nothing has changed and they don't want to lose the person because:

- It's too hard to find a new person and train them
- They do a really good job when they get there
- HR won't support them in disciplining the person

These are all valid points based on how the system is currently functioning, but how should it function (ideal behaviors) to get the results (ideal) that you want. The other thing that is starting to happen is that the employees who are doing the right things are starting to ask themselves why they are following the rules when no one else is and nothing is happening. Also, managers find that they are spending most of their times handling these issues rather than working on improvements! Eventually, this behavior becomes the expected norm, and the entire team is not reaching their full potential and their performance is degraded. This is NOT Respecting the Individual! So how would you live **Respect for the** Individual? The first step is to make sure that there are expectations (ideal behaviors) in place, and they are being met (ideal results); this is a critical point that you will hear repeated often in this chapter:

- **Are their ideal behaviors identified?**
- **Are their ideal results identified?**
- **What are the actual results?**
- **What is the gap?**
- **How do we close that gap?**

2. **Are we winning or losing?** Many times, people begin their journey without knowing if they are winning or losing in terms of satisfying the customer. Are you shipping the required product, satisfying your customer's needs, or meeting the customer's expectations? If you can

quantify this, now you can answer the question of "Are we winning or losing?" If you're losing now, you have a "gap," and with this "Gap" you have direction on what you need to do as far as systems and tools that are needed to be put in place. You also have the "why" as to why we are making these changes, and this leads to winning the hearts and minds of the teams.

3. **Shingo model – Creating transformational, sustainable change**! Once you have the first dimension of the Shingo model in place and have identified the "gaps" now you can move to the second dimension. It's important to really understand these principles, and it's important to have an open mindset. I have been involved with the Shingo model for years, and I am always seeing them in a new light as I experience different situations and understanding their meaning more fully (Figure 12.2).

4. **Creating a plan –** The next step is to create a 12–18-month plan that is tied to the company strategy. Too often companies will start doing Kaizen events not tied to their strategy, and often, I hear that "we have been doing kaizen events for years and have nothing to show for it!" In this 12–18-month strategy, you are looking at what do we need to do to move the needle:
   - **Satisfy customer needs and demand**
   - **Build market share**

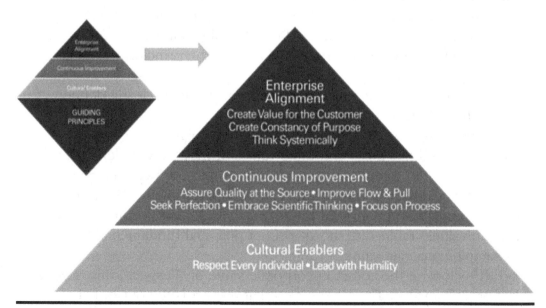

Figure 12.2   Shingo Institute model principles.

- **Improve profit margins**
- **Any market risks**
- **Meeting customer needs – safety, quality, delivery, & cost**
  Once you have done this, you can look at:
- **What are the ideal behaviors based on the principles we want?**
- **What are the ideal results we want?**
- **What are the actual results?**
- **What is the gap?**
- **How do we close that gap?**
  - What systems do we need to improve or put in place?
  - What tools will drive the right behaviors in these systems?
  - What challenges do we face?

Make it meaningful to the people – Start with Why – One of the key challenges for leaders in embedding core and consistent behaviors is moving it away from an academic statement and then making it meaningful and adding value to every individual. It is only when individuals have internalized not only what it means to them in the context of their personal values and beliefs but also how it can add value to them. Simon Sinek talks about the importance in his book "Start with Why"[1] so that people could internalize and then act in a new way. The Shingo Institute has ten core principles in their model, but to bring a much deeper understanding, they use the construct of a "fundamental truth" in the Shingo Model training courses. Table 12.1 illustrates the fundamental truths that enable a true understanding of why the principles work for individuals.

Most organizations don't have a set of core principles clearly defined; however, they do have corporate values such as customer focus, collaboration, and respect. The challenge is how to get every employee to internalize and live these corporate values. If they truly understand the "Why," we can start to internalize expectations into our personal context. An important element of respect is it can only be given and needs to be earned. Taking the fundamental truths in Table 12.1 into a common set of corporate values, Table 12.2 shows a set of potential fundamental truths for the example corporate values.

So let us look at the common corporate value of "Respect"; this is not a behavior; it is a value. The key point is that respect is the outcome but the

Table 12.1   Construct of Fundamental Truths (Shingo Model)

Shingo Model Dimension	Shingo Principle	Shingo Definition Fundamental Truth	Alternative Fundamental Truth
Enterprise alignment	Create Value for the Customer	Trust is sacred.	Customers must trust us.
	Create Constancy of Purpose	Our success depends upon a commitment to a shared understanding of why we exist.	The WHY we exist as a team/organization gives us commitment to work to this common goal.
	Think Systemically	As we see how and why everything is connected to, or part of, something else, it helps us to better understand, predict, and control outcomes.	Seeing the interconnectedness of work enables better outcomes.
Continuous improvement	Seek Perfection	People have an innate desire and ability to improve that is only limited by their expectations.	People have an innate desire and ability to improve that is only limited by their expectations.
	Improve Flow and Pull	Eliminating obstacles maximizes value creation.	Eliminating waste maximizes value creation.
	Assure Quality at Source	Quality is perfected through ownership and connectedness.	Quality is striving to get it right.
	Focus on Process	Great processes set people up to succeed.	Great processes set people up to succeed.
	Embrace scientific thinking	The best decisions are based on a clear understanding of reality.	The best decisions are based on a clear understanding of reality.
	Seek Perfection	People have an innate desire and ability to improve that is only limited by their expectations.	People have an innate desire and ability to improve.
Cultural enablers	Lead with Humility	All growth requires vulnerability.	As a leader, I do not know everything and I can learn from my team, so I need to show my vulnerability.
	Respect Every Individual	Everyone has value and untapped potential.	Everyone has more capability they can utilize.

Table 12.2 Construct of Fundamental Truths by Example Corporate Values

Corporate Value	Fundamental Truth Example
RESPECT	• Everyone has value and untapped potential. • Everyone has more capability that can be utilized. • Respect is a voluntary gift.
	• All growth requires vulnerability. • As a leader, I don't know everything and I can learn from my team and peers, so I need to show my vulnerability. • Respect has to be earned by leaders.
CUSTOMER FOCUS	• Trust is sacred. • Customers must trust us.
	• Customers define quality and is perfected through ownership and connectedness. • Quality is striving to get it right for our customers.
TRUST	• Trust is sacred. • Customers must trust us. • We need to trust each other.
COLLABORATION	• Our success depends upon a commitment to a shared understanding of why we exist. • The WHY we exist as a team/organization gives us commitment to work to this common goal.
	• As we see how and why everything is connected to, or part of, something else, it helps us to better understand, predict, and control outcomes. • Seeing the inter-connectedness of work enables better outcomes.
CONTINUOUS IMPROVEMENT	• People have an innate desire and ability to improve that is only limited by their expectations.
EMPOWERMENT	• Eliminating obstacles maximizes value creation.
	• Everyone has value and untapped potential. • Everyone has more capability that they can utilize.

behaviors that people do to show respect will differ for each person, but the outcome is the same. The complicating factor is that how the person feels respect also varies, so the intent person wanting to show respect may differ from the impact on the person they are wanting to show respect. As discussed in the previous chapter, culture and diversity can affect how respect can be shown and received.

If we start with a fundamental truth for respect as "Everyone has more capability that can be utilized." If people have this truth in mind, then they may show respect for a peer by:

■ Listen to what others have to say before expressing your viewpoint. Ask to understand. Do not speak over, butt in, or cut off another person.
■ Treating people with courtesy, politeness, and kindness, e.g., saying thank you genuinely.
■ Encourage coworkers to express themselves and share their opinions and ideas.
■ Listen to what others have to say before expressing your viewpoint. Ask to understand. Do not speak over, interrupt, or cut off another person.
■ Praise much more frequently than you challenge. Encourage praise and recognition between peers as well as from the supervisor.
■ Treat others as they wish to be treated.
■ Create an atmosphere of gratitude, as it fills the heart and mind with positive energy and a feeling of contentment.
■ Be respectful of others' time. Whenever possible, be on time—do not make others wait for you. If you say you will call someone back by a certain day or time, make every effort to do so. If you need to talk with someone, ask if it is a good time for him/her first. Be sensitive to others' schedules and time limits.
■ Respectful communication should be assertive communication that includes good listening, direct, succinct and open feedback, regular praise, paying attention to nonverbal language, and avoiding gossip.

Some people may show respect by being quite vocal in recognizing the contribution of other people in public saying why they found it insightful or great; others might just say it to the individual afterward, or even send them an email. Not only is it the WHAT message is being delivered to show respect, but it is paramount to understand HOW the message is delivered, for example, tone, pitch volume of the spoken word. Any the incongruence between WHAT the spoken words is and HOW the WHAT is delivered will always default to a negative thus having may have the wrong impact even if the intent is genuinely positive.

Demonstrating respect and be broken down into two elements, providing support and recognition contributions (Table 12.3).

Table 12.3   Examples of KBIs for Respect

High-Level Reference Behavior	Support: We invest in Everyone's Development and Encourage Them to Realize Their Potential
Example Behaviors	*Example KBIs*
1. My organization invests time and energy in developing every employee's potential.	• All new hires undergo a rigorous onboarding process. • Everyone has a PDP that they set. • PDP goals are set and achieved. • PDP goals are not specifically related to a job. • PDPs are reviewed on a regular basis. • Enterprise excellence training is ongoing at all levels. • On-the-job training is a daily occurrence.
2. My team makes personal development a priority.	• Coaching is consistent and evident throughout and at all levels. • Leaders use standard work consistently. • We cover for each other to provide time for development. • Regular time is set aside for development. • Actual time is being spent on personal development.
3. My team readily acknowledges everyone's contributions, big and small.	• Recognition is frequent, timely, and specific. • Recognition motivates a reoccurrence of the behavior. • Recognition is consistent and visible to all. • Recognition is relative to an individual's or team's maturity. • There is a formal and informal process for recognition. • Individual and team-based recognition is used when possible.

High-Level Reference Behavior	Recognition – We Honor the Contributions of Every Employee.
Example Behaviors	*Example KBIs*
1. My workgroup readily acknowledges everyone's contributions, big and small.	• Recognition is frequent, timely, and specific. • Recognition motivates a reoccurrence of the behavior. • Recognition is consistent and visible to all.

	• Recognition is relative to an individual or teams maturity. • There is a formal and informal process for recognition. • Team-based recognition is used when possible.
2. My organization values, our opinions, suggestions, and efforts.	• All employees are turning in suggestions. • Participation rate in giving improvement suggestions. • Improvement suggestions are aligned and focused. • The suggestion rate is stable with a positive trend.

An overall flowchart shows a logical process (Figure 12.3).

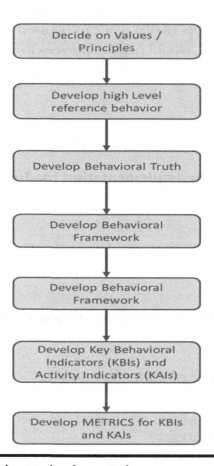

Figure 12.3   Simple flowchart to implementation.

Summary

Leaders have a sole responsibility of ensuring that the changes they implement in the work environment become successful. As a result, it would be essential for them to ensure that they seal all the loopholes that would lead to failure in one way or the other. Guiding principles dimensions discussed in this chapter and most parts of this book can help leaders to achieve the behavioral change they would want for their organizations. These dimensions involve stepwise procedures that begin with identifying a gap and then moving progressively until empowerment is achieved.

The channel of communication is quite important in the implementation of change. It is essential for leaders to know WHAT they are communicating and HOW they are communicating it to avoid misinterpretation of messages that might lead to negativity. Apart from communication, other fundamental metrics can be applied in the form of key performance indicators (KPIs) and key behavior indicators (KBIs) that can be used to foster particular organizational values that would help employees to prepare psychologically for the transformation.

Measuring Success

Traditional KPIs for the implementation roadmap are as follows:

a. Training
b. Technology
c. Leading by example
d. Teamwork

Suggested KBIs for the implementation roadmap are as follows:

a. Observe the behavior of leaders
b. Humility
c. Respect
d. Work toward expectations

Suggested key activity indicators (KAIs) for the implementation roadmap are as follows:

a. Communication plan for roadmap implementation
b. Number of training sessions
c. Number of feedback sessions, surveys, and "Do More of"

Note

1 Start with Why: How Great Leaders Inspire Everyone to Take Action, Penguin Random House Publishing, 2011 page 23.

Chapter 13

Wrap-Up

The Shingo Model formula for success requires us to define the desired culture. We define it through the use of Guiding Principles. These principles then become the yardstick by which all behaviors are measured. The external world measures us by looking at KPIs (key performance indicators). However, these are not transferable and relatable to the employees who do the work. They need metrics that guide them and define what direction they should be moving. They need KBIs (key behavioral indicators). These metrics help employees define their direction and goal. They motivate correct responses.

KBIs are incorporated into systems. These systems are required for any organization to achieve enterprise excellence. These systems are integrated into other systems, all motivating the organization's behaviors toward its Guiding Principles. Nevertheless, in order to create effective systems, two things need to be in place: Standard Work and 5S.

Systems are created and defined using tools like Lean and Six Sigma. There are over 100 different tools available in the Toyota Production System (TPS) of which Lean and Six Sigma are just a couple. It is the responsibility of the Change Manager to identify the correct tool for any improvement project.

With the correct systems in place, using the best KBIs as behavioral and motivating metrics, all of which is focused on our goal-setting Guiding Principles, we have started ourselves down a journey toward Enterprise Excellence.

DOI: 10.4324/9781003224747-13

Appendices—Summary of Behavior Frameworks

Communication Behavioral Framework

	Change Management/Effective Communication—Communicating Clearly and with Impact to Ensure Understanding, Engagement and Commitment to Action					
	Team Member	*Team Leader/ Manager*	*Executive Manager*	*General Manager*	*Executive General Manager*	*Group Executive/ CEO*
Plans and understands communication	Identifies who needs to be communicated with and determines the most appropriate approach.	Identifies stakeholders and determines the most appropriate approach.	Conducts stakeholder analysis and plans best-fit approach.	Leverages and appropriately links knowledge of the business and key stakeholders to develop communication plans and impactful key messages.	Leverages and appropriately links knowledge of the business and key internal and external stakeholders to develop strategies and compelling key messages.	Leverages and appropriately links knowledge of the organization and key internal and external stakeholders to develop strategies and compelling key messages.
	Actively reads and questions communications to ensure understanding of the impact on self and others.			Anticipates reactions and prepares potential responses.	Anticipates reactions and prepares potential responses.	Anticipates reactions and prepares potential responses.

Communication Behavioral Framework (Continued)

	Team Member	Team Leader/Manager	Executive Manager	General Manager	Executive General Manager	Group Executive/CEO
Change Management/Effective Communication—*Communicating Clearly and with Impact to Ensure Understanding, Engagement and Commitment to Action*						
Delivers clear and impactful messages	Outlines the purpose and key messages, following a logical sequence.	Outlines the purpose and key messages, following a logical sequence.	Outlines the purpose and key messages, following a logical sequence.		Takes command of a message to convey logically and succinctly.	Takes command of a message to convey logically and succinctly.
	Engages customers and other stakeholders through appropriate communication channels.	Engages team, customers and other stakeholders through considered use of different communication styles and tools.	Utilizes existing and emerging communication channels.	Utilizes existing and emerging communication channels to create impact and elicit action.	Utilizes multiple communication styles and tools to create impact and elicit action across the business/division.	Utilizes multiple communication styles and tools to create impact and elicit action across the organization.
		Simplifies complex messages to ensure fit for the audience.	Exhibits a presence that demonstrates personal impact and commitment.	Exhibits a presence that demonstrates personal impact and credibility and commitment.	Exhibits a presence that demonstrates credibility and commitment.	Exhibits a presence that demonstrates credibility and commitment.
			Applies simple and compelling language and stories to inspire commitment.	Applies simple and compelling language and stories to inspire commitment.	Applies simple and compelling language and stories to inspire commitment.	Applies simple and compelling language and stories to inspire commitment.

(Continued)

Communication Behavioral Framework (Continued)

Change Management/Effective Communication—Communicating Clearly and with Impact to Ensure Understanding, Engagement and Commitment to Action						
	Team Member	Team Leader/ Manager	Executive Manager	General Manager	Executive General Manager	Group Executive/ CEO
Ensures understanding	Seeks input from recipients and listens actively.	Seeks input from recipients and listens actively.	Invites input from others and constantly assesses reactions, adjusting messages accordingly.	Invites input from others and constantly assesses reactions, adjusting messages accordingly.	Encourages input from a diverse range of stakeholders.	Encourages input from a diverse range of stakeholders.
	Checks for understanding and clarifies points, adjusting style and language as required.	Comprehends and responds appropriately to input from others.	Comprehends and responds appropriately to input from others.	Navigates complex discussions to successful outcomes.	Constantly assesses reactions and adjusts messages accordingly.	Navigates complex discussions to successful outcomes.
	Responds appropriately to input from others.	Reinforces key messages and checks for understanding, adjusting style and language as required.			Navigates complex discussions to successful outcomes.	

Communication Behavioral Framework (Continued)

	Team Member	Team Leader/Manager	Executive Manager	General Manager	Executive General Manager	Group Executive/CEO
Influences others	Conveys own perspective in a positive and compelling manner.	Conveys own perspective in a positive and compelling manner to gain agreement from others.	Determines appropriate influencing strategies to gain genuine agreement.	Develops an influencing strategy to favorably position own agenda.	Develops an influencing strategy to favorably position the business/division.	Develops an influencing strategy to favorably position the organization.
		Determines appropriate influencing strategies to gain genuine agreement.	Adjusts approach to overcome objections.	Translates and advocates business decisions, balancing with stakeholder interests.	Translates and advocates business decisions, balancing with stakeholder interests.	Translates and advocates organizational decisions, balancing with stakeholder interests.
		Adjusts approach to overcome objections.	Steps up to conflicts and sees them as opportunities.	Utilizes appropriate negotiation techniques.	Utilizes appropriate negotiation techniques.	Utilizes appropriate negotiation techniques.
				Can hammer out tough agreements and settle disputes equitably.	Coaches and guides others through difficult conflicts.	Sets the tone for tackling tough conflicts that lead to organizational improvement.

(Continued)

Communication Behavioral Framework (Continued)

	Change Management/Effective Communication—*Communicating Clearly and with Impact to Ensure Understanding, Engagement and Commitment to Action*					
	Team Member	*Team Leader/ Manager*	*Executive Manager*	*General Manager*	*Executive General Manager*	*Group Executive/ CEO*
Engagement through communication	Seeks and listens to the views of others.	Proactively seeks the ideas, input and feedback of others.	Actively seeks to include views from a wide variety of people in their circle of advisors.	Actively seeks to include views from a wide variety of people in their circle of advisors.	Actively seeks to include views from a wide variety of people in their circle of advisors.	Actively seeks to include views from a wide variety of people in their circle of advisors.
		Creates an environment where people are safe and encouraged to speak up.	Encourages two-way communication from their stakeholders and team.	Creatively encourages two-way communication from their stakeholders and team.	Creatively encourages two-way communication from every corner of the organization.	Creatively encourages two-way communication from every corner of the organization.
			Creates an environment where people safe and encouraged to speak up.	Creates an environment where people safe and encouraged to speak up.	Creates an environment where people safe and encouraged to speak up.	Creates an environment where people safe and encouraged to speak up.

Change Management Behavior Framework

Change Management/Effective Training and Coaching—*Training and Coaching to Ensure Understanding, Engagement and Commitment to Actions That Build Proficiency in New Skills and Behaviors*					
Team Member	*Team Leader/ Manager*	*Executive Manager*	*General Manager*	*Executive General Manager*	*Group Executive/ CEO*
Identifies who needs to be trained and determines the most appropriate approach.	Identifies capability gaps and determines the most appropriate approach to training.	Conducts capability (skills and behaviors) analysis and plans, with HRM/L&D best fit approach to training	Leverages and appropriately links the purpose and values of the organization to develop, with HRM, the key competencies and behaviors	Leverages and appropriately links the purpose and values of the organization to develop, with HRM, the key competencies and behaviors	Leverages and appropriately links the purpose and values of the organization, with HRM support, to the desired skills and behaviors
Actively participates in the training to ensure understanding of new ways of working and desired behaviors on self and others.	Actively supports and participates in the training	Organizes the training and participates in the leadership training.	Actively sponsors the training and participates in the leadership training.	Actively sponsors the training and participates in the leadership training.	Actively sponsors the training and participates in the leadership training.

Analyzes and closes knowledge gaps through training

(Continued)

Change Management Behavior Framework (Continued)

Change Management/Effective Training and Coaching—*Training and Coaching to Ensure Understanding, Engagement and Commitment to Actions That Build Proficiency in New Skills and Behaviors*

	Team Member	Team Leader/ Manager	Executive Manager	General Manager	Executive General Manager	Group Executive/ CEO
Confirms understanding of training	Seeks feedback from peers and listens actively.	Seeks feedback from team and peers and listens actively.	Invites feedback from others and constantly assesses knowledge and reacts accordingly to fill gaps.	Invites feedback from others and constantly assesses knowledge and reacts accordingly to fill gaps.	Encourages feedback from a diverse range of stakeholders.	Encourages input from a diverse range of stakeholders.
	Responds appropriately to input from others.	Comprehends and responds appropriately to input from others.	Comprehends and responds appropriately to input from others.	Navigates complex discussions to successful outcomes of the training.	Constantly assesses reactions and adjusts training and delivery methods accordingly.	Constantly assesses reactions and adjusts training and delivery methods accordingly.
	Checks for understanding and closes gaps as required.	Reinforces key messages of the training and checks for understanding and comprehension.			Navigates complex discussions to successful outcomes.	

Change Management Behavior Framework (Continued)

Change Management/Effective Training and Coaching—*Training and Coaching to Ensure Understanding, Engagement and Commitment to Actions That Build Proficiency in New Skills and Behaviors*

	Team Member	Team Leader/ Manager	Executive Manager	General Manager	Executive General Manager	Group Executive/ CEO
Builds proficiency in the new skills and behaviors	Accepts assignments that build capabilities in new skills and behaviors.	Coaches others to proficiency using the appropriate leadership styles and coaching models.	Determines appropriate coaching and feedback models to develop measurable ability in the desired skills and behaviors.	Develops a learning strategy to favorably position own agenda.	Develops and maintains learning and support channels, enabling capacity for learning, building general skills and setting standards.	Provides and maintains organization-wide standards, partnerships, policies and channels for learning and support.
	Actively seeks feedback, coaching, and mentoring from those skilled and proficient in the desired skills and behaviors.	Actively seeks feedback, coaching, and mentoring from those skilled and proficient in the desired skills and behaviors.	Adjusts approach to overcome objections while establishing the desired skill and behaviors.	Translates and advocates learning decisions, balancing with stakeholder interests.	Translates and advocates business decisions, balancing with stakeholder interests.	Incorporates, with HRM, the desired competencies in the performance and development systems.
	Takes time to reflect and continuously improve.	Takes time to reflect and continuously improve.	Steps up to conflicts and sees them as opportunities.	Utilizes appropriate negotiation techniques.	Utilizes appropriate negotiation techniques.	Utilizes appropriate negotiation techniques.
				Can hammer out tough agreements and settle disputes equitably.	Coaches and guides others through difficult conflicts.	Sets the tone for tackling tough conflicts that lead to organizational improvement.

(Continued)

Change Management Behavior Framework (Continued)

Change Management/Effective Training and Coaching—*Training and Coaching to Ensure Understanding, Engagement and Commitment to Actions That Build Proficiency in New Skills and Behaviors*

Team Member	Team Leader/ Manager	Executive Manager	General Manager	Executive General Manager	Group Executive/ CEO
Visibly models the desired behaviors.	Visibly models the desired behaviors.	Communicates the culture, policies, frameworks, and processes to support sustainable change across the organization.	Monitors the culture, policies, frameworks, and processes to support sustainable change.	Monitors the culture, policies, frameworks, and processes to support sustainable change.	Provides the culture, policies, frameworks, and processes to support sustainable change across the organization.
	Uses KBI's to visibly measure and improve the desired leadership behaviors in team members.	Visibly models the desired behaviors.	Visibly models the desired behaviors.	Visibly models the desired behaviors.	Visibly models the desired behaviors.
		Communicates the agreed KBI's to hold the organization accountable to the desired leadership behaviors.	Uses appropriate KBI's to hold managers accountable to the desired leadership behaviors.	Uses appropriate KBI's to hold the organization accountable to the desired leadership behaviors.	Uses appropriate KBI's to hold the organization accountable to the desired leadership behaviors.

Reinforces the skills and behaviors through rewards and recognition

Agile Behavior Framework

Agile—Delivering Projects, Products, Services, and Organizational Improvement in a Calm Accelerating Way

	Team Member	Scrum Master	Product Owner	Scrum of Scrums master	Chief Product Owner	Executive
Fosters a culture of speed, calmness, and agility	Supporting and motivating team mates to deliver sprint goals.	Supporting and coaching team members on Scrum systems.	Participating as team member to deliver sprint goal.	Supporting Scrum masters with cultural and system challenges the team can't handle.	Supporting culture of Meta Scrum team.	Reviewing team performance and cultural measures. Supporting teams to improve.
	Celebrating and recognizing team success each sprint.	Supporting and coaching team on ideal behaviors to enhance team culture.	Supporting team members with insights on customer and stakeholder feedback.	Reviewing with Scrum masters their cultural performance and providing coaching.		Spending time with teams where they work to learn and gain insights to improve.

(Continued)

Agile Behavior Framework (Continued)

Agile—Delivering Projects, Products, Services, and Organizational Improvement in a Calm Accelerating Way

	Team Member	Scrum Master	Product Owner	Scrum of Scrums master	Chief Product Owner	Executive
Accelerates improvement speed and agility of organization at all levels	Committing to small actions and delivering these between Scrums.	Uses Yesterday's Weather to help team sprint plan.	Ensure backlog is prioritized, clean and ready to execute with a clear definition of done.	Supports the overcoming of escalated issues and roadblocks.	Analyzing backlog priorities and helping product owners align.	Supports the overcoming of escalated issues and roadblocks.
		Supports teams toward finishing the sprint backlog early and then drawing more.	Provides quality feedback from customers and stakeholders during sprint reviews to help team members learn, focus and improve.		Helping product owners keep focus on customer and stakeholder feedback.	
		Effectively runs sprint retrospectives, generating ideas from the team to improve.				

Agile Behavior Framework (Continued)

	Agile—Delivering Projects, Products, Services, and Organizational Improvement in a Calm Accelerating Way					
	Team Member	Scrum Master	Product Owner	Scrum of Scrums master	Chief Product Owner	Executive
Customer centricity and iterative innovation to deliver greater value and delight	Focus on customers with every bit of work performed.	Refer to customers during every meeting.	Collaborate with customers to gain feedback and learnings from every product release every sprint.	Refer to customers when supporting the overcoming of challenges and other decision making efforts.	Coordinate and share customer learnings form differing product owners.	Coordinate and share customer learnings form differing product owners.
		Use customer data as a point of decision-making.	Share from customers in a way that resonates and connects with the Scrum team.		Maintain absolute focus on the customer, fostering learning and adaptation from reviews.	Maintain absolute focus on the customer, fostering learning, and adaption from reviews.

(Continued)

Agile Behavior Framework (Continued)

Agile—Delivering Projects, Products, Services, and Organizational Improvement in a Calm Accelerating Way

	Team Member	Scrum Master	Product Owner	Scrum of Scrums master	Chief Product Owner	Executive
Team morale and performance improvement	Lead culture as part of the Scrum team.	Foster a culture of teamwork and collaboration. Support team in monitoring happiness metrics, learning, and adapting.	Lead culture as part of the Scrum team.	Monitor culture across different Scrum teams and support sharing and learning among teams.	Develop team culture within the product owners associated with them.	Focus on culture and teamwork as it is the primary driver. Constantly communicate and support organization focus on teamwork and culture.
	Support team mates and help them develop and grow by sharing your knowledge and skills.	Bring culture and teamwork into sprint reviews as a key topic for reflection, learning, and adaption.				Visit Scrum teams where they operate daily to learn and adapt as a leader.

Example BIP Behavior Framework

	Business Improvement *—Continuously Improving and Innovating What We Do to Make Things Simple and Easy for Our Customers and Each Other*			
	Strategic Leader	*Business Leader*	*First line Leader*	*Team Member*
Fosters a culture of continuous improvement	Encourages others to research new approaches that will deliver on strategic goals.	Invites others to challenge the status quo and envision possibilities to find better ways to achieve results.	Proactively and constructively challenges the status quo and encourages others to do the same.	Explores new ways of doing things.
	Ensures that the business delivers upon funded strategic initiatives and positive results.	Visibly supports strategic initiatives and recognizes the efforts of others.	Visibly supports strategic initiatives and recognizes the efforts of others.	Contributes and supports team initiatives that drive continuous improvement.

(Continued)

Example BIP Behavior Framework (Continued)

	Business Improvement—Continuously Improving and Innovating What We Do to Make Things Simple and Easy for Our Customers and Each Other			
	Strategic Leader	Business Leader	First line Leader	Team Member
Develops and implements solutions	Measures progress to ensure improvement efforts lead to the positive and sustainable impact.	Guides team to implement simpler ways of working considering the downstream and upstream impact.	Translates ideas into actions, considering both downstream and upstream impact.	Identifies opportunities to eliminate waste, improve and/or simplify processes, and raises with Leader/Manager as appropriate.
		Ensures improvement initiatives will deliver value before developing solutions.	Ensures improvement initiatives will deliver value before developing solutions.	
		Makes decisions about which improvement initiatives to resource.		
		Measures results and modifies solutions as required to ensure the positive and sustainable impact.		

Example BIP Behavior Framework (Continued)

	Business Improvement—Continuously Improving and Innovating What We Do to Make Things Simple and Easy for Our Customers and Each Other			
	Strategic Leader	Business Leader	First line Leader	Team Member
Leads change	Champions change initiatives across the function and support organizational change.	Leads their team through change by communicating the rationale and proactively addresses concerns.	Accepts change and encourages team to actively participate in change initiatives.	Considers change and new situations as an opportunity for learning and growth.
	Leverages relationships across the function and organization to gain commitment.	Includes others in the change process to leverage opinions and ensure commitment.	Addresses people's concerns about change.	Adaptive to new ways of doing things.
	Proactively removes roadblocks that inhibit change.	Effectively leads and coaches others through periods of change/transition.	Effectively leads and coaches others through periods of change/transition.	Understands the benefits and speak positively about change.

(Continued)

Example BIP Behavior Framework (Continued)

	Business Improvement—Continuously Improving and Innovating What We Do to Make Things Simple and Easy for Our Customers and Each Other			
	Strategic Leader	*Business Leader*	*First line Leader*	*Team Member*
Lives BIP and continuous improvement	Understands Group values and applies them regularly.	Understands Group values and applies them frequently.	Understands Group values and applies them frequently.	Understands Group values and applies them frequently.
	Continually looks for ways the function and organization can be more productive.	Actively monitors performance and output across the team and reduces variation.		
		Continually looks for ways to be more productive.		

Generic CI Behavior Framework

Continuous Improvement—*Continuously Improving and Innovating What We Do to Make Things Simple and Easy for Our Customers and Each Other*

	Team Member	Team Leader/ Supervisor	Manager	General Manager	Director/ Executive GM	Group Executive/CEO
Develops and implements solutions	Identifies opportunities to eliminate waste, improves and or simplify processes, and raises with Leader/Manager as appropriate.	Translates ideas into actions, considering both downstream and upstream impact.	Guides team to implement simpler ways of working considering downstream and upstream impact.	Provides guidance to the team on where to focus CI initiatives.	Makes decisions about which improvement initiatives to resource.	Makes decisions about which improvement initiatives to resource.
		Ensures improvement initiatives will deliver value before developing solutions.	Ensures improvement initiatives will deliver value before developing solutions.	Measures progress to ensure improvement efforts lead to the positive and sustainable impact.	Measures progress to ensure improvement efforts lead to positive and sustainable impact.	
		Measures results and modifies solutions as required to ensure the positive impact.	Measures results and modifies solution as required to ensure the positive and sustainable impact.			

(Continued)

Generic CI Behavior Framework (Continued)

	Continuous Improvement—Continuously Improving and Innovating What We Do to Make Things Simple and Easy for Our Customers and Each Other					
	Team Member	Team Leader/ Supervisor	Manager	General Manager	Director/ Executive GM	Group Executive/CEO
Leads change	Considers change and new situations as an opportunity for learning and growth.	Accepts change and encourages team to actively participate in change initiatives.	Leads their team through change by communicating the rationale and proactively addresses concerns.	Leads their teams through change by communicating the rationale and proactively addresses concerns.	Champions change initiatives across the business/division.	Champions organization wide change initiatives.
	Adaptive to new ways of doing things.	Addresses people's concerns about change.	Includes others in the change process to leverage opinions and ensure commitment.	Includes others in the change process to leverage opinions and ensure commitment.	Leverages relationships across the business/division to gain commitment.	Leverages relationships across the organization to gain commitment.
	Understands the benefits and speaks positively about change.	Effectively leads and coaches others through periods of change/transition.		Proactively removes roadblocks that inhibit change.	Proactively removes roadblocks that inhibit change.	

Generic CI Behavior Framework (Continued)

	Team Member	Team Leader/ Supervisor	Manager	General Manager	Director/ Executive GM	Group Executive/CEO
	Continuous Improvement—*Continuously Improving and Innovating What We Do to Make Things Simple and Easy for Our Customers and Each Other*					
Lives continuous improvement	Understands organization Group's CI standards and applies them constantly.	Understands organization Group's CI standards and applies them constantly.	Understands organization Group's CI standards and applies them constantly.	Champions organization Group's CI standards; reinforces the need to constantly review and optimize the business.	Advocates the CI standards to the business/ division and CI as an organizational capability.	Advocates the CI Standards to the organization and CI as an organizational capability.
	Where applicable, follows current Standard Operating Procedures.	Invests time in monitoring adherence of team members to agreed Standard Operating Procedures.	Actively monitors performance and output across the team and reduces variation.	Constantly looks for ways the business can be more productive.	Constantly looks for ways the business/ division can be more productive.	
			Constantly looks for ways to be more productive.			

Risk Behavioral Framework

Decision Making/Judgment—Making Sound Decisions Based on Understanding Business, Analyzing Data, and Applying Common Sense

	Team Member	Team Leader/ Manager	Executive Manager	General Manager	Executive General Manager	Group Executive/ CEO
Understands organization group	Understands the organization's strategies and how own role, team and department contribute.	Explains the business value and drivers for own team in relation to the organization's strategies.	Articulates the business value, drivers, and accountabilities of business units/divisions within the organization.	Understands own business operations and the organizational levers that drive profitable growth.	Understands own business operations and the organizational levers that drive profitable growth.	Articulates the shareholder value proposition of the organization to internal and external stakeholders.
	Understands the interrelationships of the Organization Group's functions/divisions.	Articulates and ensures team understands the interrelationships of the Organization Group's functions/divisions on their responsibilities.	Articulates the organizations position, products and services when compared with other organizations.	Articulates the shareholder value proposition of the business.	Articulates the shareholder value proposition of the business/division.	
		Understands the key business metrics that drive the Organization Group's results.	Optimizes business results by actively managing operational levers.	Optimizes business results by actively managing operational levers.	Optimizes business/division results by actively managing operational levers.	

Risk Behavioral Framework (*Continued*)

	Team Member	Team Leader/ Manager	Executive Manager	General Manager	Executive General Manager	Group Executive/ CEO
			Decision Making/Judgment—*Making Sound Decisions Based on Understanding Business, Analyzing Data, and Applying Common Sense*			
Understands the Industry	Understands how the Organization Group is differentiated from competitors.	Monitors industry trends and articulates the potential impact.	Monitors industry trends and articulates the potential impact.	Monitors and anticipates global trends that impact being a leading provider of financial services.	Monitors and anticipates global trends.	Monitors and anticipates global trends that impact being a leading provider of financial services.
		Understands how the Organization Group is differentiated from competitors.	Integrates understanding of the industry into decision-making.	Plans for impact of regulatory or commercial changes.	Manages financial impact of regulatory or commercial changes and proposes strategies to mitigate.	Anticipates the impact of economic policy issues and/or industry regulations.

(*Continued*)

Risk Behavioral Framework (*Continued*)

Decision Making/Judgment—Making Sound Decisions Based on Understanding Business, Analyzing Data, and Applying Common Sense						
Team Member	Team Leader/ Manager	Executive Manager	General Manager	Executive General Manager	Group Executive/ CEO
			Integrates understanding of the industry into decision-making.	Incorporates industry best practice into business/division plans.	Incorporates industry best practice and understanding of the external environment into organizational strategy.
			Knowledgeable in current and possible future policies, practices, trends, technology, and information that impact the organization.	Knowledgeable in current and possible future policies, practices, trends, technology and information that impact the organization.	Knowledgeable in current and possible future policies, practices, trends, technology, and information that impact the organization.

Risk Behavioral Framework (*Continued*)

	Decision Making/Judgment—*Making Sound Decisions Based on Understanding Business, Analyzing Data, and Applying Common Sense*					
	Team Member	*Team Leader/ Manager*	*Executive Manager*	*General Manager*	*Executive General Manager*	*Group Executive/ CEO*
Reaches measured decisions	Identifies important information and data relevant to role.	Identifies and analyzes important data relevant to role and recommends actions.	Analyzes data to shape business decisions; separates the important from the unimportant.	Analyzes complex data and metrics to shape business decisions; gets to the heart of issues.	Analyzes complex data and metrics with rigor; is decisive in adjusting business/ division strategies.	Demonstrates decisiveness and commitment in order to pursue organizational advantage.
	Considers broader implications of actions.	Considers broader implications of actions.	Considers broader implications and practicality of decisions.	Evaluates options considering depth and breadth of impact and consequences.	Evaluates options considering depth and breadth of impact and consequence.	Actively seeks to simplify complicated issues by isolating the most important elements and creates clarity when in ambiguous situations.
				Actively seeks to create clarity and simplicity in complex or ambiguous situations.	Actively seeks to create clarity and simplicity in complex or ambiguous situations.	

(Continued)

Risk Behavioral Framework (Continued)

Decision Making/Judgment—Making Sound Decisions Based on Understanding Business, Analyzing Data, and Applying Common Sense

	Team Member	Team Leader/ Manager	Executive Manager	General Manager	Executive General Manager	Group Executive/ CEO
Enhances brand and reputation	Understands organization brand proposition and the importance of reputation to the organization's success.	Understands organization brand proposition and the importance of reputation to the organization's success and encourages team to do the same.	Actively supports the brand proposition and understands the importance of mitigating the risk of erosion.	Proactively sponsors the brand proposition and the importance of mitigating the risk of erosion.	Cascades the brand proposition and proactively sponsors the importance of mitigating the risk of erosion.	Ensures that the organization has a clear brand proposition that will deliver shareholder value.
	Considers organization's reputation and potential risks when taking action or making decisions.	Considers organization's reputation and potential risks when taking action or making decisions.	Manages reputational risk with internal and external stakeholders, escalating as required.	Proactively manages reputational risk with internal and external stakeholders, escalating as required.	Objectively manages reputation risk in consideration of business/division and organization brand.	Proactively manages reputational risks to the organization through expert judgment in critical decision making.

Risk Behavioral Framework (Continued)

	Team Member	Team Leader/ Manager	Executive Manager	General Manager	Executive General Manager	Group Executive/ CEO
Decision Making/Judgment—*Making Sound Decisions Based on Understanding Business, Analyzing Data, and Applying Common Sense*						
Applies good judgment	Makes good decisions based on a mixture of analysis, wisdom, experience, and judgment.	Makes good decisions based on a mixture of analysis, wisdom, experience, and judgment	Makes good decisions based on a mixture of analysis, wisdom, experience, and judgment.	Makes good decisions based on a mixture of analysis, wisdom, experience, and judgment.	Makes good decisions based on a mixture of analysis, wisdom, experience, and judgment.	Makes good decisions based on a mixture of analysis, wisdom, experience, and judgment.
		Aware of the importance of the perception when making good decisions.	Understands that good decisions need to be perceived as in the best interest of customers, organisation, and employees.	Ensures good decisions are perceived as in the best interest of customers, organization and employees.	Balances the conflicting interests of multiple stakeholders to an equitable outcome.	Balances the conflicting interests of multiple stakeholders to an equitable outcome.

Customer Focus Behavior Framework

Customer Experience—Delivering Value across the Total Customer Experience from the Customer Need Arising Trough to the Need Being Satisfied

Lifecycle Stage	Team Member	Team Lead/Supervisor	Manager	General Manager	Executive General Manager	Group Executive/CEO
Awareness	Generates and reinforces customers understanding.	Identifies CX Improvements.	Negotiates improvement priorities across teams and stakeholders.	Coordinates and collaborates with peers and the C suite to connect the dots between strategy and execution.		
Buy-in	Encourages information access and provides supporting advice.	Negotiates with stakeholders' improvement implementation.	Provides guidance and support by connecting the dots and drawing the lines across the organization and its operations.	Provides directional support to ensure priorities are understood and acted upon.	Links everything and everybody to understanding customer's obsession.	
Acquisition	Provides the means to purchase/access the product or service.	Supports implementation of improvements.	Oversees and reports on multiple experiences to ensure alignment to the North Star.	Manages the politics of change throughout the organization and its stakeholders.	Supports and assists CX discussions at the top table.	Provides internal and external leadership to establish North Star principles and alignment.

Customer lifecycle

Customer Focus Behavior Framework (Continued)

Lifecycle Stage	Team Member	Team Lead/ Supervisor	Manager	General Manager	Executive General Manager	Group Executive/CEO
		Customer Experience—Delivering Value across the Total Customer Experience from the Customer Need Arising Trough to the Need Being Satisfied				
Customization	Understands the customer need(s) to align the product or service.	Tracks and reports CX performance.	Determines how to implement the strategy and enable operations to deliver on those strategic objectives.	Develops initiatives and gains support for maturing customer experiences.	Identifies and gain support for business wide CX improvements across people, processes, and technology.	Leads from the front with the customer-obsessed mantra.
Use	Ensures the customer understands and uses the product/service efficiently and effectively.	Collaborates with stakeholders to mature the experience(s).	Facilitates internal and external discussions to continually improve process, systems, and experience.	Presents strategic and operational options to enhance organization effectiveness.	Provides infrastructure support to ensure the appropriate attitudes, behaviors, and culture.	Liaises with industry and partners to ensure ongoing improvements/ innovations of strategy and operations.

(Continued)

Customer Focus Behavior Framework (Continued)

Lifecycle Stage	Customer Experience—Delivering Value across the Total Customer Experience from the Customer Need Arising Trough to the Need Being Satisfied					
	Team Member	Team Lead/ Supervisor	Manager	General Manager	Executive General Manager	Group Executive/CEO
Share	Creates the means to socialize the experience.	Communicates across teams and the organization the evolution of their experience(s).	Maintains the CX real-time dashboards.		Agrees resource allocations and effective utilization of those resources.	
Repeat	Reinforces the customer relationship to ensure greater product/service penetration.	Identifies "in the moment" risks and ensures necessary actions to mitigate failure.	Creates visibility of dashboards across all stakeholders.			

Customer Focus Behavior Framework (Continued)

Lifecycle Stage	Customer Experience—Delivering Value across the Total Customer Experience from the Customer Need Arising Trough to the Need Being Satisfied					
	Team Member	Team Lead/ Supervisor	Manager	General Manager	Executive General Manager	Group Executive/CEO
Creates value	Ensures every customer interaction delivers Triple Crown Plus benefits.	Breaks value of Triple Crown Plus into team metrics.	Identifies Triple Crown Plus dependencies.	Focuses attention on the Triple Crown Plus to guide all behaviors.	Determines the strategic and operational focus to delivering congruently Triple Crown Plus benefits and North Star alignment.	Faces off to external stakeholders by sharing, explaining and clarifying the organization CX strategy as embodied in North Star alignment.
	Reports and Acts upon misalignment against Triple Crown Plus objectives.	Tracks and reports on value past/ present and future.	Implements action in the moment capability across the value streams.	Co-ordinates and collaborates with peers and the C suite to connect the dots across Triple Crown Plus objectives.	Reinforces the creation of shareholder value is determined by consistently delivering Triple Crown Plus benefits.	

(Continued)

Customer Focus Behavior Framework (Continued)

Customer Experience—Delivering Value across the Total Customer Experience from the Customer Need Arising Trough to the Need Being Satisfied

Lifecycle Stage	Team Member	Team Lead/Supervisor	Manager	General Manager	Executive General Manager	Group Executive/CEO
Identifies opportunities	Participates in Innovation thinking and actions to implement opportunities to improve the CX.	Coordinates and provides guidance to team members through the chosen innovation approach.	Utilizes "innovation approaches" to identify and prioritize potential improvements.	Connects the strategic objectives with execution actions to ensure opportunities are identified and realized.	Balances across stakeholder groups the prioritization of opportunities.	Establishes the culture to ensure opportunities are identified and acted upon "from the board room to the lunch room."
Resolves issues	Collaborates with colleagues to understand and share issues.	Highlights and prioritizes challenges.	Provides a forum for negotiating and managing challenges.	Liaises with other GMs to ensure a coordinated approach to overcoming issues.	Maintains a long-sighted view of issue resolution to balance immediate challenges with long-term goals and objective.	Demonstrates that the learning organization embraces challenges as opportunities to make things progressively better.
	Practices "Action in the Moment" to overcome immediate issues.	Agrees resolution actions and enables "Action in the Moment" capability.				

Customer Focus Behavior Framework *(Continued)*

Customer Experience—Delivering Value across the Total Customer Experience from the Customer Need Arising Trough to the Need Being Satisfied

Lifecycle Stage	Team Member	Team Lead/ Supervisor	Manager	General Manager	Executive General Manager	Group Executive/CEO
Customer obsession	Ensures every interaction is informed by customer-obsessed goals and outcomes.	Guides team members in the day-to-day management of customer obsessive goals and outcomes.	Provides a customer obsession framework to link the principles, measures, and mechanisms across teams and individuals.	Co-ordinates and collaborates with peers and the C suite to connect the dots with customer obsession objectives.	Develops the measures and mechanisms to make customer obsession actionable.	Articulates the principles associated with customer obsession.
						Lives, eats, and breathes customer obsession across all internal and external relationships.

Customer Experience Behavior Framework

Customer Focus—Creating Value in Each Customer Interaction and Focusing on the Total Customer Experience

	Team Member	Team Leader/ Supervisor	Manager	General Manager	Executive General Manager	Group Executive/CEO
Understands the customer	Actively listens to customers and other stakeholders.	Leverages the voice of customers and other stakeholders in understanding customer information to anticipate their needs.	Leverages the voice of customers and other stakeholders understanding customer information to anticipate their needs and future priorities.	Maintains an understanding and current knowledge of customer's needs and potential issues.	Maintains an understanding and current knowledge of customer's needs and potential issues.	Analyzes domestic and global data to anticipate changing customer expectations.
	Proactively asking questions to understand their needs.	Stays abreast of customer service best practices.	Understands the key end-to-end processes that create value for the customer.	Evaluates internal and external data to anticipate changing customer expectations.	Analyzes domestic and global data to anticipate changing customer expectations.	Gathers and responds to stakeholder feedback on expectations of organization.
			Stays abreast of customer service best practices.	Articulates the key end-to-end processes that create value for the customer.	Articulates the key end-to-end processes that create value for the customer.	Articulates the organization's customer value proposition.

Customer Experience Behavior Framework (Continued)

Customer Focus—Creating Value in Each Customer Interaction and Focusing on the Total Customer Experience

	Team Member	Team Leader/ Supervisor	Manager	General Manager	Executive General Manager	Group Executive/CEO
Creates value	Demonstrates a positive attitude, builds rapport and treats customers with care and courtesy.	Establishes and grows strong, value add relationships with customers and stakeholders.	Develops a partnering relationship with customers and stakeholders and adopts a long-term perspective.	Develops a partnering relationship with customers and stakeholders and adopts a long-term perspective.	Structures the business to best serve customer needs and build sustainable relationships.	Structures the organization to best serve customer needs and build sustainable relationships.
	Provides solutions that meet the customers' needs.	Creates win/win solutions with customers and other stakeholders.	Creates win/win solutions with customers and other stakeholders.	Uses understanding of customer needs and supporting data to institute products, processes, and services that will ensure customer satisfaction.	Ensures products, processes, and services will assure customer satisfaction.	Ensures products, processes, and services will assure customer satisfaction.
		Encourages team to consider the impact on customers when making decisions.	Monitors customer satisfaction to ensure high levels are being achieved.	Champions a customer-first approach to business decisions.	Champions a customer-first approach to business decisions.	Champions a customer-first approach to business decisions.
			Encourages team to consider impact on customers when making decisions.			

(Continued)

Customer Experience Behavior Framework (Continued)

Customer Focus—Creating Value in Each Customer Interaction and Focusing on the Total Customer Experience

	Team Member	Team Leader/ Supervisor	Manager	General Manager	Executive General Manager	Group Executive/CEO
Resolves issues	Empathizes and takes personal responsibility for resolving issues.	Recognizes potential service issues and takes corrective action.	Recognizes potential service issues and takes corrective action.	Resolves complex customer issues that have been escalated.	Resolves complex customer issues where reputational damage is at risk.	Resolves escalated, complex customer issues where reputational damage is at risk.
	Escalates customer concerns when required.	Identifies and removes root causes of locally generated issues.	Identifies systemic issues to remove root causes.	Identifies systemic issues to remove root causes.		
		Resolves customer issues escalated by team in a timely manner.	Resolves customer issues escalated by team in a timely manner.			
Lives sales and service	Consistently demonstrates group sales and service principles.	Demonstrates the sales and service principles and ensures team applies them effectively.	Embeds sales and service principles in their business.	Champions sales and service principles within the business.	Champions sales and service principles across the business/division.	Champions sales and service principles across the organization.

Customer Experience Behavior Framework (Continued)

Customer Focus—Creating Value in Each customer Interaction and Focusing on the Total Customer Experience

	Team Member	Team Leader/Manager	Executive Manager	General Manager	Executive General Manager	Group Executive/CEO
Understands the customer	Actively listens to customers and other stakeholders.	Leverages voice of customers and other stakeholders in understanding customer information to anticipate their needs.	Leverages voice of customers and other stakeholders understanding customer information to anticipate their needs and future priorities.	Maintains an understanding and current knowledge of customer's needs and potential issues.	Maintains an understanding and current knowledge of customer's needs and potential issues.	Analyzes domestic and global data to anticipate changing customer expectations.
	Proactively asking questions to understand their needs.	Stays abreast of customer service best practices.	Understands the key end-to-end processes that create value for the customer.	Evaluates internal and external data to anticipate changing customer expectations.	Analyzes domestic and global data to anticipate changing customer expectations.	Gathers and responds to stakeholder feedback on expectations of organisation.
			Stays abreast of customer service best practices.	Articulates the key end-to-end processes that create value for the customer.	Articulates the key end-to-end processes that create value for the customer.	Articulates the organization's customer value proposition.

(Continued)

Customer Experience Behavior Framework (Continued)

Customer Focus—Creating Value in Each customer Interaction and Focusing on the Total Customer Experience

	Team Member	Team Leader/ Manager	Executive Manager	General Manager	Executive General Manager	Group Executive/CEO
Creates value	Demonstrates a positive attitude, builds rapport, and treats customers with care and courtesy.	Establishes and grows strong, value-added relationships with customers and stakeholders.	Develops a partnering relationship with customers and stakeholders and adopts a long-term perspective.	Develops a partnering relationship with customers and stakeholders and adopts a long-term perspective.	Structures the business to best serve customer needs and build sustainable relationships.	Structures the organization to best serve customer needs and build sustainable relationships.
	Provides solutions that meet the customers' needs.	Creates win-win solutions with customers and other stakeholders.	Creates win-win solutions with customers and other stakeholders.	Uses understanding of customer needs and supporting data to institute products, processes, and services that will ensure customer satisfaction.	Ensures products, processes, and services will assure customer satisfaction.	Ensures products, processes, and services will assure customer satisfaction.
		Encourages team to consider impact on customers when making decisions.	Monitors customer satisfaction to ensure high levels are being achieved.	Champions a customer-first approach to business decisions.	Champions a customer-first approach to business decisions.	Champions a customer-first approach to business decisions.
			Encourages team to consider impact on customers when making decisions.			

Customer Experience Behavior Framework (Continued)

Customer Focus—*Creating Value in Each customer Interaction and Focusing on the Total Customer Experience*

	Team Member	Team Leader/ Manager	Executive Manager	General Manager	Executive General Manager	Group Executive/CEO
Resolves issues	Empathizes and takes personal responsibility for resolving issues.	Recognizes potential service issues and takes corrective action.	Recognizes potential service issues and takes corrective action.	Resolves complex customer issues that have been escalated.	Resolves complex customer issues where reputational damage is at risk.	Resolves escalated, complex customer issues where reputational damage is at risk.
	Escalates customer concerns when required.	Identifies and removes root causes of locally generated issues.	Identifies systemic issues to remove root causes.	Identifies systemic issues to remove root causes.		
		Resolves customer issues escalated by team in a timely manner.	Resolves customer issues escalated by team in a timely manner.			
Lives sales & service	Consistently demonstrates group sales and service principles.	Demonstrates the sales and service principles and ensures team applies them effectively.	Embeds sales and service principles in their business.	Champions sales and service principles within the business.	Champions sales and service principles across the business/ division.	Champions sales and service principles across the organization.

Safety Behavioral Framework

Safety (Management)—Creating a Physically and Psychologically Safe Environment for All Employees to Reduce the Risk to a Level That Is as Low as Is Reasonably Practicable to Prevent Harm to People or the Environment

	Team Member	Team Leader/ Manager	Executive Manager	General Manager	Executive General Manager	Group Executive/CEO
Fosters a culture of safety	Explores new ways of doing things.	Challenges the status quo among the team members by encouraging them to try out the new safety measures.	Oversees the implementation of safety measures.	Drafts the strategies that would be used to foster a safety culture in the organization.	Collaborate with the CEO and the board to create policies for a safer work environment.	Provides strategic and operational leadership that would help to create a safer environment for work.
	Works hard to implement the safety measures in place by being observant of any loopholes. In other words, he/she sets expectations and observes them.	The team leader supports the strategic initiatives and recognizes the efforts of his/her team members.	He is responsible for ensuring that all the measures put in place are followed adequately in his department.	Manages the staff to ensure that they conform to the standards of safety guidelines developed.	Works closely with other managers to foster a new safety culture.	He sets goals and ensures that they are executed separately using other manager down the hierarchy.

Safety Behavioral Framework (Continued)

	Team Member	Team Leader/Manager	Executive Manager	General Manager	Executive General Manager	Group Executive/CEO
Safety (Management)—Creating a Physically and Psychologically Safe Environment for All Employees to Reduce the Risk to a Level That Is as Low as Is Reasonably Practicable to Prevent Harm to People or the Environment						
Develops and implements solutions	Identifies safety opportunities to eliminate workplace injuries.	Translates the safety policies from the upstream managers to actions that would be adopted downstream.	Oversees the implementation of safety policies and guides the downstream members on other simpler ways of achieving success using the new strategies.	Oversees the implementation of safety policies and guides the downstream members on other simpler ways of achieving success using the new strategies.	Measures the results and modifies the solution to ensure that the change is within the parameters of sustainability and capable of leading to positive outcome.	Measures the results from the reports received and modifies the solution to ensure that the change is within the parameters of sustainability and capable of leading to positive outcomes.
	Improves and simplifies the process of adopting safety measures by being positive about the change.	Ensures safety improvement among the team members while aiming for a solution and considering the impact that would be experienced both upstream and downstream	Ensures that the new strategies will deliver optimum outcomes and solve the safety issues facing the organization.	Decides on which improvement initiatives to resource.	Monitors the progress of policy implementation to ensure it is within the niche of sustainability and positivity.	

(Continued)

Safety Behavioral Framework (Continued)

Safety (Management)—Creating a Physically and Psychologically Safe Environment for All Employees to Reduce the Risk to a Level That Is as Low as Is Reasonably Practicable to Prevent Harm to People or the Environment

	Team Member	Team Leader/ Manager	Executive Manager	General Manager	Executive General Manager	Group Executive/CEO
Leads safety	Shows readiness in adopting safety measures by acknowledging that it is the only way to grow.	Accepts the changes brought about by safety policies by participating actively in the process while showing respect to his team members.	Actively monitors performance and output across the leaders downstream and reduces the variability that would lead to undesired outcomes.	Actively monitors performance and output across the leaders downstream and reduces the variability that would lead to undesired outcomes.	Understands the values of the group and applies them frequently when developing policies and making decisions. Continuously looks for ways of making the organization more functional and productive.	Understands the values of the group and applies them frequently when developing policies and making decisions. Continuously looks for ways of making the organization more functional and productive.

Safety Behavioral Framework (*Continued*)

Safety (Management) *— Creating a Physically and Psychologically Safe Environment for All Employees to Reduce the Risk to a Level That Is as Low as Is Reasonably Practicable to Prevent Harm to People or the Environment*

	Team Member	*Team Leader/ Manager*	*Executive Manager*	*General Manager*	*Executive General Manager*	*Group Executive/CEO*
Lives safety	Understands the values of the group and applies them frequently.	Understands the values of the group and applies them quite often.	Understands the values of the group and regularly applies them. Monitors the performance of the employees actively in terms of output as related to safety output measures. Continuously looks for other ways of being productive.	Understands the values of safety policies and finds a way of ensuring they are implemented efficiently.	Understands the values of the new policies and continuously looks for ways of enhancing the organizational functionality to make it more productive.	Understands the values of the new policies and continuously looks for ways of enhancing the organizational functionality to make it more productive.

Leadership Decision-Making Behavior Framework

Drive Results—Initiating Action and Committing to Achieving Business Outcomes by Taking Accountability for Goals

	Team Member	Team Leader/ Manager	Executive Manager	General Manager	Executive General Manager	Group Executive/ CEO
Sets goals and drives accountability	Understands personal accountabilities and expected results.	Understands personal and team accountabilities and expected results.	Understands personal and team accountabilities and expected results.	Understands personal and business accountabilities and expected results.	Sets the strategies and goals for the business, translating them into short- and long-term goals.	Sets the organizational vision and strategic priorities that will result in sustainable growth.
	Accepts responsibility for outcomes.	Cascades goals and sets expectations.	Translates the department's goals and expected results.	Communicates organization goals and translates them for their business.	Articulates expected business/ division results and challenges the team to take accountability.	Articulates expected results and challenges the team to take accountability.
		Aligns resources and communicates accountabilities.	Aligns resources and holds others accountable.	Aligns resources and holds others accountable.		

Leadership Decision-Making Behavior Framework (Continued)

Drive Results—*Initiating Action and Committing to Achieving Business Outcomes by Taking Accountability for Goals*

	Team Member	Team Leader/ Manager	Executive Manager	General Manager	Executive General Manager	Group Executive/ CEO
Stays focused to execute	Plans work and prioritizes tasks.	Plans and prioritizes work, leveraging resources to complete work on time, to agreed quality and within budget.	Prioritizes work, leveraging resources, and adjusting as circumstances change.	Prioritizes goals and leverages resources across the business to deliver results.	Prioritizes goals and leverages resources across the business/ division to deliver results.	Leverages resources across the organization to remove systemic obstacles to delivering results.
	Overcomes obstacles, finds solutions and persists to completion.	Anticipates and removes obstacles.	Proactively removes obstacles.	Works relentlessly to overcome obstacles.	Measures and tracks performance and takes corrective action.	Measures and tracks organizational performance and takes corrective action.
			Measures and tracks progress and outcomes, taking corrective action when required.	Measures and tracks progress and outcomes, taking corrective action when required.		

(Continued)

Leadership Decision-Making Behavior Framework (Continued)

Drive Results—Initiating Action and Committing to Achieving Business Outcomes by Taking Accountability for Goals

	Team Member	Team Leader/ Manager	Executive Manager	General Manager	Executive General Manager	Group Executive/ CEO
Manages risks prudently	Identifies and manages risk when appropriate; escalates where required.	Identifies, manages, and mitigates risk; escalates where required.	Identifies, manages, and mitigates risk; escalates where required.	Practices and actively promotes culture of risk awareness and risk management.	Practices and actively promotes culture of risk awareness and risk management.	Practices and actively promotes culture of risk awareness and risk management.
		Makes decisions in consideration of organisation risk practices.	Makes decisions in consideration of organisation risk practices.	Makes decisions in consideration of the organisation Group risk appetite.	Makes decisions in consideration of the organisation Group risk appetite.	Determines the organization's risk appetite.
		Observes the business and ensures products, processes, and services are within the risk appetite of the business.	Observes the business and ensures products, processes, and services are within the risk appetite of the business.	Observes the business and ensures products, processes, and services are within the risk appetite of the business.	Observes the business and ensures products, processes, and services are within the risk appetite of the business.	

Leadership Decision-Making Behavior Framework (Continued)

Customer Focus—Creating Value in Each Customer Interaction and Focusing on the Total Customer Experience

	Team Member	Team Leader/ Manager	Executive Manager	General Manager	Executive General Manager	Group Executive/ CEO
Understands the customer	Actively listens to customers and other stakeholders.	Leverages voice of customers and other stakeholders in understanding customer information to anticipate their needs.	Leverages the voice of customers and other stakeholders understanding customer information to anticipate their needs and future priorities.	Maintains an understanding and current knowledge of customer's needs and potential issues.	Maintains an understanding and current knowledge of customer's needs and potential issues.	Analyzes domestic and global data to anticipate changing customer expectations.
	Proactively asking questions to understand their needs.	Stays abreast of customer service best practices.	Understands the key end-to-end processes that create value for the customer.	Evaluates internal and external data to anticipate changing customer expectations.	Analyzes domestic and global data to anticipate changing customer expectations.	Gathers and responds to stakeholder feedback on expectations of organisation.
			Stays abreast of customer service best practices.	Articulates the key end-to-end processes that create value for the customer.	Articulates the key end-to-end processes that create value for the customer.	Articulates the organization's customer value proposition.

(Continued)

Leadership Decision-Making Behavior Framework (Continued)

Customer Focus—Creating Value in Each Customer Interaction and Focusing on the Total Customer Experience

	Team Member	Team Leader/ Manager	Executive Manager	General Manager	Executive General Manager	Group Executive/ CEO
Creates value	Demonstrates a positive attitude, builds rapport and treats customers with care and courtesy.	Establishes and grows strong, value add relationships with customers and stakeholders.	Develops a partnering relationship with customers and stakeholders and adopts a long-term perspective.	Develops a partnering relationship with customers and stakeholders and adopts a long-term perspective.	Structures the business to best serve customer needs and build sustainable relationships.	Structures the organization to best serve customer needs and build sustainable relationships.
	Provides solutions that meet the customers' needs.	Creates win/win solutions with customers and other stakeholders.	Creates win/win solutions with customers and other stakeholders.	Uses an understanding of customer needs and supporting data to institute products, processes and services that will ensure customer satisfaction.	Ensures products, processes and services will assure customer satisfaction.	Ensures products, processes and services will assure customer satisfaction.
		Encourages team to consider impact on customers when making decisions.	Monitors customer satisfaction to ensure high levels are being achieved.	Champions a customer-first approach to business decisions.	Champions a customer-first approach to business decisions.	Champions a customer-first approach to business decisions.
			Encourages team to consider impact on customers when making decisions.			

Leadership Decision-Making Behavior Framework (Continued)

Customer Focus—Creating Value in Each Customer Interaction and Focusing on the Total Customer Experience

	Team Member	Team Leader/ Manager	Executive Manager	General Manager	Executive General Manager	Group Executive/ CEO
Resolves issues	Empathizes and takes personal responsibility for resolving issues.	Recognizes potential service issues and takes corrective action.	Recognizes potential service issues and takes corrective action.	Resolves complex customer issues that have been escalated.	Resolves complex customer issues where reputational damage is at risk.	Resolves escalated, complex customer issues where reputational damage is at risk.
	Escalates customer concerns when required.	Identifies and removes root causes of locally generated issues.	Identifies systemic issues to remove root causes.	Identifies systemic issues to remove root causes.		
		Resolves customer issues escalated by the team in a timely manner.	Resolves customer issues escalated by the team in a timely manner.			
Lives sales and service	Consistently demonstrates group sales and service principles.	Demonstrates the sales and service principles and ensures the team applies them effectively.	Embeds sales and service principles in their business.	Champions sales and service principles within the business.	Champions sales and service principles across the business/division.	Champions sales and service principles across the organization.

References

Acur, N. and Bititci, U. S., 1999. Process oriented, performance headed strategy. *International Conference on Advances in Production Management Systems*, Berlin.

Aidla, A. 2003. Interrelationships between personality traits and organisational culture. In: Maaja Vadi (ed.), *Organisational Culture in Estonia: Manifestations and Consequences*, edition 1 vol. 16, University of Tartu, pp. 82–100.

Albliwi, S., Antony, J., Lim, S. and Wiele, T. 2014. Critical failure factors of Lean Six Sigma: A systematic literature review. *International Journal of Quality & Reliability Management*, 31(9), pp. 1012–1030.

Aljohani, M. 2016. Change management. *International Journal of Scientific & Technology Research*, 5(5), pp. 319–323.

Amah, E. and Ahiauzu, A., 2013. Employee involvement and organizational effectiveness. *The Journal of Management Development*. 32(7), DOI.10.1108/JMD-09-2010-0064

Ambrus, A. and Suszter, G., 2019. Quality control and quality assurance. In: Tadeo JL (ed.), *Analysis of Pesticides in Food and Environmental Samples*, CRC Press, Boca Raton, FL, pp.135–174.

Antony, J. and Gupta, S. 2019. Top ten reasons for process improvement project failures. *International Journal of Lean Six Sigma*, 10(1), pp. 367–374.

Antony, J., Fabiane Letícia, L., Marcelo Machado, F., Mary, D., Attracta, B. and Julie, M. 2019. A study into the reasons for process improvement project failures: Results from a pilot survey. *International Journal of Quality & Reliability Management*, 36(10), pp. 1699–1720.

Badawy, M., El-Aziz, A.A., Idress, A., Hefny, H.A., & Hossam, S. (2020). A survey on exploring key performance indicators. *Future Computing and Informatics Journal*, 1, 47–52.

Bauer, T. and Erdogan, B. 2012. An Introduction to Organizational Behavior, College Textbook Revolution: The Case of Unnamed Publisher, Creative Commons, Mountain View, CA.

Beheshtifar, M., Mazrae-Sefidi, F. and Moghadam, M. N., 2011. Role of perfectionism at workplace, *European Journal of Economics, Finance and Administrative Sciences*, 38, pp. 167–171

Benders, J. 2011. Lean human resources; Redesigning HR processes for a culture of continuous improvement, by C. M. Jekiel. *International Journal of Production Research*, 50(4), pp. 1237–1238.

Bhatti, M., Awan, H. and Razaq, Z., 2013. The key performance indicators (KPIs) and their impact on overall organizational performance. *Quality & Quantity*, 48(6), DOI: 10.1007/s11135-013-9945-y.

Bird, A., Lichtenau, T. and Michels, D., 2016. Three questions to spur corporate change efforts [online]. *Bain & Company*. Viewed 13 Jan 2021, https://www.bain.com/insights/three-questions-to-spur-corporate-change-efforts-forbes

Brethower, D. 2004. Understanding behavior of organizations to improve behavior in organizations. *The Behavior Analyst Today*, 5(2), pp. 170–181.

Burrill, G., Parker, J. and Fitzgerald, E., 2019, *Creating a culture of excellence*, KPMG's international health practice report no. 135998-G [online], KPMG, Viewed 12 Jan 2021, https://assets.kpmg/content/dam/kpmg/xx/pdf/2019/03/creating-a-culture-of-continuous-improvement-kpmg-global-healthcare.pdf

By, R., 2005. Organizational change management: A critical review. *Journal of Change Management*, 5, pp. 369–380.

Change Synergy. 2016. Our change management methodology overview: How changefirst helps you implement change [online]. Viewed 17 Mar 2021, https://changesynergy.com.au/wp-content/uploads/2016/10/PCI-Our-Change-Management-Methodology.pdf

Cherry, K. 2020. Ego as the rational part of personality [Online]. Viewed 26 Mar 2021, https://www.verywellmind.com/what-is-the-ego-2795167

Cox, R., Issa, R. and Koblegard, K. 2005. Management's perception of key behavioral indicators for construction. *Journal of Construction Engineering and Management* 131(3), DOI: 10.1061/(ASCE)0733-9364(2005)131:3(368)

Daryani, S. M., Ali, S. and Asli-zadeh, A. 2012. Organizational theory, systemic thinking and system management. *International Journal of Organizational Leadership*, 1(2), pp. 71–79.

Delatoura, G., Laclémencea, P., Calceib, D. and Mazric, C. 2014. Safety performance indicators: A questioning diversity. *Chemical Engineering Transactions*, 36, pp. 55–60. DOI: 10.3303/CET1436010

Deming, W. E. 2000. *Out of the Crises*, reprint ed., The MIT Press, Cambridge, MA.

Dewar, C., Blackburn, S., Nielsen, A., Irons, E., Keller, S., Meaney, M., Ulosevich, G. and Wood, C., 2011. *How do I transform my organization's performance?* [online]. Viewed 12 Jan 2021, https://www.mckinsey.com/~/media/mckinsey/dotcom/client_service/public%20sector/pdfs/how_do_i_transform_my_organizations_performance.ashx

Dinner, I., Johnson, E. J., Goldstein, D. G. and Liu, K. 2011. Partitioning default effects: Why people choose not to choose. *Journal of Experimental Psychology Applied*, 17(4), DOI: 10.1037/a0024354.

Dolan, P., Hallsworth, M., Halpern, D., King, D. and Vlaev, I. 2009. MINDSPACE: influencing behavior through public policy. Cabinet office. Available at: https://www.instituteforgovernment.org.uk/sites/default/files/publications/MINDSPACE.pdf

Dominici, G. 2013. Organizational systems: Managing complexity with the viable system model. *Kybernetes*, 42(2), pp. 340–348.

Dunbar, K. N. and Klahr, D., 2012. *Scientific Thinking and Reasoning*. In: The Oxford Handbook of Thinking and Reasoning, DOI: 10.1093/oxfordhb/9780199734689.013.0035

Eckes G. 2007. *Making Six Sigma Last: Managing the Balance Between Cultural and Technical Change*. Wiley.

Edgeman, R. 2018. Excellence models as complex management systems: An examination of the shingo operational excellence model. *Business Process Management Journal*, 24(2), DOI: 10.1108/BPMJ-02-2018-0049.

Edmondson, A. C. 2003. *Psychological Safety, Trust, and Learning in Organizations: A Group-Level Lens*, Harvard Business School, Boston, MA.

Ey, 2020. *Operational excellence 2.0 How digital supply chain transformation is affecting operational excellence* [online]. Viewed 12 Jan 2021, https://assets.ey.com/content/dam/ey-sites/ey-com/de_de/topics/industrial-products/ey-operational-excellence-20-032020.pdf

Forbes, 2018. The science behind adopting New Habits (And Making Them Stick) [online]. Viewed 17 Jan 2021, https://www.forbes.com/sites/joewalsh/2021/01/15/us-has-no-covid-19-vaccine-reserve-despite-trump-administrations-claims-report-says/?sh=78bce7e6173b

Gardner, W. L., Reithel, B., Cogliser, C., Walumbwa, F. and Foley, R. 2012. Matching personality and organizational culture effects of recruitment strategy and the five-factor model on subjective person—Organization fit, *Management Communication Quarterly*, 24(4), pp. 585–622. DOI:10.1177/0893318912450663

George, J. M., 2014. *Understanding and Managing Organizational Behavior*, 6th ed., Prentice Hall, Boston, MA.

Giffen, R. 2015. Organizational culture and personality type: relationship with person-organization fit and turnover intention. Graduate Theses and Dissertations. 14387. Iowa State University.

Giulioni, J. W., 2015. Risky business: Strategies to encourage employee risk-taking [online]. *Juliewinklegiulioni*. Viewed 21 Jan 2021, https://www.juliewinklegiulioni.com/blog/leadership-matters/risky-business-strategies-to-encourage-employee-risk-taking/

Glaser, S. and Halliday, M. 1980. Organisations as systems. *Human Relations*, 33(12), pp. 917–928.

Gorenak, M. and Košir, S., 2012. *The importance of organizational values for organization*. Management Knowledge and Learning International Conference.

Grant, A. Persuading the unpersuadable [online]. Harvard Business Review. Viewed 26 Mar 2021, https://hbr.org/2021/03/persuading-the-unpersuadable

Gutierrez, J., 2016. How to form new habits using proven science [Online]. *Themonklife*. Viewed Henderson 17 Jan 2021, http://www.themonklife.net/how-to-form-new-habits/

Hiatt, J. M. 2006. The Essence of ADKAR: a model for individual change management. Prosci. Available at: http://www.dpac.tas.gov.au/__data/assets/pdf_file/0017/273140/Document_-_The-essence-of-adkar.pdf

Hines, P. and Butterworth, C. 2019. *The Essence of Excellence: Creating a Culture of Continuous Improvement.* edition 2, SA Partners, Caerphilly, Wales.

Hines, P. and Jekiel, C., 2021. Understanding the people value stream [online]. People Value Stream. Viewed 17 Mar 2021, https://www.peoplevaluestream.com/papers

Hines, P., Taylor, D. and Walsh, A. 2018. The lean journey: Have we got it wrong? *Total Quality Management & Business Excellence*, 31(3–4), pp. 389–406.

Takeuchi, H. and Nonaka, I. 1986. The new new product development game – Stop running the relay race and take up rugby, *Harvard Business Review*, January-February, pp. 137–146.

Jiju, A., Snee, R., and Hoerl, R., 2017. *Lean Six Sigma: Yesterday, Today and Tomorrow*, vol. 34, pp. 1073-1093. DOI.10.1108/IJQRM-03-2016-0035

Jones, M., Butterworth, C. and Harder, B. 2018. *4 + 1: Embedding a Culture of Continuous Improvement in Financial Services*, Action New Thinking Limited, Terrigal, NSW.

Jørgensen, F., Laugen, B. T. and Boer, H. 2007. Human Resource management for continuous improvement. *Creativity and Innovation Management*, 16 (4), pp. 363–375. DOI: 10.1111/j.1467-8691.2007.00452.x

Jung, K. B., Kang, S. and Choi, S. B., 2020. Empowering leadership, risk-taking behavior, and Employees' commitment to organizational change: The mediated moderating role of task complexity. *Sustainability*, 12(6), doi:10.3390/su12062340

Kaniški, I. and Vincek, I. 2018. Business processes as business systems. *Tehnički Glasnik*, 12(1), pp. 55–61.

Karahanna, E., Evaristo, J. R. and Srite, M. 2005. Levels of culture and individual behavior. *Journal of Global Information Management*, 13(2), pp. 1–20.

Karmes, J. A. 2014. *Lead With Humility: 12 Leadership Lessons from Pope Francis.* AMACOM, New York, NY.

Khera, S., 2018. Psychological research on habit formation [online]. *Youthincmag.* Viewed 17 Jan 2021, https://youthincmag.com/psychological-research-habit-formation

Kocaoglu, B. and Demir, E. 2019. The use of McKinsey s 7S framework as a strategic planning and economic assestment tool in the process of digital transformation. *Pressacademia*, 9 (9), pp. 114–119. DOI: 10.17261/Pressacademia.2019.1078

Komulainen, E., Meskanen, K., Lipsanen, J., Lahti, J. M., Jylhä, P. and Melartin, T., et al. 2014. The effect of personality on daily life emotional processes. *PLoS ONE*, 9(10), e110907. https://doi.org/10.1371/journal.pone.0110907

Kortian, V. and Harrison, N. 2018, 'Has machine learning and artificial intelligence removed the need to have black belts?'.

Kotterinc. 2021. The 8-step process for leading change [online]. Viewed 17 Mar 2021, https://www.kotterinc.com/8-steps-process-for-leading-change/

KPMG, 2019, Agile transformation [online]. Viewed 13 Jan 2021, https://assets.kpmg/content/dam/kpmg/be/pdf/2019/11/agile-transformation.pdf

Kurniatia, N., Yehb, R. and Linc, J., 2015. Quality inspection and maintenance: The framework of interaction. *Procedia Manufacturing*, 4, pp. 244–251.

Lazzeri, F., 2014. On defining behavior: Some notes. *Behavior and Philosophy*, 42, pp. 65–82.

Lloyd, J., 2012. The Myers-Briggs Type Indicator® and mainstream psychology: Analysis and evaluation of an unresolved hostility. *Journal of Beliefs & Values-studies in Religion & Education*, vol.33, pp. 23–34. DOI.10.1080/13617672.2012.650028.

M, V. S. and Prashar, A. 2020. Empirical examination of critical failure factors of continuous improvement deployments: Stage-wise results and a contingency theory perspective. *International Journal of Production Research*, 58(16), pp. 4894–4915.

Mallinger, M. 2001. Personality traits and workplace culture. *Graziadio Business Review*, 4 (1). Available at: https://gbr.pepperdine.edu/2010/08/personality-traits-and-workplace-culture /

Marchant, T., 1999. Strategies for improving individual performance and job satisfaction at Meadowvale Health, *Journal of Management Practice*, 2(3) pp. 63–70.

McGee, A. and McGee, P. 2020. *Whoever You Want Me to Be: Personality and Incentives, IZA Discussion Papers, No. 13809*, Institute of Labor Economics (IZA), Bonn.

McKinsey and Company, 2011. Lean management: new frontiers for financial institutions [online]. Viewed 13 Jan 2021 https://www.mckinsey.com/~/media/mckinsey/dotcom/client_service/financial%20services/latest%20thinking/reports/lean_management_new_frontiers_for_financial_institutions.pdf

McKinsey. 2008. Enduring ideas: The 7-S framework. McKinsey Quarterly. Available at: https://www.mckinsey.com/business-functions/strategy-and-corporate-finance/our-insights/enduring-ideas-the-7-s-framework#

Mclean, R. and Antony, J. 2014. Why continuous improvement initiatives fail in manufacturing environments? A systematic review of the evidence. *International Journal of Productivity and Performance Management*, 63(3), pp. 370–376.

McLean, R. S., Antony, J. and Dahlgaard, J. 2017. Failure of continuous improvement initiatives in manufacturing environments: A systematic review of the evidence. *Total Quality Management & Business Excellence*, 28(3–4), pp. 219–237.

Middlesworth, M. 2018. A short guide to leading and lagging indicators of safety performance [online]. ErgoPlus. Viewed 17 Mar 2021, https://ergo-plus.com/leading-lagging-indicators-safety-preformance/

Miller, D. 2001. Successful change leaders: What makes them? What do they do that is different? *Journal of Change Management*, 2(4), pp. 359–368.

Minculete, G. and Olar, P. 2016. "Push" and "pull" systems in supply chain management: Correlative approaches in the military field. *Journal of Defense Resources Management*, 7(2) (13), pp. 165–172.

Mohammed, S., Mathieu, J. E. and Bartlett, L. B. 2002. Technical-administrative task performance, leadership task performance, and contextual performance: Considering the influence of team- and task-related composition variables, *Journal of Organizational Behavior*, 23, pp. 795–814.

Morcos, M. 2018. Organisational culture: definitions and trends.

Muniyappa, M., Prasad, S., Kumar, K. and Puthran, D. 2014. Value stream mapping: A lean tool. *The International Journal of Business & Management*, 2(4), pp. 100–104.

Murata, K. and Katayama, H. 2009. An evaluation of factory performance utilized KPI/KAI with data envelopment analysis. *Journal of the Operations Research*, 52(2), pp. 204–220.

Myers-Briggs. 2021a. MBTI basics [Online]. Viewed 26 Mar 2021. https://www.myersbriggs.org/my-mbti-personality-type/mbti-basics/

Myers-Briggs. 2021b. The 16 MBTI types [Online]. Viewed 26 Mar 2021. https://www.myersbriggs.org/my-mbti-personality-type/mbti-basics/the-16-mbti-types.htm

Neill, M. S. 2018. Change management communication: Barriers, strategies & messaging. *Public Relations Journal*, 12(1), pp. 1–26.

Ngucha, M. 2019. Leading & lagging indicators. Integrate sustainability. Available at: https://www.integratesustainability.com.au/wp-content/uploads/2019/01/ISPL-Insight-Leading-Lagging-Indicators.pdf

Nordlund, M. 2009. *The Effects of Priming on Personality Self-Reports: Challenges and Opportunities*. University of Akron, Akron, OH.

Northwestern Medicine, 2019. 11 Fun facts about your brain [online]. Viewed 21 Jan 2021, https://www.nm.org/healthbeat/healthy-tips/11-fun-facts-about-your-brain

Palmquist, M. 2015. A culture of personality [Online]. Strategy + Business. Viewed 26 Mar 2021, https://www.strategy-business.com/blog/A-Culture-of-Personality?gko=a7df2

Peeters, M., Rutte, C., Harrie, T. and Reymen, I. 2006. The big five personality traits and individual satisfaction with the team, *Small Group Research*, 37(2), pp. 187–211. DOI: 10.1177/1046496405285458

Prime, J. and Salib, E., 2014. The best leaders are humble leaders [online], *Harvard Business Review*. Viewed 21 Jan 2021, https://hbr.org/2014/05/the-best-leaders-are-humble-leaders

Prosci. 2021a. Prosci change management methodology [online]. Viewed 17 Mar 2021, https://www.prosci.com/resources/articles/change-management-methodology

Prosci. 2021b. Applying ADKAR [online]. Viewed 17 Mar 2021, https://www.prosci.com/adkar/applications-of-adkar

Quaquebeke, N. V., Zenker, S. and Eckloff, T 2009. Find out how much it means to me! The importance of interpersonal respect in work values compared to perceived organizational practices. *Journal of Business Ethics*, 89(3), pp. 423–431.

Richmond, J., 2020. Risk-takers believe in the unlimited possibilities [online]. *Business*. Viewed 21 Jan 2021, https://www.business.com/articles/hire-risk-takers/

Rogers, K. M. and Ashforth, B. E. 2014. Respect in organizations: Feeling valued as "We" and "Me". *Journal of Management*, 43(5), pp. 1–31.

Rudd, J. 2020. What is an empathy map? [online]. Accenture. Viewed 17 Mar 2021, https://www.accenture.com/us-en/blogs/bloglandingpage/blogpostpage?wppreview=45257#:~:text=An%20empathy%20map%20is%20a,popularity%20within%20the%20agile%20community.

Schein, E. H. 2010. *Organizational Culture and Leadership*. 4th ed. Jossey-Bass, San Francisco, CA.

Sharma, P. 2017. Six sigma-a case study of amazon.Com. *International Journal of Research in Management, Economics and Commerce*, 7(8), pp. 131–135.

Sheikh, M. 2013. The role of communication in change management (Masters thesis, University of Gothenburg).

Shingo Institute, 2016. *The Shingo model handbook* [online]. Viewed 12 Jan 2021, https://shingo.org/shingo-model/

Shingo Institute, 2020. *The Shingo model handbook* [online]. Viewed 12 Jan 2021, https://shingo.org/shingo-model/

Shingo Institute, 2021. *The Shingo model handbook* [online]. Viewed 12 Jan 2021, https://shingo.org/shingo-model/

Singh, S. 2011. Creating and sustaining customer value. *IMS Manthan*, 5(2), pp. 57–60.

Son, S. 2016. How to work with the 16 different Myers-Briggs personality types [Online]. Tinypulse. Viewed 26 Mar 2021. https://www.tinypulse.com/blog/sk-how-to-work-with-different-myers-briggs-personality-types

Soto, C. 2018. Big five personality traits. In M. H. Bornstein, M. E. Arterberry, K. L. Fingerman, and J. E. Lansford (eds.), *The SAGE Encyclopedia of Lifespan Human Development*. Sage Publications, Thousand Oaks, CA, pp. 240–241.

Stormboard. 2021. What is empathy mapping and how do you use it? [online]. Viewed 17 Mar 2021, https://stormboard.com/blog-archive/what-is-empathy-mapping

The RBL Group and Dave Hanna. 2013. *The organizational systems model: A tool for developing high performance* [online]. Viewed 17 Jan 2021, https://rblip.s3.amazonaws.com/Articles/Organizational+Systems+Model+-+Dave+Hanna.pdf

Thompson-Atlassian, J. 2020. A practical guide to working remotely with all 16 personality types [online]. Fast Company. Viewed 26 March 2021. https://www.fastcompany.com/90582809/a-practical-guide-to-working-remotely-with-all-16-personality-types

Verplanken, B. and Aarts, H. 2011. Habit, attitude, and planned behavior: Is habit an empty construct or an interesting case of automaticity? *European Review of Social Psychology*, 10(1), pp. 101–134.

Ward-Dutton, M., 2008, *BPM case study: The Carphone Warehouse*, Continues advisory service report [online]. Viewed 13 Jan 2021, http://services.mwdadvisors.com

Wyles, G. 2013. The eight personalities involved in change management programmes [online]. HR Zone. Viewed 26 Mar 2021, https://www.hrzone.com/lead/change/the-eight-personalities-involved-in-change-management-programmes

Yeh, Y., Li, P. and Lin, C. 2020. The interactive effects of associative effects of associative response priming and response priming and personality traits on insight problem solving over time. *Journal of Global Education Research*, 4(1), pp. 14–32. https://www.doi.org/10.5038/2577-509X.4.1.1023

Ziapour, A., Khatony, A., Jafari, F. and Kianipour, N. 2017. Correlation between personality traits and organizational commitment in the staff of Kermanshah University of Medical Sciences in 2015. *Annals of Tropical Medicine and Public Health*, 10, pp. 371–376.

Index

Note: Page references in *italics* denote figures and in **bold** denote tables.

A

A-B-C model 121, 122
Ability
    and change management 46
    to influence 212
    technical 140
Achievement
    orientation 212
    striving 193
Activity level, as personality trait 192
ADKAR model 45–46, 48, 50
Adventurer (ISFP) 201, 205
Adventurousness, as personality trait 193
Advocate (INFJ) 200, 205
Affect 209–210
Agile 1, 9–10, 42–43, 91, **269–272**
    behavior framework **87–90**
    described 74–77
    and leadership 77–79
    overview 73
    patterns of behaviors and systems 80–86
Agile Manifesto 73
Agreeableness
    and commitment 210
    and conscientiousness 194–195
    vs. disagreeableness 192
    and extraversion 194
    scores 194
Ali, S. 37
Altruism 192
Amazon 9, 150, 156, 215

Ambassadors, as personality type 195–196
Ambiguity 212
Antony, J. 4
Apple 149–150
Apple World Developers conference 150
Architect (INTJ) 200–201, 205
Arrogance, as barrier to change 211
Artifacts 190
Artificial intelligence (AI) 8, 106, 215–226
Ashforth, B. E. 30
Asli-zadeh, A. 37
Assumptions, and organizational culture 191
A.T. Kearney (ATK) consulting firm 95–96
Atlanta Journal-Constitution 141
Autonomous teams 82
Awareness, and risk-defining behavior 139

B

Banking Royal Commission 142–143
Barriers to change
    arrogance 211
    narcissism 211–212
    stubbornness 211
Behavior(s)
    affect 209–210
    assessing 57–58
    commitment 210
    and communication 6
    defaults 208
    defined 16
    deploying 57

desired 15–40
ego 210–211
and habits 24
incentives 207
influences on 206–211
messenger 206–207
norms 207–208
priming 209
principles guiding 19, 30–38, 137
and risk-taking mindset 38–39
salience 208–209
setting 57
suggested KBIs for 214
and systems 27–29, 137
traditional KPIs for 214
Behavioral change
impact of personalities on 190
making real 244–253
Behavioral framework
Agile **87–90**
BIP 102–107
CI program **113–115**
Behavioral risk 119–120
Behavior-based safety 176–177
Behavioural patterns 80–86
Beliefs, and organizational culture 190–191
Benefit realization framework (BRF) 95
Bezos, Jeff 150, 151
Big Five Personality Traits model 191–195
Boer, H. 52–53
Brand recognition
enhancing 136–137
ideal risk behaviors 136–137
Brand reputation 107
Breskvar, Alexander 152
Bright flag system 101
Business improvement program (BIP) **273–276**
achievements in Suncorp Group 94–95
competencies behavioral framework 102–107, **103–104**
improved business performance and services 98
lessons learned 101–102
shortfall in Suncorp Group 99–101
Suncorp Group 93–94
Business process 32, 97, 101

Business transformation 153–154
Butterworth, C. 22, 27

C

Campaigner (ENFP) 202, 205
Carphone Warehouse 10
Case study
continuous improvement (CI) program 93–118
in financial services 93–118
Suncorp Group 93–118
Cautiousness, as personality trait 193
Challenge management 123
Challengers, as personality type 196
Champions, as personality type 195
Change 49–50
and BIP 105
fatigue 65
leading 116
Change management 10–12, *12*, 41–72, **260–268**
approach tools 41
assessing behaviors 57–58
assessing performance 58
and continuous improvement programs 42
deploying behaviors 57
disconnected bridge 42–44
effective communication for 58–65
execution of strategy 55–58
lag KPIs 54
lead KPIs 54–55
methodologies 44–51
setting behaviors 57
setting principles 56
understanding principles 56–57
Claims benefit framework 96
Coaching **67–70**, 178, **260–263**, **269**
Collectivism *vs.* individualism 213
Color coding of safety spectrum *185*
Commander (ENTJ) 203–204, 206
Commitment 210
and agreeableness 210
and reciprocity 210
Communication
and behavior 6

effective, for change management 58–65,
        60–64
poor and CI program 5–6
Competencies behavioral framework
        102–107, **103–104**, **260–264**
Conscientiousness
    and agreeableness 194–195
    vs. unconscientiousness 192–193
Constancy of purpose 36
Consul (ESFJ) 203, 206
Continuous improvement (CI) program
        277–279
    behavior framework **113–115**
    and BIP 106
    business process 32
    case study 93–118
    challenges 1–13
    competency framework 107–117
    contextual reasons 8
    failure, reasons for 2–9
    flow and pull value 33
    focus on performance 4
    HRM department role in 52
    inadequate infrastructure 7–8
    inexperienced managers and team
            members 6–7
    lack of motivation 4–5
    and poor communication 5–6
    previous approaches 9–10
    and productivity 117
    quality assurance 34
    scientific thinking 32–33
    seeking perfection 34–35
    short-term results 8–9
    tool-oriented approach 3–4
    traditional approach of *2*, 2–3
Cooperation 192
Core behaviors
    defined 17–18
    ideal 18–20, *19*
    organizations 17–20
Corporate values **250**
Critical business systems 28
Cross-functional team 80–82
Cultural enablers 30–31
    lead with humility 31
    respect every individual principle 30–31

Culture
    CI 8, 11–12, 105
    emphasis on 43–44
    risk-defining behavior 139
Customer(s)
    create value for 220
    interactions 152
    satisfaction 151, 158
Customer experience (CX) 9, 72, 95, 98,
        147–171, **292–297**
    as another functional silo 151
    approaching 151
    becoming distracted by digitization 152
    and business transformation 153–154
    challenges with 151–152
    customer interactions 152
    discipline and science of 151
    evolving to customer-centric view
            152–153
    hiring consultants 152
    improving customer satisfaction 151
    leadership 154–155
    measuring success 171
    as new religion 151–152
    and organization structures 152
    overview 147–149
    as a report to executives 151
    research 151
    strategy for CX success 154–158
Customer focus **286–297**, **305–307**
    behavior framework **159–170**
CX initiatives or programs
    suggested KAIs for 171
    suggested KBIs for 171
    traditional KPIs for 171
Cybersecurity 121, 144

D

Daryani, S. M. 37
Das, Sanchoy 141
Debater (ENTP) 202–203, 205
Decision-making 106–107, **280–285**
    risk-defining behavior 139
Defaults 208
Defender (ISFJ) 200, 205
De Rycke, Thomas 9

Dewar, C. 4
Disidentification 58
Dodkins, James 150
Doerr, John 184
Drucker, Peter 21

E

Eckes, George 43
Effective communication **264–268**; *see also*
    Communication
    barriers to 65–71, **67–70**
    change fatigue 65
    for change management 58–65, **60–64**
    lack of leader 65
    lack of planning 65
    and multiple cultures 66–71
    participatory communication 59–65
    programmatic communication 59
    strategies for 58–65
    and technology issues 66
Ego 210–211
Empowerment 20, **250**, 254
Enterprise alignment 35–38
    constancy of purpose 36
    think systemically 37–38
    value creation 35–36
Entertainer (ESFP) 202, 205
Entrepreneur (ESTP) 202, 205
Ethical role modeling 122–123
Evaristo, J. R. 16
Executive (ESTJ) 203, 205–206
Executive Action Team (EAT) 78
Executive Meta Scrum (EMS) 78
Extraversion 198
    and agreeableness 194
    vs. introversion 191–192

F

Financial services
    compliance governing and
        management 121
    cybersecurity 121
    risk in 120–121
    risks beyond 141–142
    third party 121

5S 1, 16, 42, 176, 179, 188, 232, 257
Flow and pull value 33
4+1 Embedding a Culture of Continuous
        Improvement in Financial Services
        (Jones, Butterworth, and Harder) 22
Frameworks
    behavior **113–115**
    benefit realization framework (BRF) 95
    BIP behavioral 102–107
    competencies behavioral 102–107,
        103–104
    competency 107–117
    leadership decision-making behavior
        235–240
    safety behavioral **180–183**
    Suncorp Group 95–96
    total experience management 155
Freud, Sigmund 210
Friendliness, as personality trait 192

G

Gartner 155
General Motors 243
General respect 30
Giulioni, J. W. 38
Good judgment, and ideal risk
        behaviors 137
Governance program 95–96
Grant, A. 211
Gregariousness, as personality trait 192
Grove, Andy 184
Gutierrez, J. 24

H

Habits
    and behaviors 24
    defined 22
    formation 22–24
    same habits cycle 24
Happiness metric 85–86
Harder, B. 22
Harrison, N. 8
Hemsley, Richard 9
Hiatt, Jeffery 45
Hibino, Shozo 244

Hierarchies, and system 26–27
High-level system map 28
High neuroticism
    vs. low neuroticism 193
    and skeptics 196
Hines, P. 27, 42–43, 52
Human resource management (HRM)
        department 51
    role in continuous improvement 52
Humility 219, 244–246
    and leadership 31
    leading with 31, 176
    lead with 229–234, 241

I

Ideal behaviors
    core 18–20, *19*
    and ideal results 20–24
Ideal risk behaviors 128–137
    defining 137–138
    enhancing brand recognition 136–137
    framework 136–137
    good judgment, applying 137
    and ideal results 137
    measured decisions 136
    steps for defining 129
    understanding the organization 136
    understand the industry 136
IIoT (Industrial Internet of Things) 216
Implementation 243–255
    simple flowchart to *253*
    suggested KAIs for 255
    suggested KBIs for 254
    traditional KPIs for 254
Incentives 12, 207
Individualism *vs.* collectivism 213
Individual respect 30
Industrial Revolution 216
Industry
    ideal risk behaviors 136
    understanding 136
Industry 4.0 216, *216*
    suggested KAIs for 226
    traditional KBIs for 226
    traditional KPIs for 225–226
Infrastructure, and CI program 7–8

Integrated Cultural Framework (ICF)
    ability to influence 212
    achievement orientation 212
    comfort with ambiguity 212
    individualism *vs.* collectivism 213
    space orientation 213
    time orientation 213
Introversion *vs.* extraversion 191–192
IoT (The Internet of Things) 216–217

J

Jekiel, C. 42–43, 52
Jobs, Steve 150, 151
Jones, M. 22
Jørgensen, F. 52–53
Judgment 107, **130–135**, 137

K

Karahanna, E. 16
Karmes, J. 31
Key activity indicators (KAIs) 22
    anatomy of 39
    for CX initiatives/programs 171
    for implementation roadmap 255
    for Industry 4.0 226
    as measure of behavioral transition 40
    for respect **252–253**
    for risk behaviors 145
    for safety initiatives/programs 188
    suggested 145, 171, 188, 226, 255
Key behavioral indicators (KBIs) 21–22, 29,
        55, 142, 171, 257
    anatomy of 39
    and change management 52–53
    for CX initiatives or programs 171
    for implementation roadmap 254
    for Industry 4.0 226
    for leadership responsibility 242
    for personality and behavior 214
    for respect **252–253**
    for risk behavior 142, 145
    for safety initiatives/programs 188
    suggested 142, 145, 171, 188, 214,
        242, 254
    traditional 142, 226

Key performance indicators (KPIs) 21–22, 28, 257
  anatomy of 39
  and change management 52–53
  for CX initiative or programs 171
  for implementation roadmap 254
  for Industry 4.0 225–*226*
  lag 54
  lead 54–55
  for leadership responsibility 241–242
  for personality and behavior 214
  for risk behaviors 145
  for safety initiatives or programs 188
  traditional 145, 171, 188, 214, 225–226, 241–242, 254
Khera, S. 23
Knowledge 45–46, 209
Kortian, V. 8
Kotter's theory of change 48–50

L

Lag KPIs 54
Laugen, B. T. 52–53
Leaders 5–6, 11, 21, 31–33, 65, 100, 101–102, 105, 116; *see also* Leadership
Leadership 178–179, 227–242
  and Agile 77–79
  CX 154–155
  decision-making behavior framework **235–240**
  and humility 31, 229–234, 241
  Respect for the Individual 228–229, 241
  and Scrum 77–79
  servant 234
  suggested KBIs for 242
  team, alignment of 233
  traditional KPIs for 241–242
Leading with humility 229–234, 241
Lead KPIs 54–55
  decision-making 54
  variability of measurement 55
Lean champions/influencers 232
Lean practitioners
  and psychological safety 186–187
  and technology 216
Lean programs 1, 9, 42, 74
Liberalism 193

Live Flow model 98
Logician (INTP) 201–202, 205
Logistician (ISTJ) 200, 205

M

Machine learning 8
Mallinger, M. 191, 212
Mallinger, R. 212
Management behavior 15
Mangat, Gurmeet 215
Maslow's hierarchy of needs 173–174, *174*, 187
McGee, A. 207
McGee, P. 207
Mckinsey 7-S model 46–48, 50
  shared values 47–48
  skills 47
  staff 47
  strategy 47
  structure 47
  style 46
  systems 47
Mclean, R. 4
Measured decisions, and ideal risk behaviors 136
Mediator (INFP) 201, 205
Messenger 206–207
Motivation 83–86; *see also* Incentives
  and CI program 4–5
  intrinsic 12
Multigenerational workforce 234
Myers & Briggs 16 personalities 198–204
  adventurer 201
  advocate 200
  architect 200–201
  campaigner 202
  commander 203–204
  consul 203
  debater 202–203
  defender 200
  entertainer 202
  entrepreneur 202
  executive 203
  logician 201–202
  logistician 200
  mediator 201
  protagonist 203
  virtuoso 201

N

Narcissism, as barrier to change
211–212
Neill, M. S. 65
Noguchi, Kouichiro 243
Nonaka, I. 84
Nonblame behavior 123
Norms 207–208
North Star Alignment
migrating organization to 155–157
template (NSAT) 156, *157*
North Star metric 156–158
Northwestern Medicine 22
NUMMI 243–244

O

O Coplien, James 80
Ohno, Taiichi 229
Openness *vs.* closeness to experience 193
Organization(s)
core behaviors 17–20
CX approaches and structures 152
health of 4
ideal risk behaviors 136
North Star Alignment, migrating to
155–157
performance 53
system 20
understanding 136
Organizational culture 190–191, 204
artifacts 190
and behavior of employees 16–17
beliefs and values 190–191
importance of 16–17
underlying assumptions 191

P

Participatory communication 59–65
Passengers, as personality type 198
Peeters, M. 194
People
barriers to change 211–212
emphasis on 43–44
persuading 211–212
Perfectionism, seeking 34–35

Performance
and CI program 4
measurements 53
Personalities
ambassadors 195–196
challengers 196
champions 195
impact on behavioral change 190
and imposing change 204–206
passengers 198
prisoners 197
saboteurs 196–197
skeptics 196
suggested KBIs for 214
thieves 197
traditional KPIs for 214
Personality traits
agreeableness *vs.* disagreeableness 192
conscientiousness *vs.*
unconscientiousness 192–193
extraversion *vs.* introversion 191–192
high neuroticism *vs.* low neuroticism 193
openness *vs.* closeness to experience 193
predictions for work outcomes 194–195
Physical safety 174–177
Plenert, Gerhard 244
Prime, J. 31
Priming 209
Principles
and behaviors 19, 30–38
CI 31–35
cultural enablers 30–31
defined 19
enterprise alignment 35–38
guiding behaviors 137
importance of 56
setting 56
understanding 56–57
Prisoners, as personality type 197
Process risk controls 121
Production process 53
Productivity, and continuous improvement 117
Programmatic communication 59
Prosci Change Framework 45–46
future 46
prepare approach 45
transition 45–46
Protagonist (ENFJ) 203, 206

Psychological safety 179, 184–186
  and lean practitioner 186–187
Pull/flow system 219
Purpose statement 28

Q

Quality assurance 34, 205

R

Reciprocity, and commitment 210
Regular product increment 84–85
Reidentification 58
Reinforcement 46
Relationship 53
  external 26
  internal 26
Respect
  KAIs for **252–253**
  KBIs for **252–253**
Respect for the Individual 175, 219, 228–229,
    241, 244–246
Ringelmann, Maximilien 80–81
Ringelmann effect *81*
Risk(s)
  behavioral 119–120
  beyond financial services 141–142
  in financial service 120–121
  inevitable 124
  manageable 124
  matters 124
  as opportunity 124
  as responsibility of all people 124
Risk attitude 122
Risk behaviors 122–125, **130–135**
  A-B-C model 122
  behavioral risk 119–120
  challenge management 123
  developing risk mindset 125
  ethical role modeling 122–123
  measuring success 145
  nonblame behavior 123
  process risk controls 121
  risk culture 125–145
  risk in financial service 120–121
  risk mindset 123–125

  suggested KAIs for 145
  suggested KBIs for 142
  traditional KPIs for 142
Risk culture 122, 125–145
  Banking Royal Commission 142–143
  benefits of risk-defining behavior
    138–139
  bottom-to-top approach 127
  definition 125–127
  developing 127–128
  effects of 126
  ideal risk behaviors 128–138
  measuring success 142
  practical case 139–141
  risks beyond financial services 141–142
  top-to-bottom approach 126–127
Risk-defining behavior
  awareness 139
  benefits of 138–139
  decision-making 139
  improved culture 139
  learning and improvement 138
  projection of performance results 139
  reducing uncertainty 138
  regulatory requirements 138
Risk mindset 123–125
Risk-taking behaviors 38–39
  consistency 38–39
  enabling giving 38
  modeling 38
  support 38
Rogers, K. M. 30
Royal Commission into Misconduct in the
    Banking, Superannuation, and
    Financial Services Industry, *see*
    Banking Royal Commission
Rudd, J. 50

S

Saboteurs, as personality type 196–197
Safety 173–188
  behavioral framework **180–183**
  behavior-based safety 176–177
  and coaching 178
  goal of 177–179
  keys to success 179–187

leadership 178–179
management **298–301**
observation card *177*
physical 174–177
psychological 179, 184–186
real-life example 177
set expectations and observe 178
stabilization ladder *187*
and technology 178
Safety initiatives or programs
suggested KAIs for 188
suggested KBIs for 188
traditional KPIs for 188
Salib, E. 31
Salience 208–209
Scaled daily Scrums (SDSs) 78
Schein, E. H. 190
Schwarber, Ken 73–74
Scientific thinking 32–33, 219
Scrum 73–74
defined 84
described 74–77
and leadership 77–79
patterns of behaviors and systems 80–86
sprint cycle *75*
A Scrum Book: The Spirit of the Game
(O Coplien) 80
Scrum master 74, 76
Scrum of Scrums master (SoS Master) 79
Scrum@Scale approach 78, 79, *79*
Sedgwick, Steve 143
Self-consciousness 193
Self-efficacy 193
Sensei Moment 224–225
Servant leadership 234
Shared values 47–48
Sheikh, M. 58
Shingo, Ritsuio 229
Shingo Institute 2, 16
definition of respect for every
individual 30
definition of system 25
model of excellence 20
Shingo model *245*, 257
construct of fundamental truths **249**
creating transformational/sustainable
change 247

lead with humility 229–234, 241
principles *220*, *247*
Respect for the Individual 228–229, 241
Shingo model bridge 3, *3*
Shingo Prize
creating a plan 247–251
respect for the individual/humility
244–246
Shingo model 247
winning/losing 246–247
Six Sigma 1, 9, 42, 72, 257
Skeptics
and high neuroticism 196
as personality type 196
Skills, and change management 47
Small-item Scrum pattern 82
Small teams 80–82
Space orientation 213
Sprint goal 82–83
Srite, M. 16
Staff, *see* Workforce/staff
Standard Work 1
Strategy 47
for CX success 154–158
Structures 47
and system 26–27
Stubbornness, as barrier to change 211
Style, and change management 46
Suncorp Group 40, 93, 106
BIP achievements 94–95
BIP behavioral framework 102–107
BIP shortfall 99–101
business improvement program (BIP)
93–94
case study 93–118
enhanced customer experience 98–99
financial outcomes 96–97
improved business performance and
services 98
initiatives and frameworks 95–96
lessons learned from BIP 101–102
previous transformation attempts 94
Sutherland, Jeff 73–74, 78, 80
Swarming Scrum pattern 84
System 47
and behavior 27–29
defined 25

defining purpose of 24, 27
designing 26–27
internal and external relationships 26
structures and hierarchies 26–27
Systematic approach *vs.* tool-oriented
approach 43
Systems drive behaviors 137
System theory 20

T

Takeuchi, H. 84
Tanner, Obert 184
Taylor, John C., Jr. 227
Technology 178
and lean practitioner 216
TFSD model 50–51, 59
Thieves, as personality type 197
Think systemically 37–38
Third party, and financial services 121
Time orientation 213
Tool-oriented approach
and CI program 3–4
vs. systematic approach 43
Total experience management
framework 155
Total experience model (TEM)
approaches *153*
Toyota 243–244
Toyota Production System (TPS) 56, 74, 175,
189, 224, 230, 244, 257
Toyota's Global Marketing Strategy:
Innovation through
Breakthrough Thinking and Kaizen
(Noguchi) 243
Traditional key performance indicators (KPIs)
for CX initiative or programs 171
for implementation roadmap 254

for Industry 4.0 225–226
for leadership responsibility 241–242
for safety initiatives or programs 188
Trust 186–187, 192, **250**

U

Uncertainty
reducing 138
risk-defining behavior 138
Unconscientiousness *vs.* conscientiousness
192–193
USA Today 227

V

Values
and behaviors 19
corporate **250**
creation 35–36
defined 19
organizational culture 190–191
Value stream mapping (VSM) 1, 29
Virtuoso (ISTP) 201, 205

W

Wind farms
Sensei Moment 224–225
traditional approach 216–224
Workforce/staff 47
multigenerational 234
"Working Backwards (2021)" 150
Wyles, G. 195

Y

Yesterday's Weather Scrum pattern 83–84